IMAGES
of America

AROUND JEFFERSON AND ROAMING SHORES

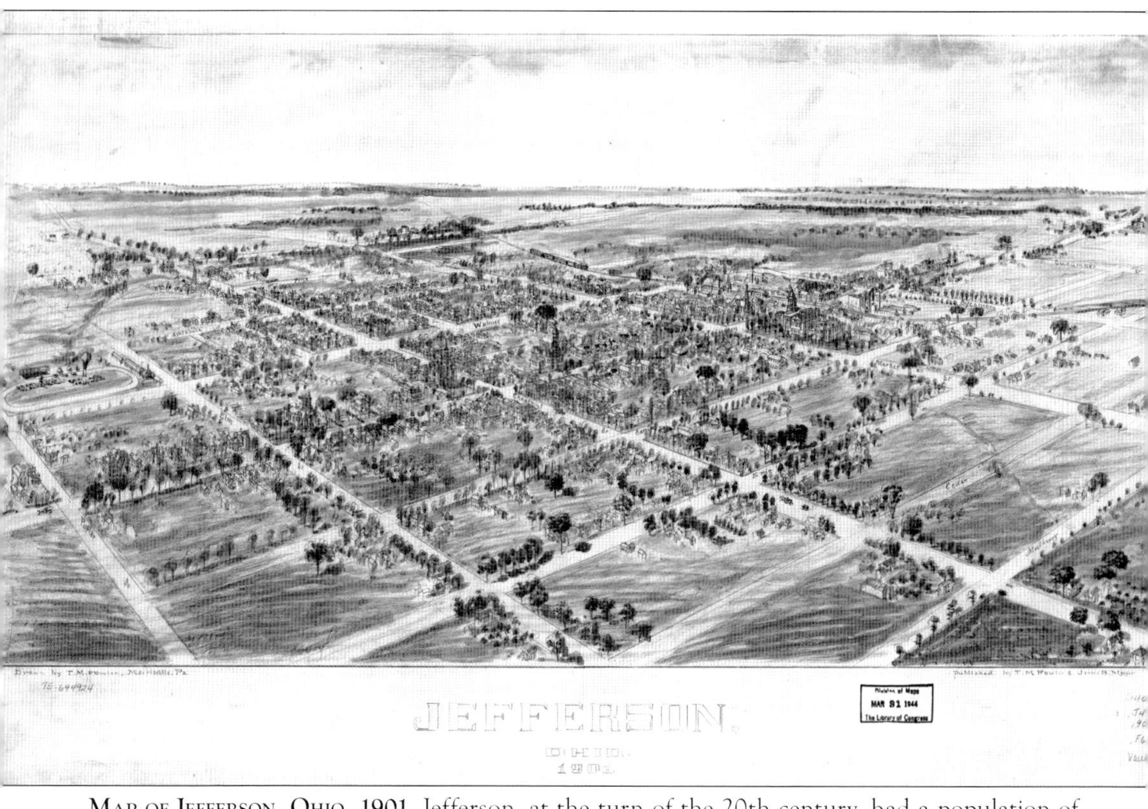

MAP OF JEFFERSON, OHIO, 1901. Jefferson, at the turn of the 20th century, had a population of 1,319 (according to the US Census Report). At that time, the village had five churches, three law offices, and a dozen retailers. (Library of Congress.)

ON THE COVER: OUTSIDE THE GIDDINGS LAW OFFICE, 1960. The Giddings Law Office, once located on North Chestnut Street adjacent to the Giddings family home, was saved from being razed in the 1930s by a group of dedicated citizens. It is currently owned by the Ashtabula County Historical Society, an organization that dates to 1838. (Jefferson Historical Society.)

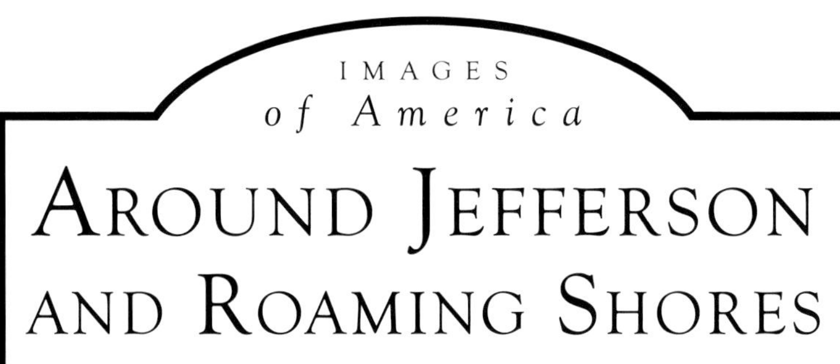

Sandy Mitchell Pavick

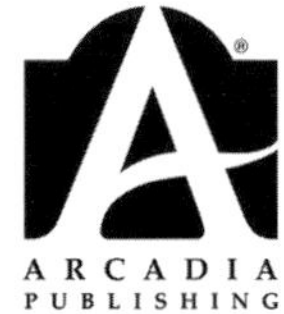

ISBN 978-1-4671-6312-5

Published by Arcadia Publishing
Charleston, South Carolina

Printed in the United States of America

Library of Congress Control Number: 2025946959

For all general information, please contact Arcadia Publishing:
Telephone 843-853-2070
Fax 843-853-0044
E-mail sales@arcadiapublishing.com

Visit us on the Internet at www.arcadiapublishing.com

To the people of Jefferson and Rock Creek, past and present

Contents

Acknowledgments

To the people of Jefferson, past and present, thank you for sharing your stories, your memories, and your passion and affection for your city.

Thank you also to Caroline Vickerson, my editor at Arcadia Publishing, who kindly guides me in the right direction.

Special thanks to Norma Waters and the Jefferson Historical Society, Barb Pruden, the Platt R. Spencer Historical Society, Carrie Wimer and the staff at the Ashtabula County District Library in Ashtabula, the Ashtabula Historical Society, Judy Pallutch, Elizabeth Piwkowski, and Annette Sheldon for their help in gathering historic images for this book.

Thanks to my husband, Steve, who encourages me and never tires of hearing about "what I learned today."

And, above all, thank you to the readers who, by your interest, keep Ashtabula County history alive for future generations.

A portion of the profits from this book will be donated to Ashtabula County food pantries.

INTRODUCTION

Jefferson, the county seat of Ohio's largest county, Ashtabula County, is rich in history. The area that would become the village of Jefferson was originally home to wandering tribes of Erie, Chippewa, and Wyandot Native Americans, who used this area for a seasonal hunting ground. In 1795, when the area became part of the Connecticut Western Reserve, it attracted land speculators who invested in the Connecticut Land Company and drew lots for the parcels of land they would receive. Two of the largest investors were Gideon Granger and Oliver Phelps. These two East Coast gentlemen became owners of most of the land that would become Jefferson Township and the surrounding area.

Neither gentleman hurried to live in the Western Reserve. Phelps promptly went bankrupt, and Granger sent a proxy, Eldred Smith, to build a log cabin here and establish residency. At the same time, Granger enticed other East Coast families to venture west for a new life in the Western Reserve. These intrepid new landowners bought their properties sight unseen. By most accounts, Granger vastly oversold the amenities of this new property. When early landowners arrived, instead of a village, they found blazes on trees where Granger intended to clear roads. Instead of cleared farmland, they found dense forest.

Granger, however, stuck to his vision of building a city that resembled Philadelphia. By 1811, Jefferson had become the Ashtabula County seat of government, had an elegant courthouse (thanks to land and building funds from Granger), and supported a host of retailers and businesses.

The village of Jefferson was the center of national abolitionist sentiment in the pre–Civil War years, led by Congressman Joshua R. Giddings and Sen. Benjamin Wade, both Jefferson residents. Together, they kept the abolitionist cause in front of Congress. So much so that Giddings was censured by the House of Representatives for discussing slavery on the House floor, something that was prohibited in the early 1860s. Abolitionist John Brown had strong ties to the county and traveled to Jefferson to meet with Giddings at least once.

Jefferson is also reputed to have had several stations along the Underground Railroad. Ashtabula County was a natural route for escaping slaves seeking freedom across Lake Erie in Canada. The county is only 100 miles from the panhandle of Virginia (now West Virginia), and five separate Underground Railroad lines crossed the county.

Jefferson was prominent in the women's suffrage cause, with the Congregational Church being the site of one of the first suffrage conventions. Jefferson has an eclectic array of museums, ranging from the Jefferson Depot Village, with its collection of historic homes and buildings, to the closed but not forgotten Victorian Perambulator Museum, with its vintage dolls and baby carriages.

Nearby Rock Creek, Ohio, to the west of Jefferson, was founded in 1798. The village never grew as big as neighboring Jefferson, Geneva, and Ashtabula. However, during the early days of automobile travel, the village was a popular stop for travelers making the trek from Lake Erie to the Ohio River via State Route 45. At that time, Rock Creek boasted two hotels, two gas stations, and several popular restaurants.

Rock Creek is home to a cemetery with more than 100 Civil War veterans' graves, a picturesque downtown, a creek-side park, and a diverse collection of Victorian and Western Reserve architecture. The village has been home to several interesting people. Among these are landscape artist David Birdsey Walkley, evangelist Lewis Chafer, and psychologist Theodore Newcomb.

Roaming Shores, located southwest of Jefferson, is a planned community formed by damming Rock Creek in 1966–1967. The development, originally called Roaming Rock, was incorporated as the village of Roaming Shores in 1979. The collection of more than 800 homes there, many of them located directly on the lake, includes some of the most picturesque and sought-after real estate in the county. Today, more than 1,500 people call Roaming Shores home.

One

Jefferson

Jefferson, Ohio, with a 2020 population of 3,226 residents, is the county seat of Ashtabula County, Ohio's largest county. The village is known as the site of the annual Ashtabula County Fair, the headquarters for the county's Covered Bridge Festival, and as the corporate headquarters of Bissell Maple Farms and the *Gazette* newspapers.

While there is a city called Jefferson in all the 48 continental United States, Ohio's Jefferson has arguably the best claim to naming itself after the nation's third president, Thomas Jefferson. Gideon Granger, a Revolutionary War veteran who purchased the land on what would become Jefferson, Ohio, was the postmaster general under President Jefferson. That land cost him 70¢ an acre. Granger proceeded to lay out the design for the village after the city of Philadelphia and to donate the land and money for the first courthouse.

Jefferson had electric streetcars from 1898 until 1924, when cars and buses made streetcars obsolete. In 1902, the fare between Jefferson and Ashtabula was 20¢ one way or 35¢ round-trip. Approximately 600–700 persons rode the streetcars daily. The daily record was on August 25, 1908, when 5,600 people rode the cars to visit the Ashtabula County Fair.

Dairy farming was the largest source of agricultural income in the greater Jefferson area up until the early 1970s. In 1966, Jefferson area dairy farmers, such as Hamilton and Musgrave Dairy Farms, produced an average of 10,500 pounds of milk per cow, higher than the Ohio state average. Ashtabula County as a whole led the state for decades in dairy production.

Two of Jefferson's most notable citizens were Joshua R. Giddings and Benjamin F. Wade. Both were staunch abolitionists and helped to shape the national sentiment toward the cause. For a time in the pre–Civil War years, the center of the national abolitionist movement was in the unlikely small town of Jefferson. Giddings, a lawyer, was a US congressman. He was censured by Congress in 1842 for violating that body's "gag rule" that prohibited discussion of slavery in Congress. Wade, also a lawyer and law partner to Giddings, was a US senator. He came within one vote of becoming president (albeit for a short term) during the impeachment trial of Pres. Andrew Johnson.

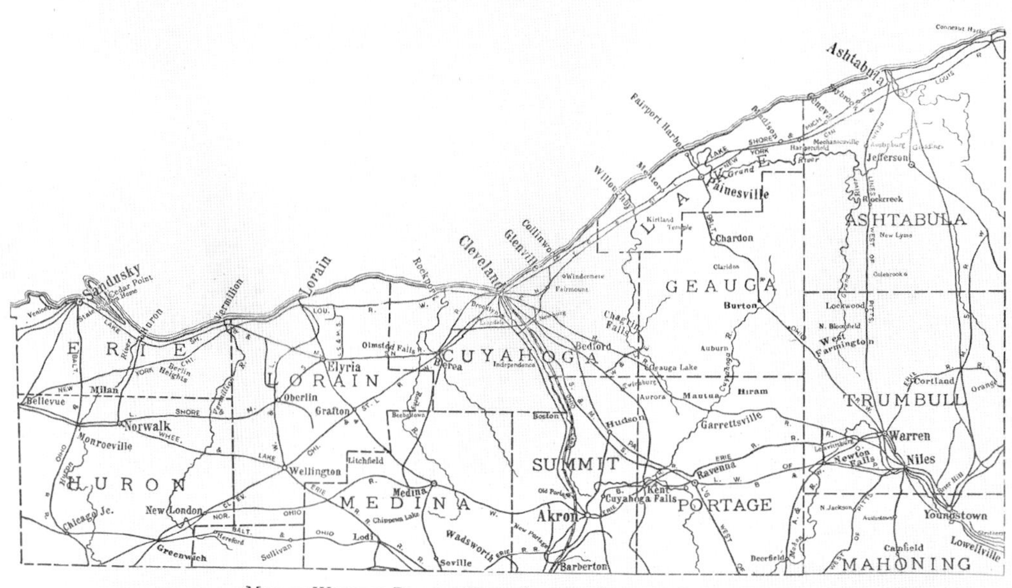

MAP OF WESTERN RESERVE WITH PRESENT COUNTIES PROJECTED ON IT

CONNECTICUT LAND COMPANY. The area that would eventually become Ashtabula County was once part of the Connecticut Western Reserve. This 3,366,921-acre tract of land was awarded to Connecticut by the US government in 1795 in exchange for that state relinquishing its "sea-to-sea" claim from an earlier treaty. The Western Reserve stretched from the Pennsylvania/Ohio state line 120 miles west and south to the 41st parallel. It included today's Ashtabula, Lake, and Geauga Counties. The State of Connecticut, not knowing what to do with its western lands, sold the Western Reserve to a group of real estate investors called the Connecticut Land Company in 1796. (Ashtabula County District Library.)

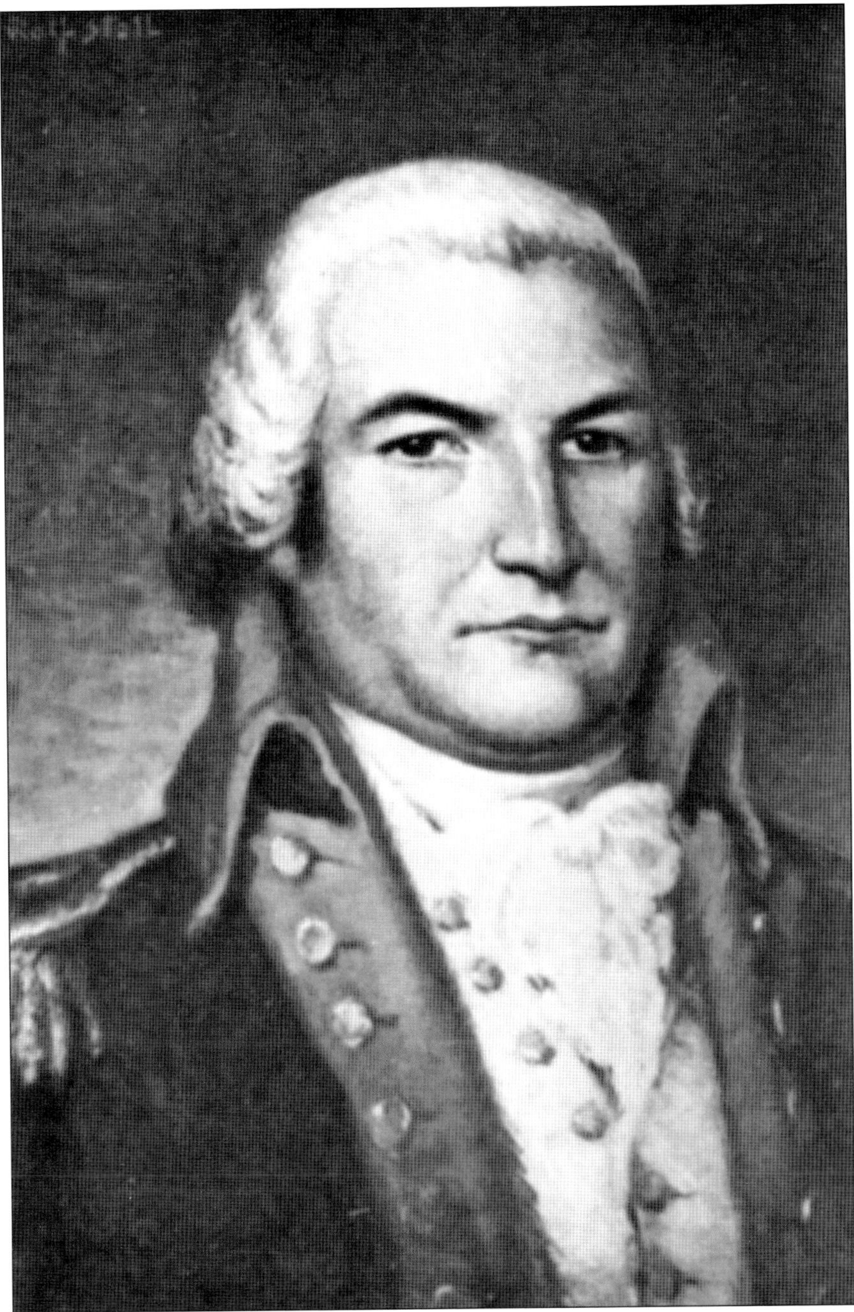

Moses Cleaveland. The Connecticut Land Company sent lawyer and surveyor Gen. Moses Cleaveland, an investor himself, with a group of 50, including two women, to map the Western Reserve and divide the land into five-mile-square parcels. Those parcels remain as today's townships. Each township was divided into 36 individual plots. Cleaveland first set foot in the territory in 1796 when he and his party landed at the mouth of the Conneaut River, in the extreme northeast corner of what is now Ashtabula County. (Cleaveland would later travel to the Cuyahoga River and lend his name—without the "a"—to the village that became Cleveland, Ohio, roughly 70 miles to the east of Conneaut.) (Ashtabula County District Library.)

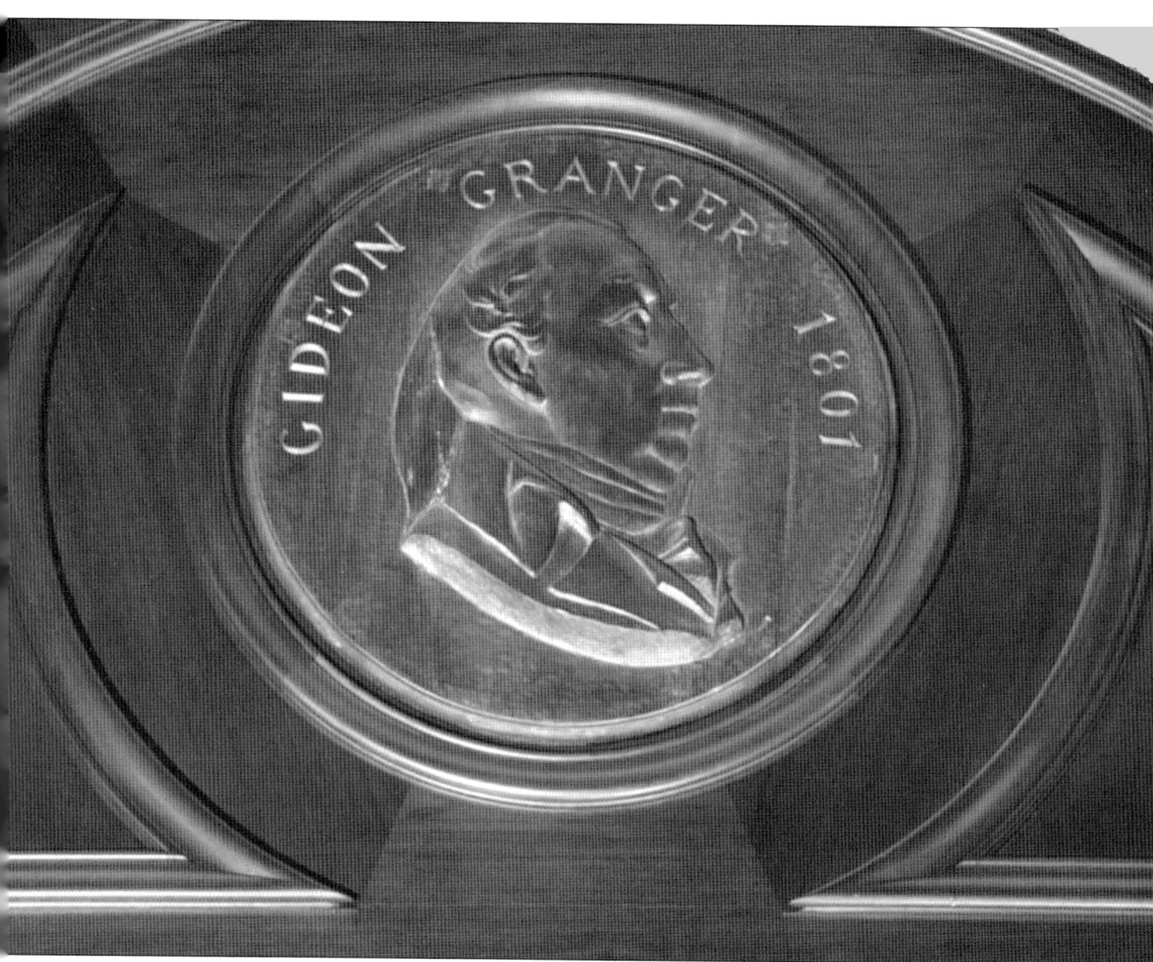

Gideon Granger. Granger is credited with founding the settlement that would become Jefferson, Ohio, in 1805. Granger, a Connecticut native, was one of the original shareholders in the Connecticut Land Company and purchased all the plots in Jefferson Township as well as some in Wayne, Harpersfield, and Lenox Townships. He was a Yale graduate, a political essayist, and a member of the Connecticut House of Representatives. A 19th-century issue of the *Jefferson Gazette* describes Granger as "a man of commanding appearance, of striking physiognomy, of talents equally brilliant and profound, and of a kind and benevolent heart." Granger served as the US Postmaster General under Pres. Thomas Jefferson from 1801 to 1814 and named the village and township he founded after the third president. Granger sent Eldred Smith, an employee, to build the first home in Jefferson Township, a log cabin, in 1804. Granger secured Jefferson as the county seat before Ashtabula County was even duly organized by donating the land for and promising to fund the construction of the first county courthouse. (Library of Congress.)

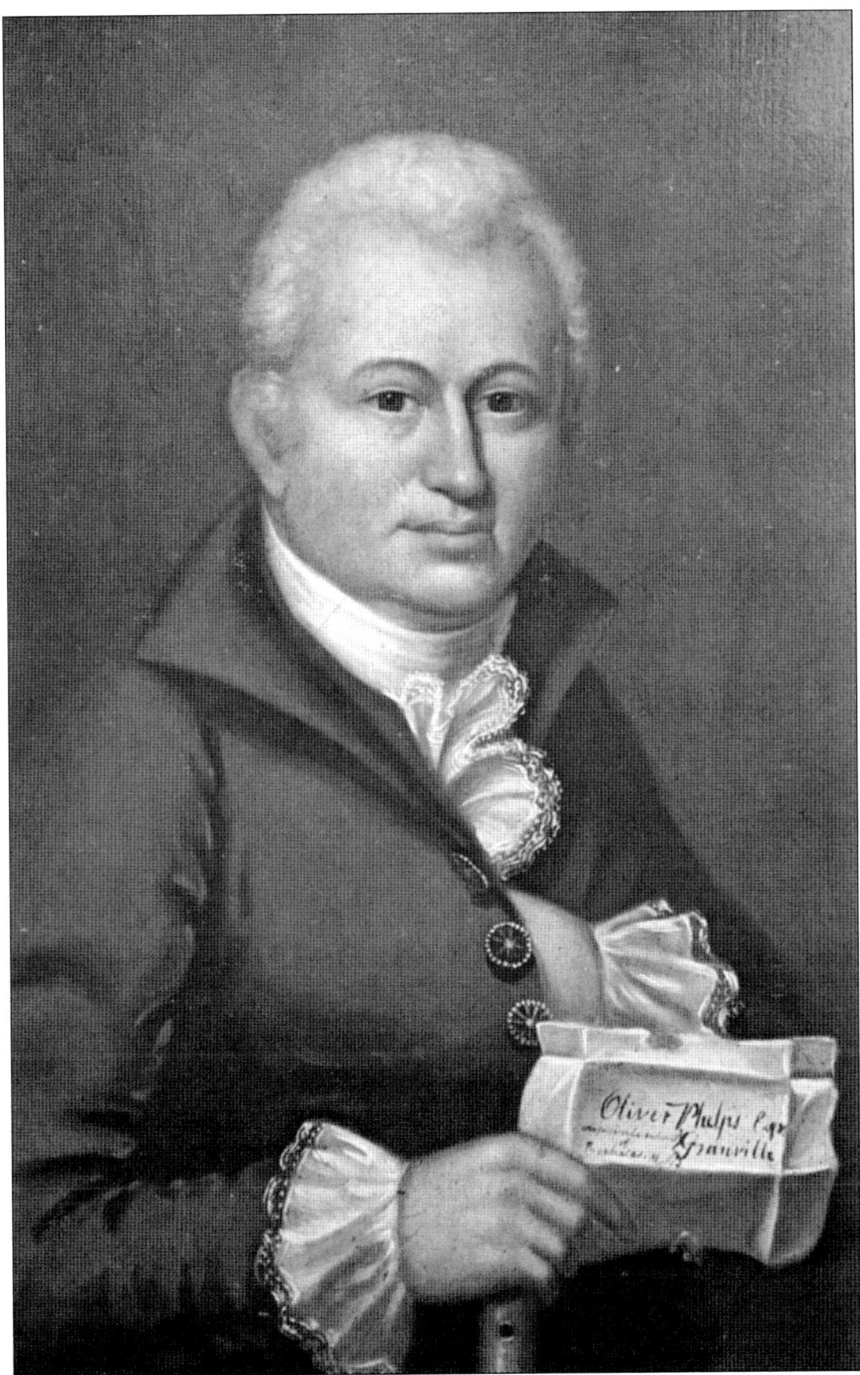

Oliver Phelps. Gideon Granger's business partner, Oliver Phelps, was one of the largest investors in the Connecticut Land Company. A Connecticut native, he was a Revolutionary War veteran. After the war, he was appointed a judge and was elected to the US House of Representatives. Phelps died in 1809 at age 59, owing substantial debts to Granger. At his death, his holdings in the Western Reserve, including lots in Jefferson Township, transferred to Granger to settle that debt. Phelps never lived in the Western Reserve. He is buried in Canandaigua, New York. (Author's collection.)

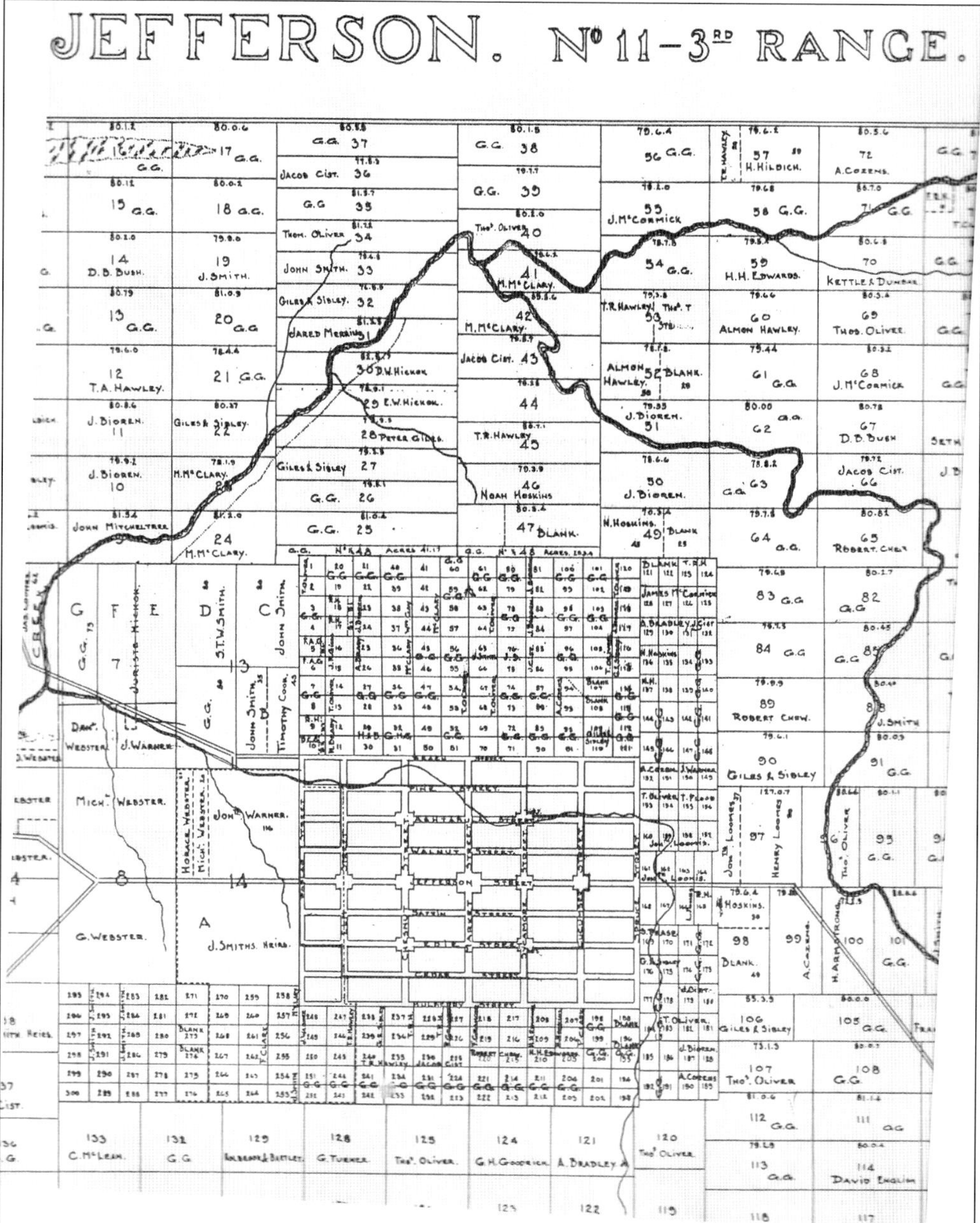

MAP OF JEFFERSON, 1830. Granger laid out the plots and the streets of the village of Jefferson based on the layout of the city of Philadelphia. The original plan had seven east-west streets, intersected by nine north-south streets. Granger planned for the center of town to be at the intersection of Jefferson and Market Streets, but village activity was drawn toward the courthouse, and the true center evolved into the juncture of Jefferson and Chestnut Streets. In 1830, Jefferson had a population of around 300 residents. That number would grow to 453 in the 1850 census. On this 1830 plat map, one can see the initials "GG" for Gideon Granger on most of the parcels around the courthouse. (Author's collection.)

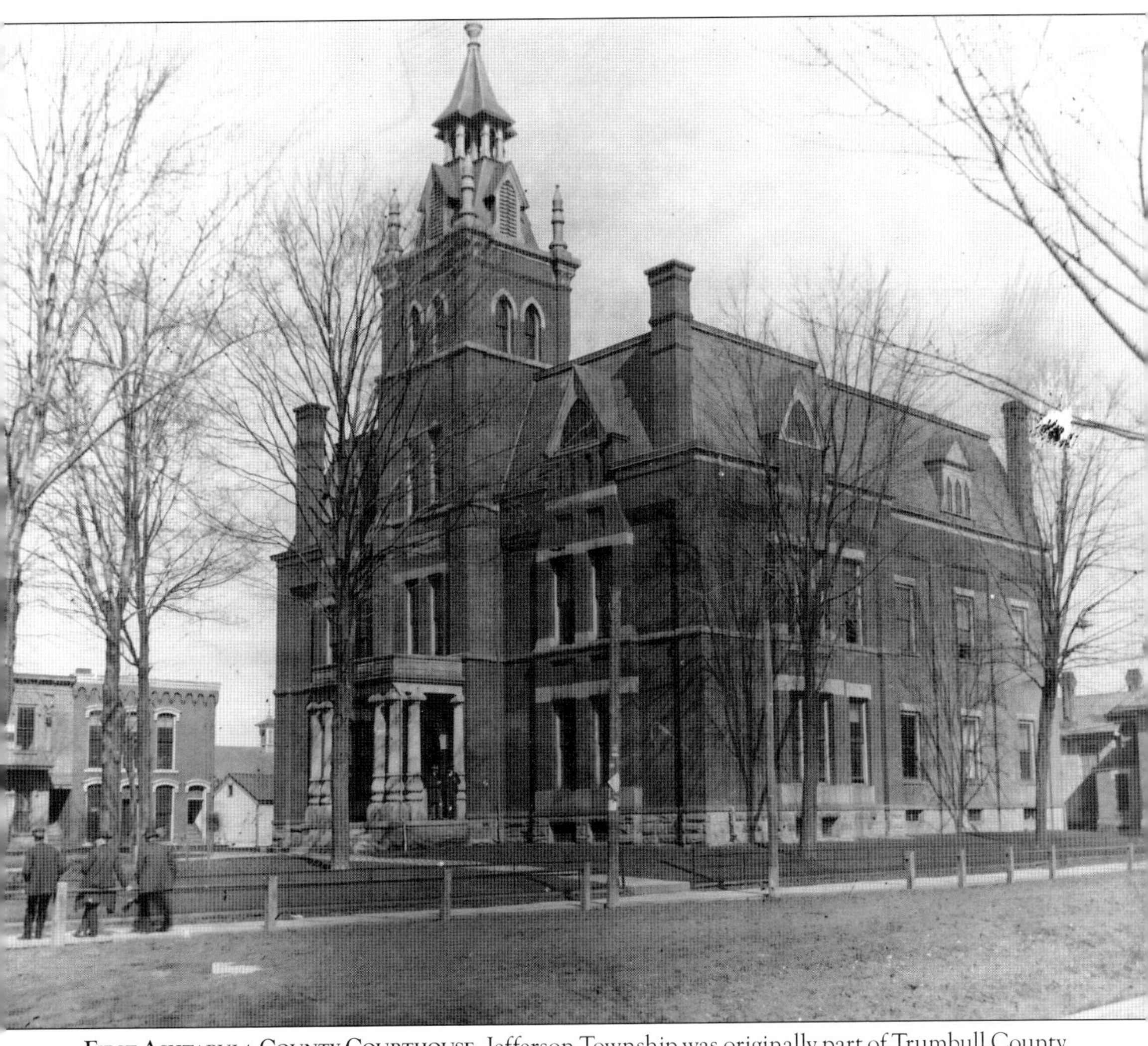

First Ashtabula County Courthouse. Jefferson Township was originally part of Trumbull County. Ashtabula County was formed in 1807, carved out of parts of Trumbull and Geauga Counties. The settlement that would become the village of Jefferson was named as the county seat in 1811, just as Gideon Granger had predicted and lobbied for, beating out nearby Austinburg for the honor. The first Ashtabula Courthouse opened in 1811, shortly after Ashtabula became a county. It was funded by Gideon Granger as a gift to the city he founded and loved. A second courthouse was constructed in 1836 but was partially destroyed by fire in 1850. It was subsequently rebuilt, and the original 1836 date can still be seen above the doorway. The courthouse was lit by natural gas and kerosene lamps until 1892. Telephone service was added to the courthouse in 1902. (Ashtabula District Library Archives.)

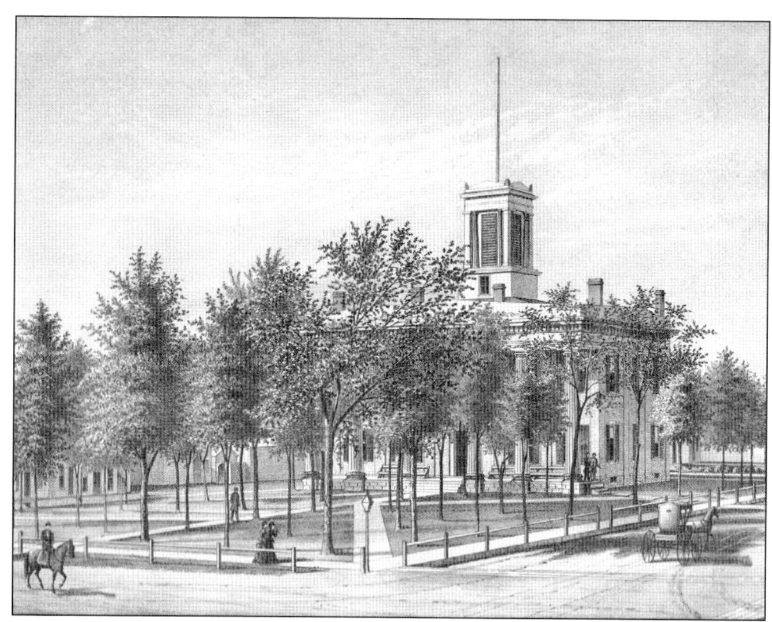

Ashtabula County Courthouse. The original courthouse had two floors and measured 30 feet by 40 feet. The downstairs consisted of a large courtroom, and the upstairs was divided into four offices that surrounded a central wood stove. (Author's collection.)

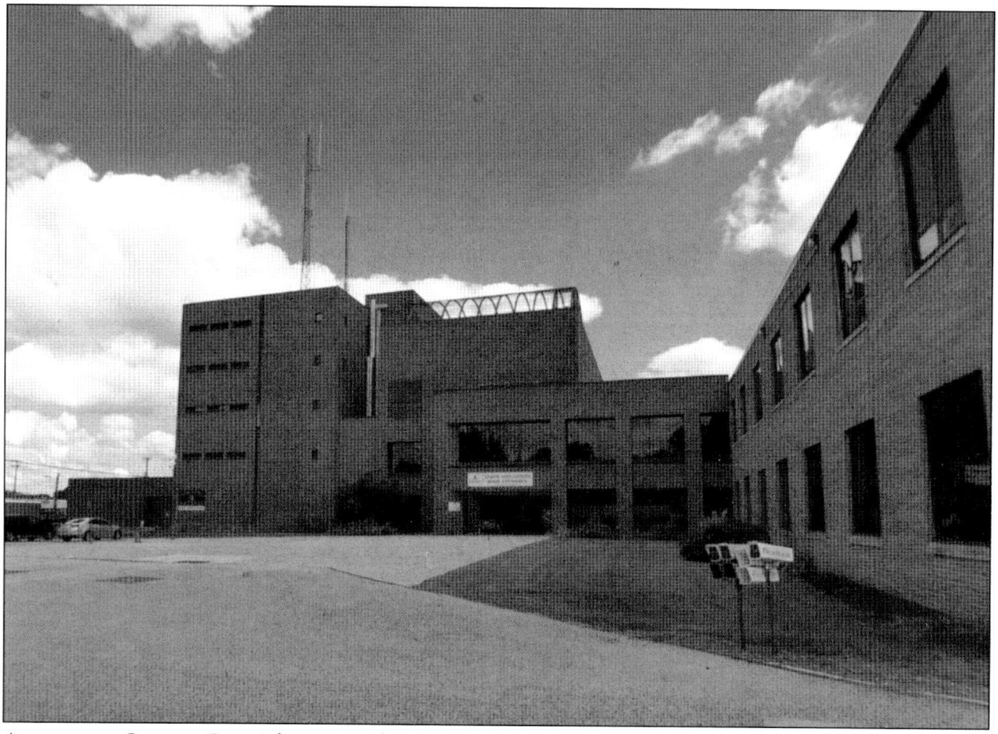

Ashtabula County Jail. The original courthouse had a two-story jail behind it, measuring 20 feet by 30 feet, and included a "dungeon" and a debtor's cell. The justice wing of today's courthouse was added in 1970 with courtroom space, judges' chambers, and a law library. The present five-story county jail was added in 1979 at a cost of $7 million. It has a capacity of 97 inmates. (Author's collection.)

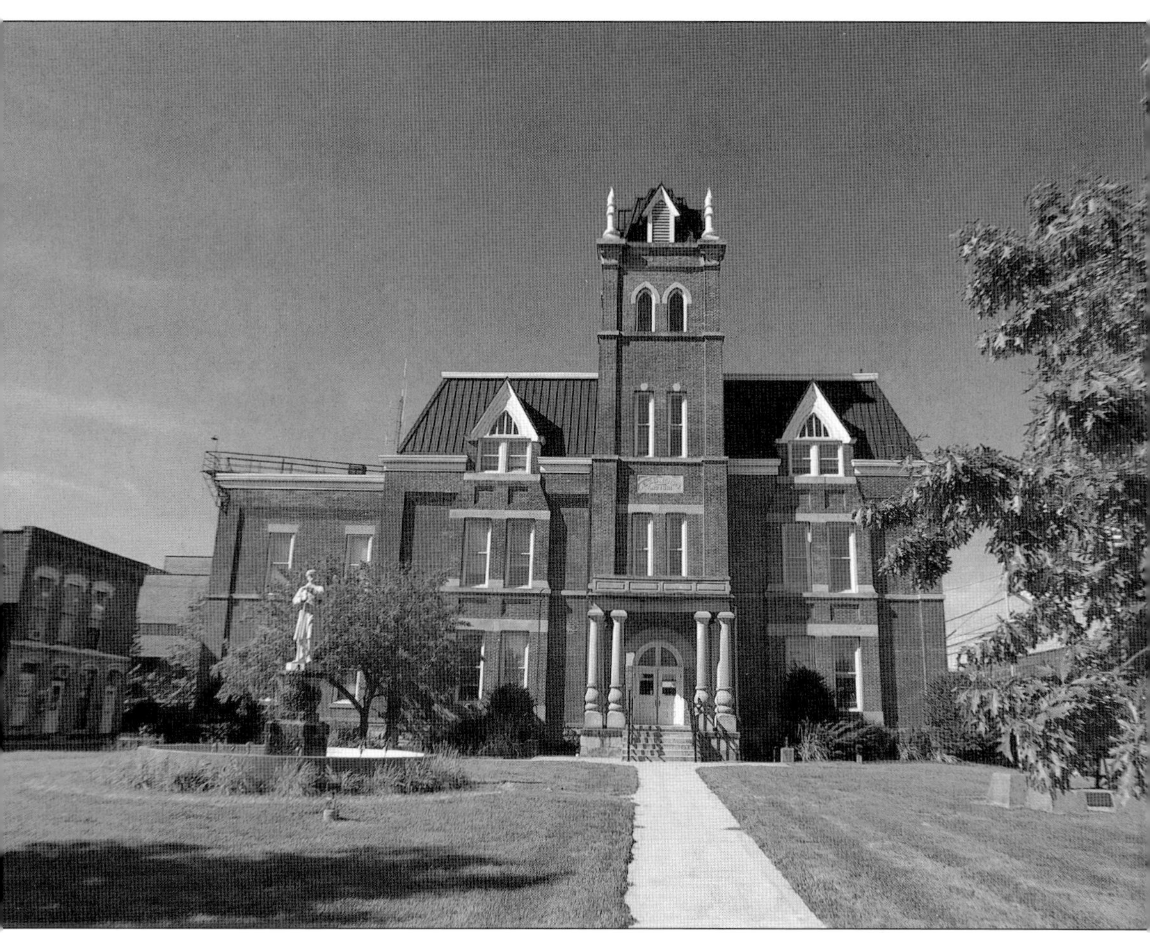

THE ASHTABULA COUNTY COURTHOUSE TODAY. The current Ashtabula County Courthouse was constructed in 1850, begun shortly after the fire that took down the second courthouse, at a cost of $3,650. Today's courthouse is a prime example of Victorian Italianate architecture. It was added to the National Register of Historic Places in 1975. The 1850 courthouse building houses the offices for the Covered Bridge Festival, among other offices. (Author's collection.)

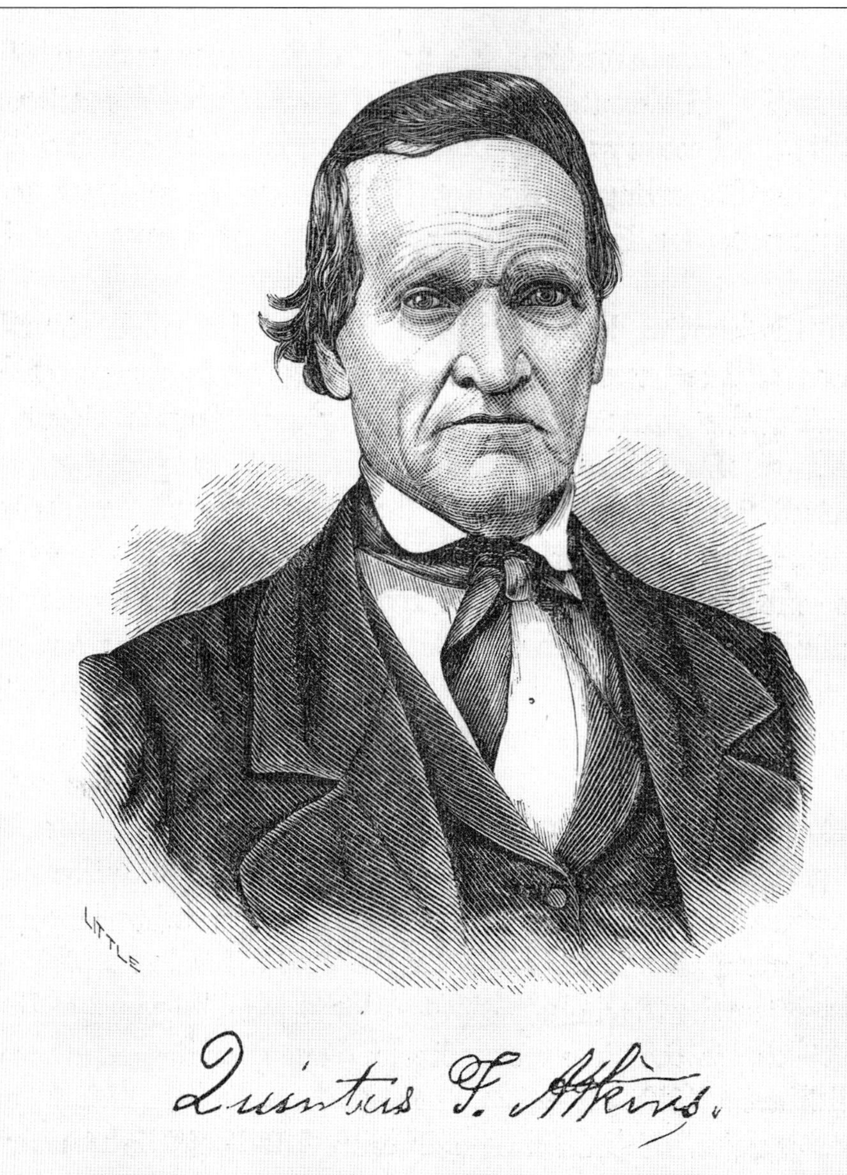

QUINTUS ATKINS. Quintus Atkins was born in Wolcott, Connecticut, in 1782 and headed west to the Connecticut Western Reserve as a young man. He settled in Morgan Township in 1802 and signed on to be a mail carrier, traveling between Cleveland and Sandusky. He married Sarah Wright in 1803. The deeply religious couple would join Rev. John Badger, an early itinerant preacher, as missionaries among the indigenous Wyandot people in the Sandusky area. They remained there for around 18 months. When Ashtabula County was established in 1811, Atkins was elected sheriff, a post he held for two years before he resigned to go to war during the War of 1812. After the war, he was reelected sheriff. Atkins later became an associate common pleas judge in Cuyahoga County. He died in 1859 at the age of 77. (Ashtabula County District Library.)

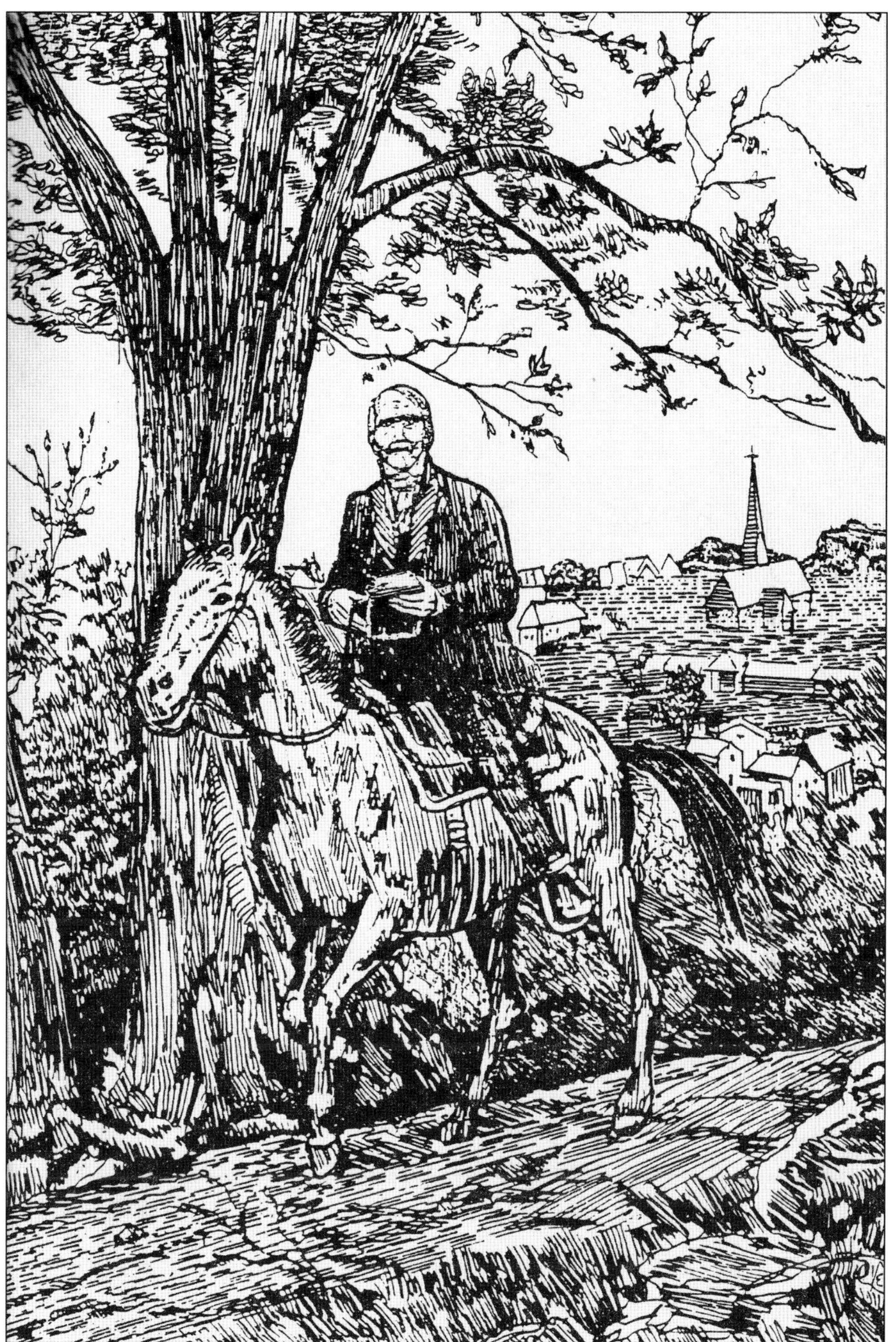

Rev. Joseph Badger. Reverend Badger was a fascinating person and a key figure in the development of churches in Ashtabula County. A native of Connecticut, Badger served with Gen. George Washington at the crossing of the Delaware. After the Revolutionary War, he graduated from Yale and served as a pastor in Connecticut for 10 years before being called to see if there was a need for churches in the Western Reserve. In that, Badger found his life's work, and more than a dozen area churches, including First United Church of Christ (UCC) in Austinburg, trace their roots back to Reverend Badger's work. (Ashtabula County District Library.)

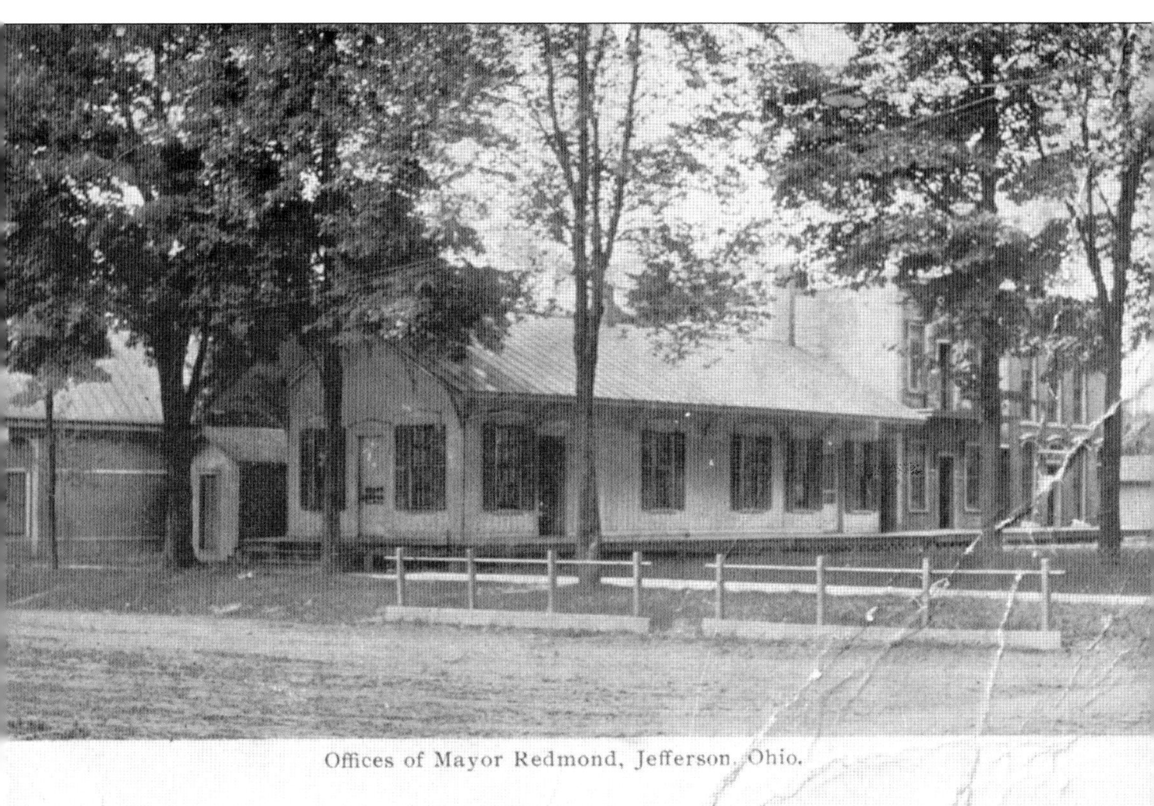
Offices of Mayor Redmond, Jefferson, Ohio.

MAYOR REDMOND'S OFFICE. The area west of the courthouse, now called "Lawyer's Row," was once home to the village mayor's office. One of the gentlemen to occupy this office was Canadian-born Howard James Redmond, the mayor of Jefferson between 1905 and 1917. Redmond was also a lawyer and a partner with S.A. Northway and E.H. Fitch. Howard Redmond died in 1936 and is buried at Oakdale Cemetery. Lawyer's Row was added to the National Register of Historic Places in 1976. (Jefferson Historical Society.)

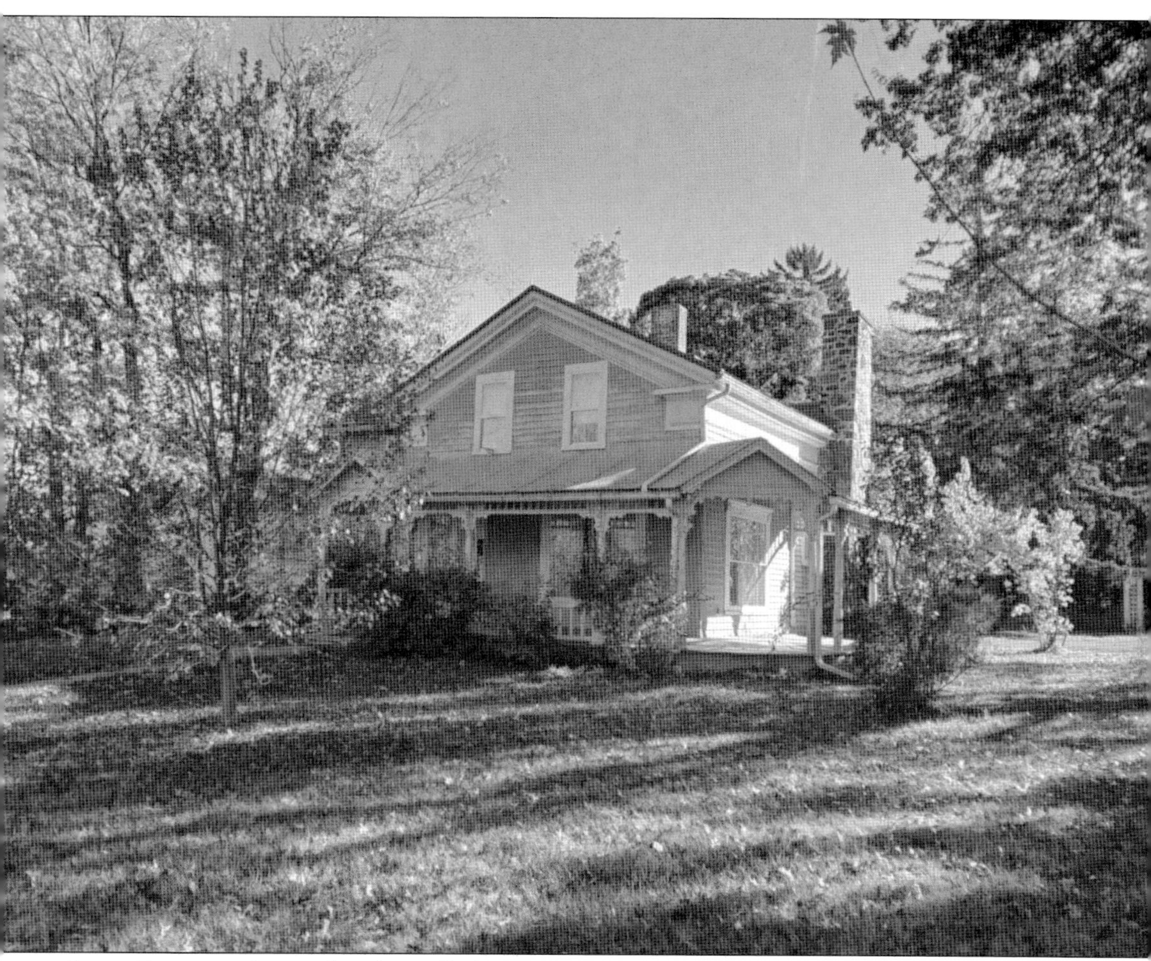

Clara Redmond. Howard Redmond's daughter Clara became the first female deputy sheriff in Ashtabula County and the first woman to carry a weapon as part of her duties. Clara Redmond died in 2003 at the age of 96. She never married and lived most of her life at the family home at 306 North Chestnut Street (pictured). She is also buried at Oakdale. (Author's collection.)

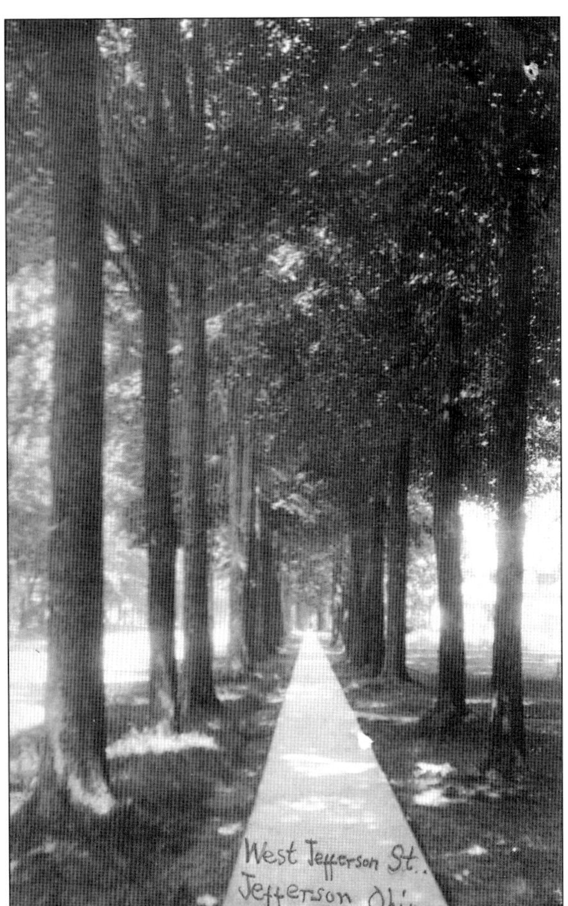

Trees along West Jefferson Street. The row of maple trees along West Jefferson Street originated with the Ladies Literary Class in the mid-19th century. This group planted trees in memory of their members who had passed. The first tree was planted in memory of Eliza Howells in 1924. Eliza Howells was the wife of Joseph A. Howells, the brother of author William Dean Howells. (Judy Pallutch.)

"Dean Howell" Elm. The elegant elm and chestnut trees that once lined Jefferson streets and graced its parks have since gone, victims of different invasive predators. One of these trees, called erroneously the "Dean Howell" elm in the postcard, helped provide shade at Oakdale Cemetery. The tree was most likely named for author and onetime Jefferson resident William Dean Howells. (Judy Pallutch.)

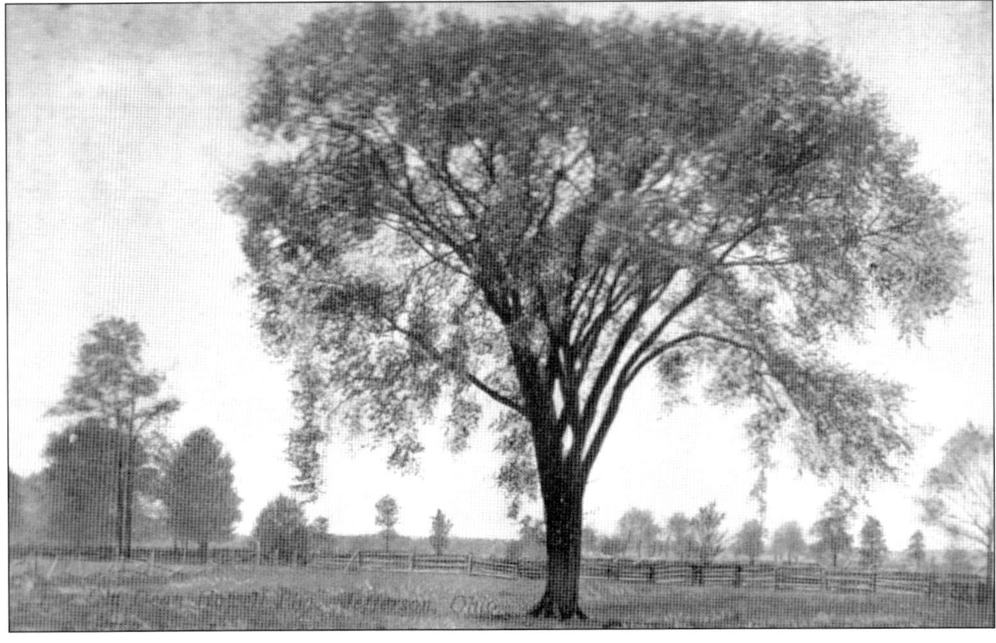

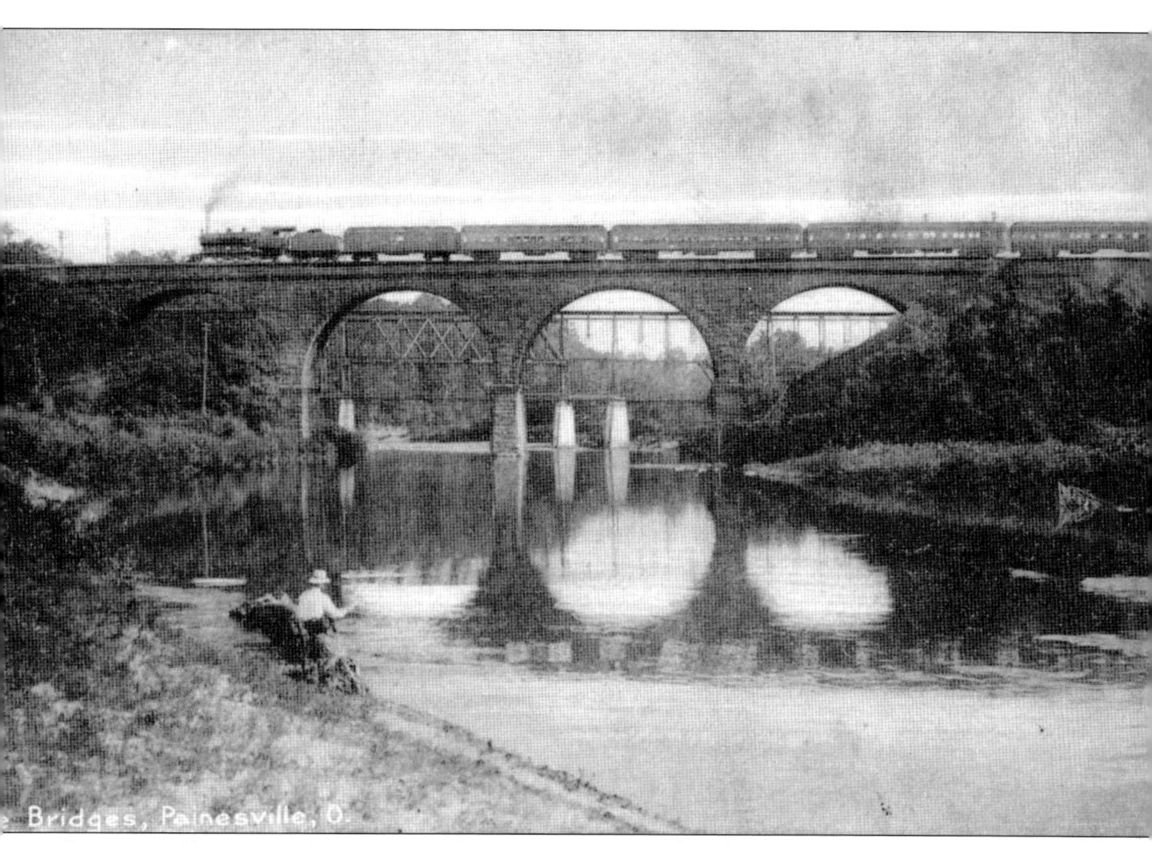

Cleveland, Painesville & Ashtabula Railroad Company. The Cleveland, Painesville & Ashtabula (CP&A) Railroad line was connected to Jefferson in 1872, with the rails constructed by the Lake Shore & Michigan Southern Railroad (later the New York City Railroad). Passenger service to Jefferson ended in August 1956, although freight service continued for several more years. The Cleveland, Painesville & Ashtabula Railroad Company, sometimes called the Lake Shore Railway, was the last rail link built between Buffalo, New York, and Chicago. (Author's collection.)

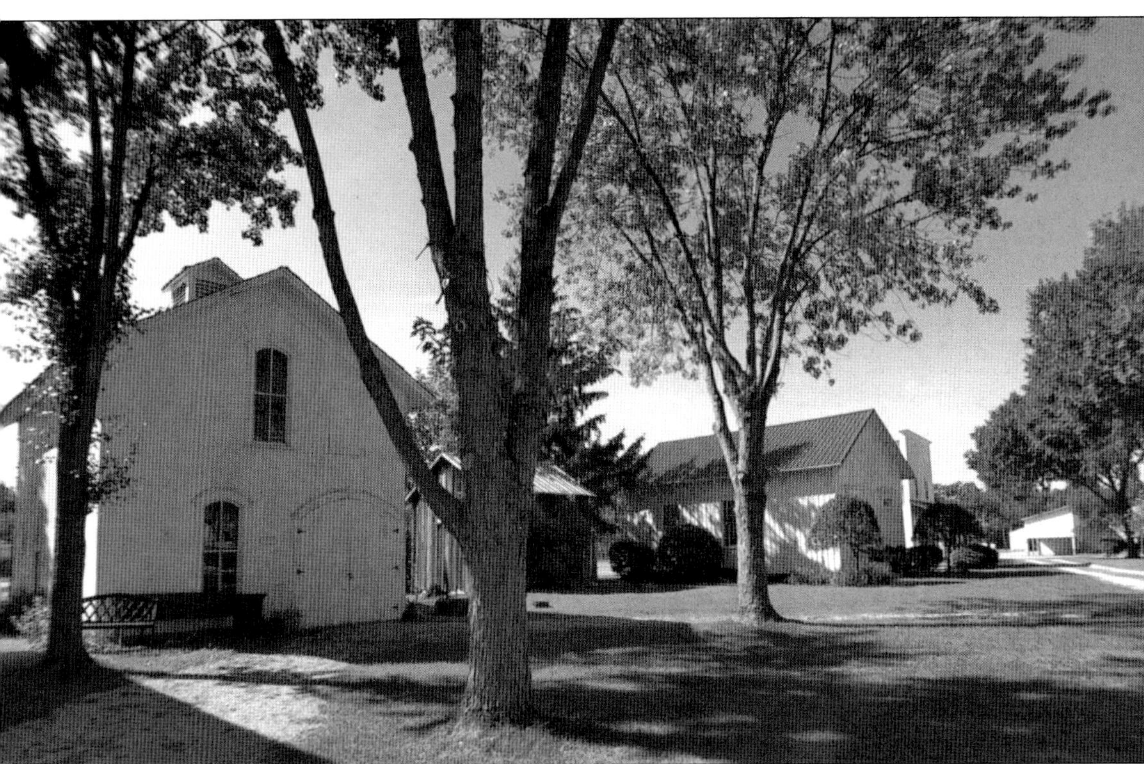

Jefferson Depot Village. Jefferson Depot Village is a living history museum in the heart of Jefferson. Located at the former Jefferson train station and the surrounding property, it features more than a dozen historic buildings that have been moved to the site. Included are the original Jefferson Methodist Church and its parsonage, an 1838 one-room schoolhouse, and an 1845 post office. (Author's collection.)

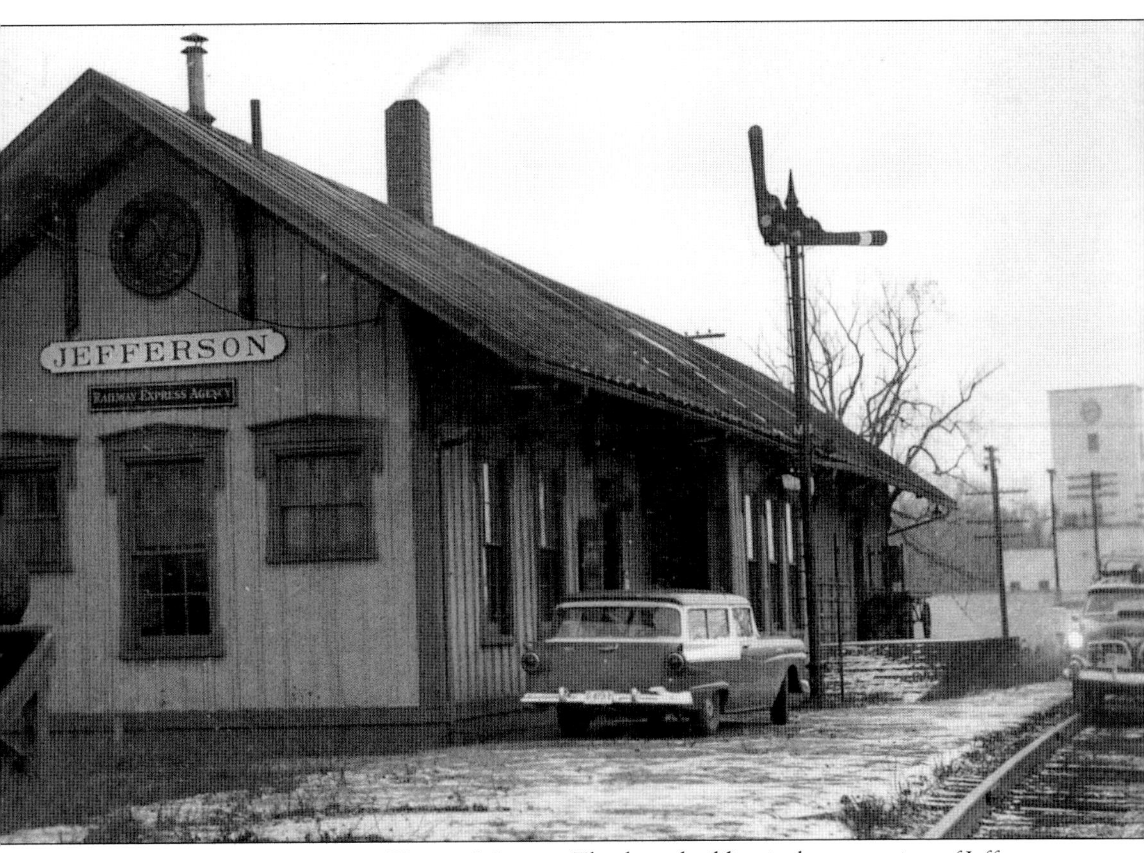

Jefferson Depot Village Living History Museum. The depot building is the centerpiece of Jefferson Depot Village. This building was constructed in 1872, with the freight room added in 1912. The building was purchased by the Jefferson Garden Club for $300, and the club started gradually to restore it. In 1981, the club purchased the 1.5 acres of land surrounding the depot from Conrail for $13,500 and formed the museum. (Author's collection.)

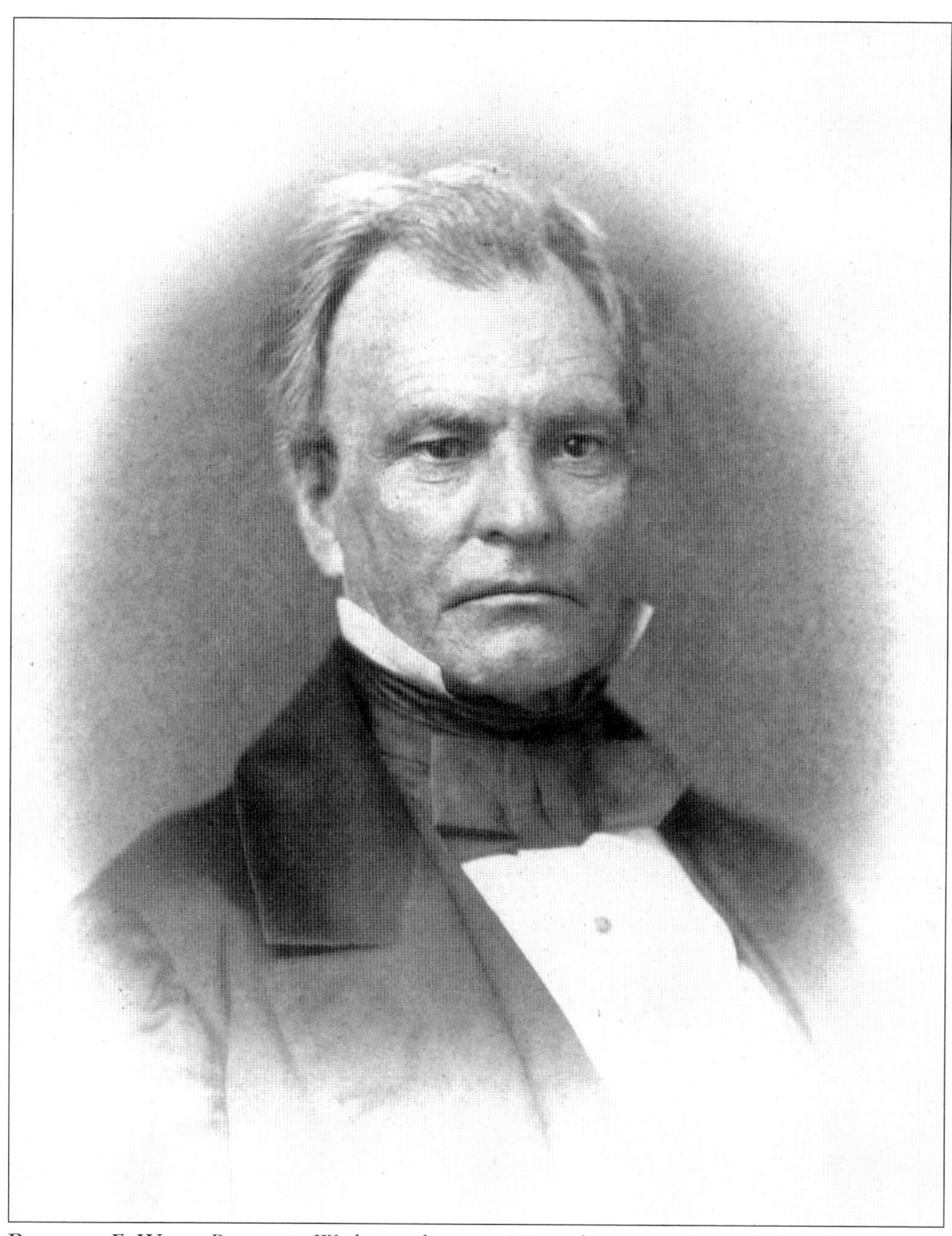

Benjamin F. Wade. Benjamin Wade was born in Massachusetts and traveled to the Western Reserve as a young man. One of his first jobs was as a laborer on the Erie Canal that connected Lake Erie to the Hudson River at Albany. He was a self-made man who became a local judge and a member of the Ohio State Senate before being elected to the US Senate in 1851. He was a vocal opponent of the Fugitive Slave Act and a supporter of women's suffrage and equality for African Americans. He served in the US Senate for 14 years. Wade and his wife, Caroline, were members of First Congregational Church in Jefferson. The couple had two sons, James and Henry. James was a career soldier who rose to the rank of major general in the US Army and served in the Civil and Spanish-American Wars. (Jefferson Historical Society.)

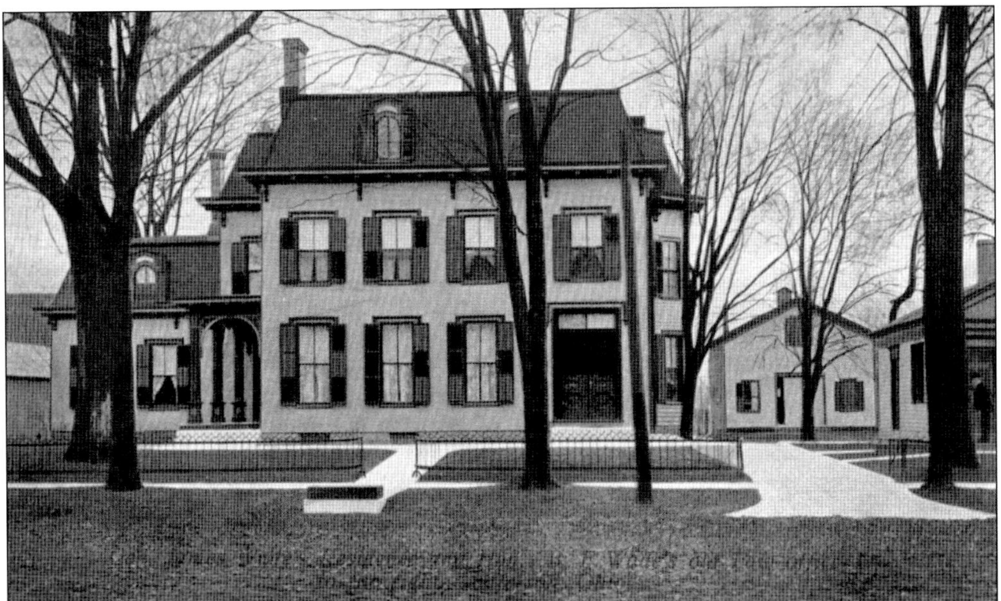

Benjamin Wade House. Located at 22 Jefferson Street across from the courthouse, the Benjamin Wade House was the home of the senator and his family. His son, James F. Wade, a Civil War and Spanish-American War veteran, and his family also lived in the house. (Library of Congress.)

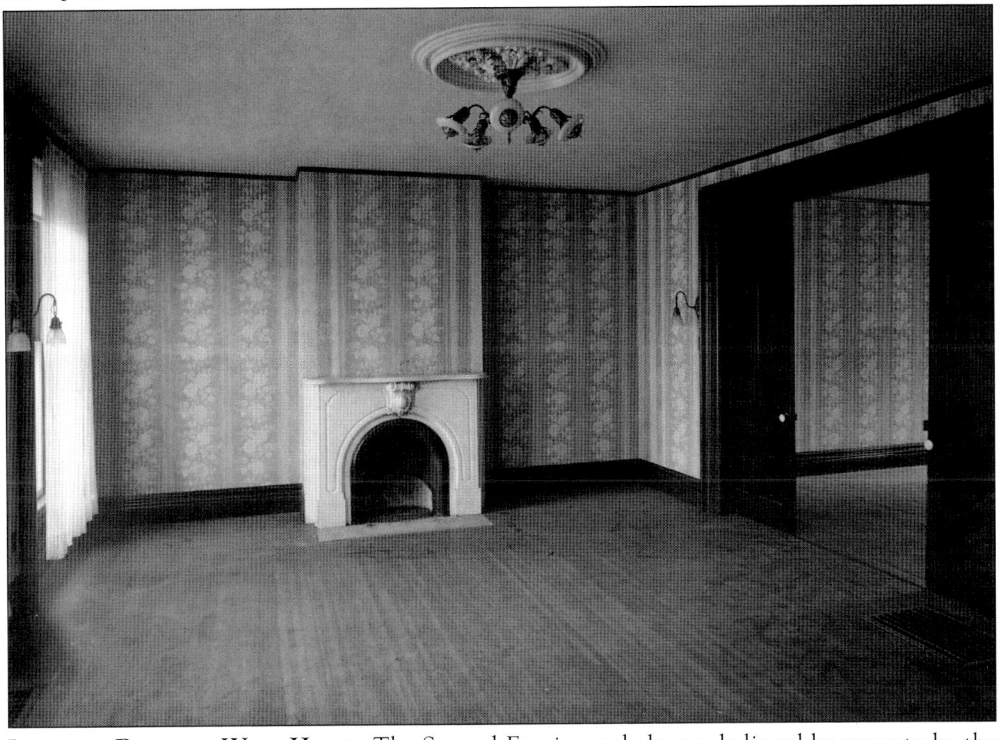

Interior, Benjamin Wade House. The Second Empire–style home, believed by many to be the most beautiful residence in Jefferson, was designed by John Watters. It was noted for its graceful lines and mansard roof. The house was razed in 1968, despite an enthusiastic, grassroots effort to save the structure. (Library of Congress.)

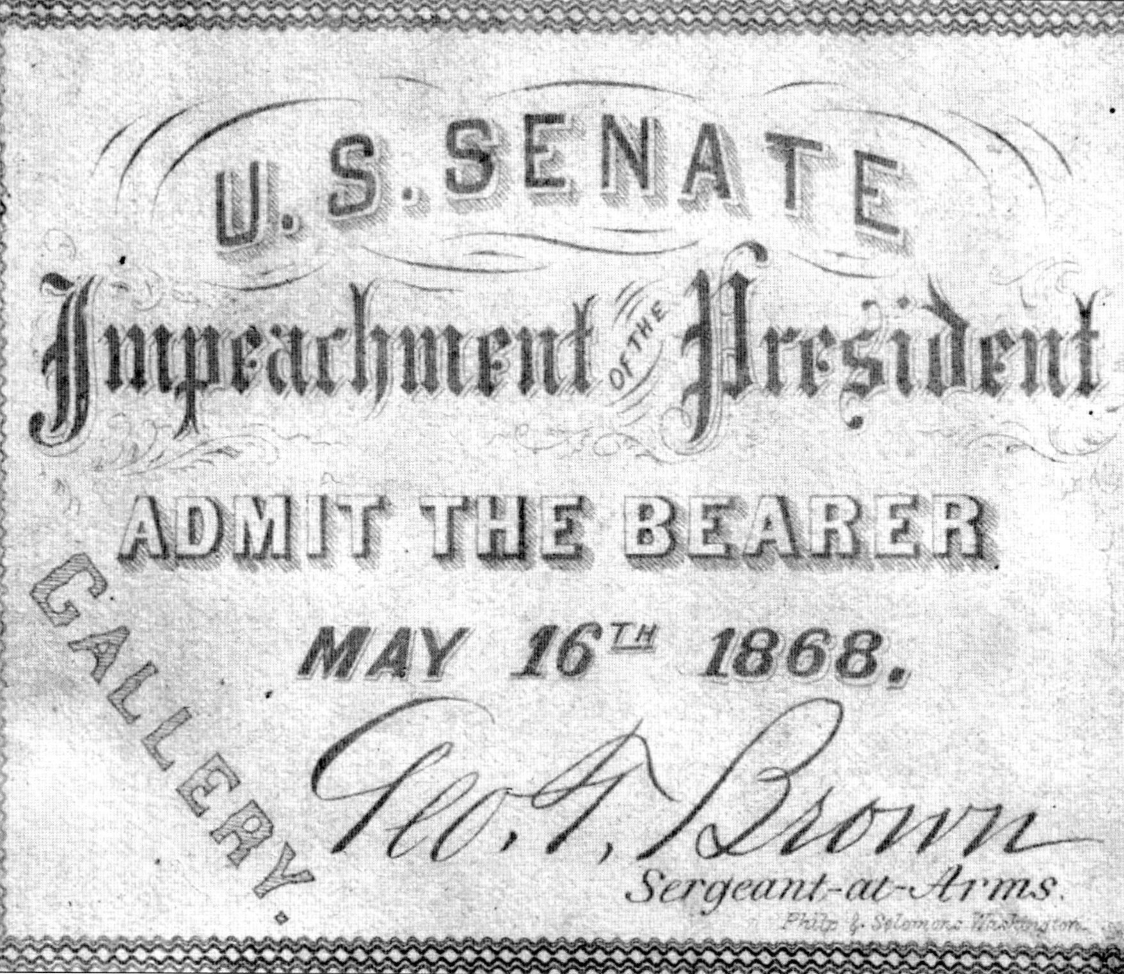

ANDREW JOHNSON SENATE IMPEACHMENT ADMISSION TICKET. Benjamin Wade served as president pro tempore of the Senate from 1867 to 1869. As such, he was in line to succeed Andrew Johnson had Johnson been impeached during his trial in 1868. If one more senator had voted for impeachment, Wade would have become president of the United States for the remaining nine months of Johnson's term. Admission to the proceedings was limited to members of Congress and ticket holders. (Ashtabula Historical Society.)

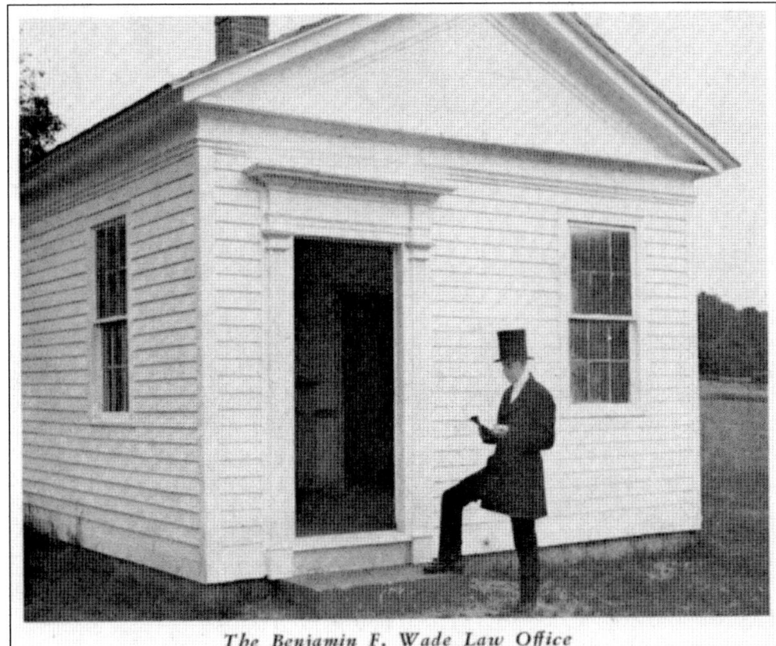

The Benjamin F. Wade Law Office

WADE LAW OFFICE. Unlike the Gidding Law Office, which stayed in Jefferson, the Wade Law Office, built in 1825, was moved to Hale Farm, a living history museum in Bath, Ohio, in 1977. The small, Federalist-style office was originally located adjacent to the Wade mansion on West Jefferson Street. (Ashtabula Historical Society.)

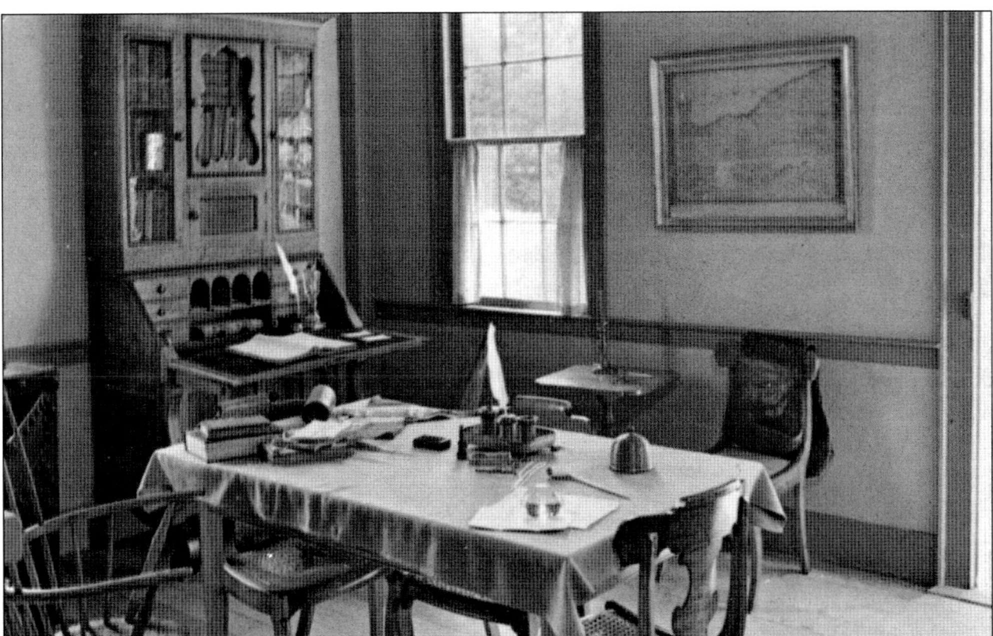

WADE LAW OFFICE INTERIOR. The Wade Law Office is open for the public to visit as part of Hale Farm's living history exhibits. The office is furnished with period-correct furniture and artifacts, several of which belonged to Senator Wade and the Wade family. (Author's collection.)

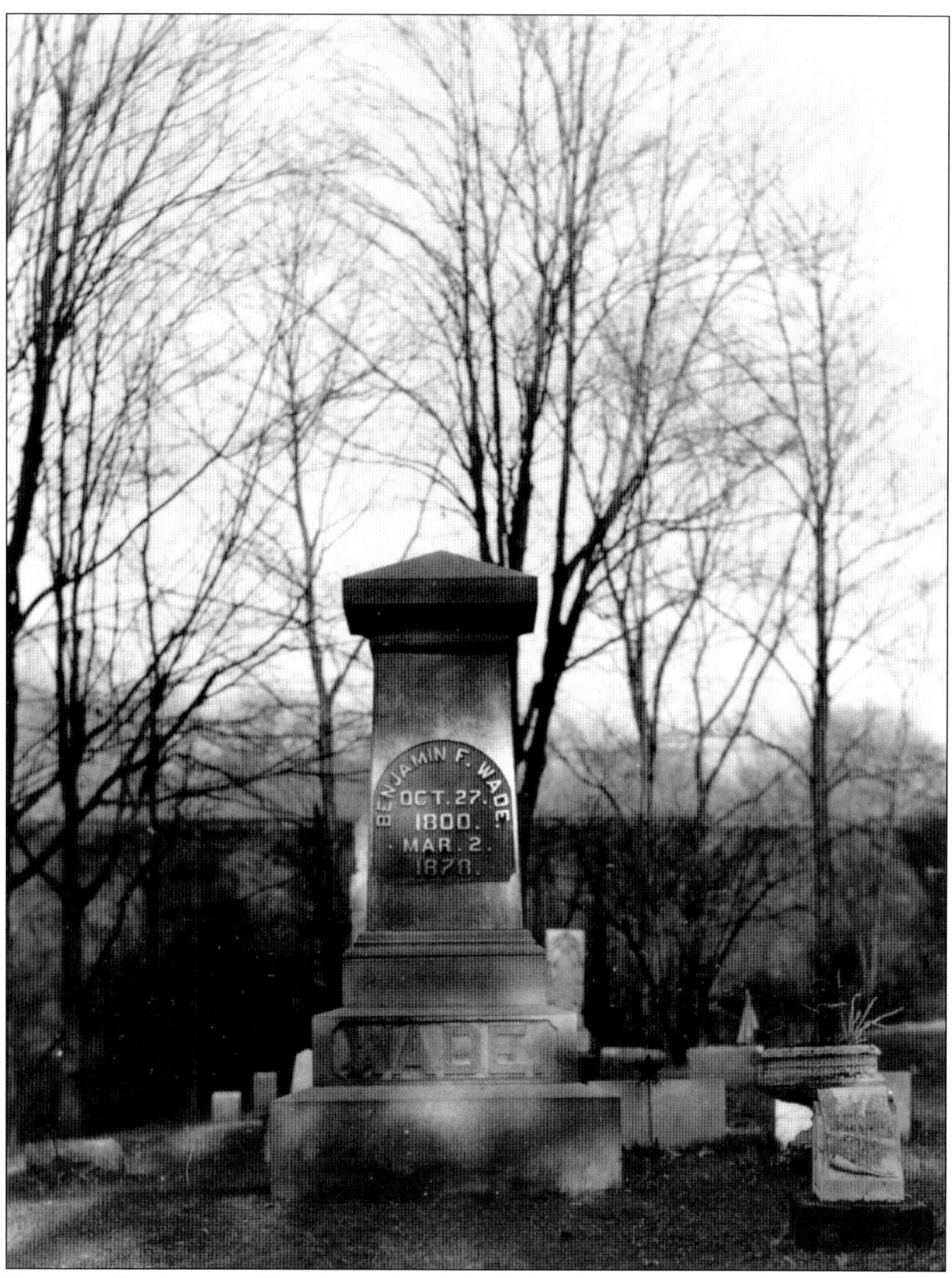

Benjamin Wade's Grave. Wade died on March 2, 1878, in Jefferson of typhoid fever. He is buried at Oakdale Cemetery in Jefferson alongside his wife, Caroline, and numerous relatives. The *New York Times*, a longtime critic of Wade, titled his obituary, "The Last of the Congressional Champions of Freedom." (Ashtabula Historical Society.)

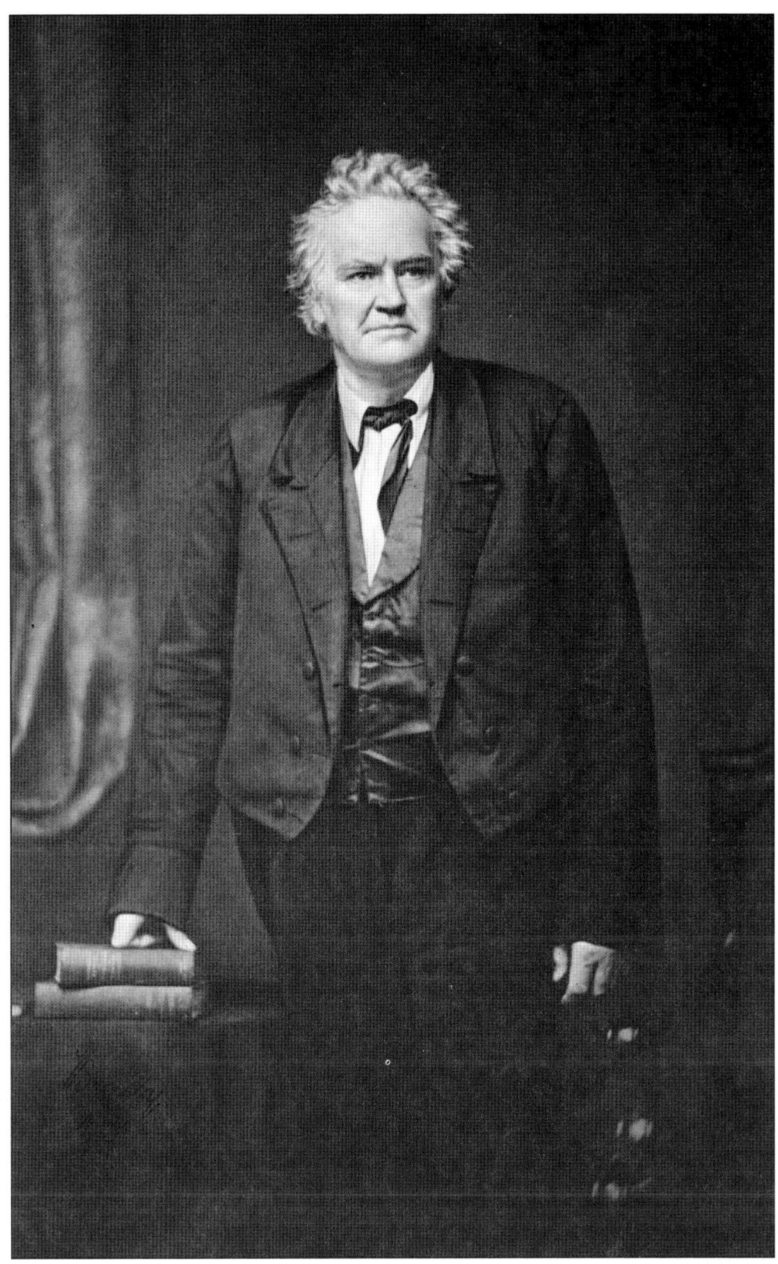

Joshua Reed Giddings. Joshua Reed Giddings was a prominent Ashtabula County lawyer and US congressman from 1838 to 1855. He was an ardent abolitionist and, with his friend and business partner Benjamin Wade, was largely responsible for Ashtabula County being a hotbed of antislavery sentiment in the years leading up to the Civil War. Giddings was also a founding member of the Republican Party. Giddings and his wife, Sarah, were founding members of First Congregational Church in Jefferson, and he served as a ruling elder (lay leader) of the church. The couple had eight children, five of whom survived into adulthood. After 20 years in Congress, Giddings was appointed by President Lincoln in 1861 to be the consul general in Montreal, Canada. Giddings held that position until his death in 1864. He is buried with his wife and many other relatives at Oakdale Cemetery in Jefferson. (Library of Congress.)

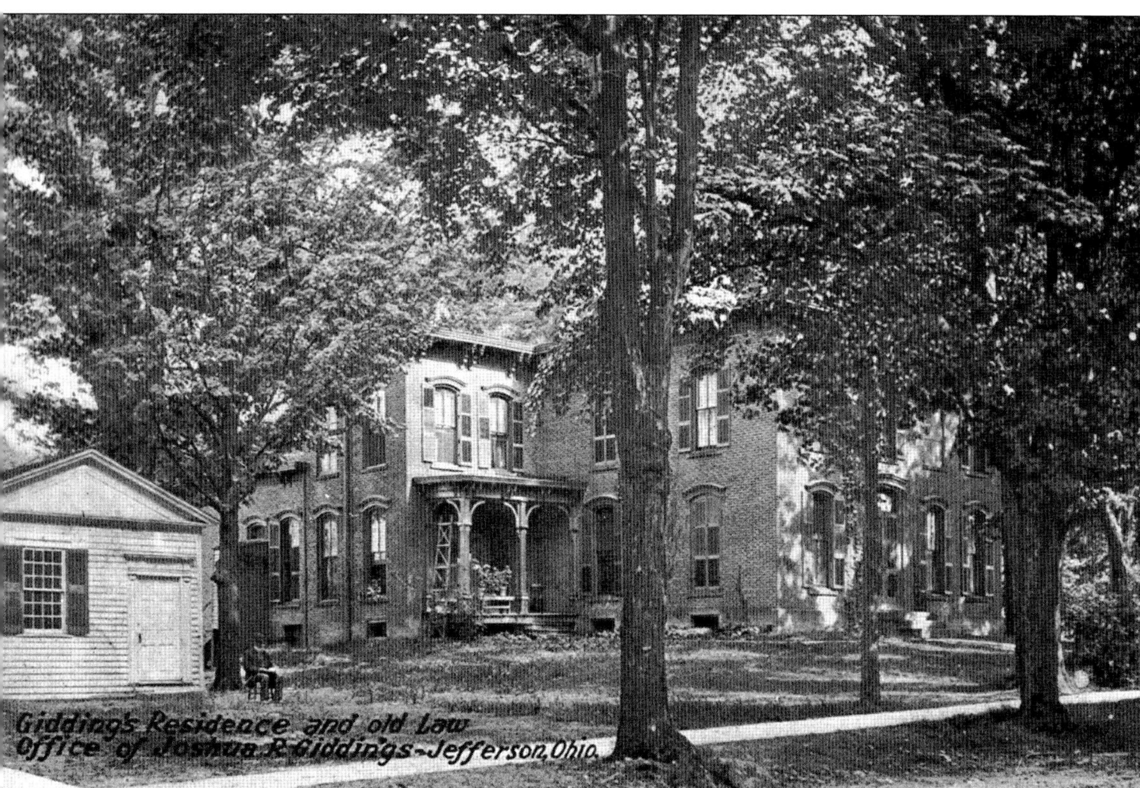

Joshua A. Giddings Home, c. 1910. Located on the northeast corner of North Chestnut and East Walnut Streets, the Giddings home was a modest, wood-frame structure. It was destroyed by fire in the 1870s, shortly after Giddings's death. His son J.A. Giddings built a large, two-story brick Italianate home on the lot. That house, too, no longer exists. (Jefferson Historical Society.)

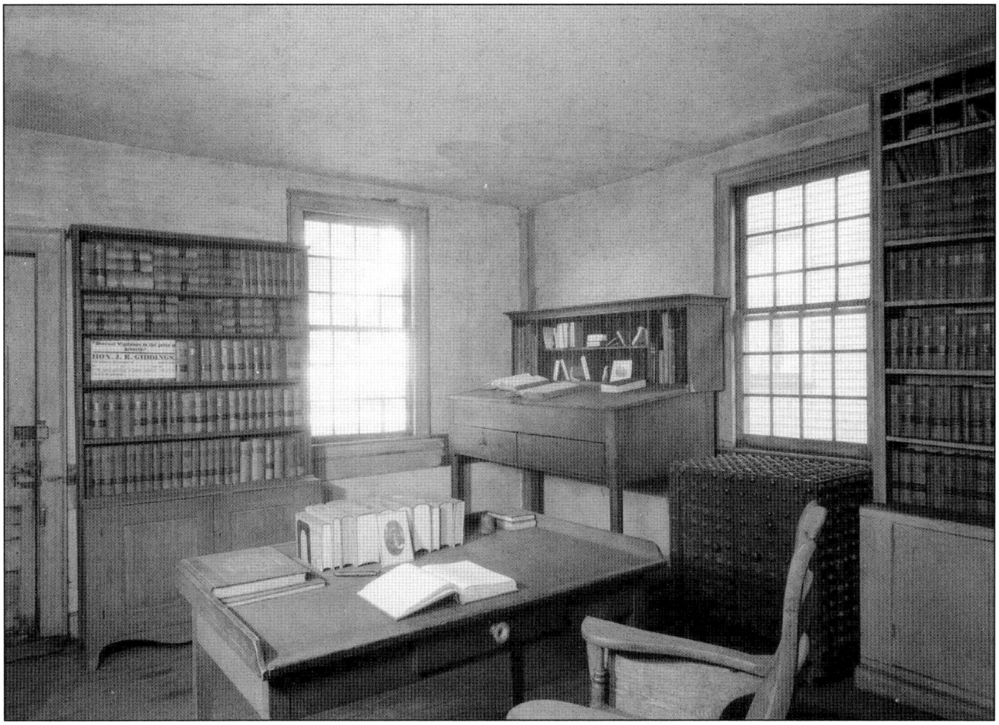

Gidding Home and Law Office, 1960. Joshua Giddings's law office, constructed in 1823, was originally located on North Chestnut Street, where McDonald's now sits. The modest law office was saved through a private fundraising effort in 1932. Despite being in the middle of the Great Depression, individuals donated between 50¢ and $25 to preserve the building. It was moved to Giddings Park on the east side of town and has been preserved as a museum. The office, a national historic landmark, is now owned by the Ashtabula County Historical Society and is open to the public during the summer months. (Above, Library of Congress; below, Jefferson Historical Society.)

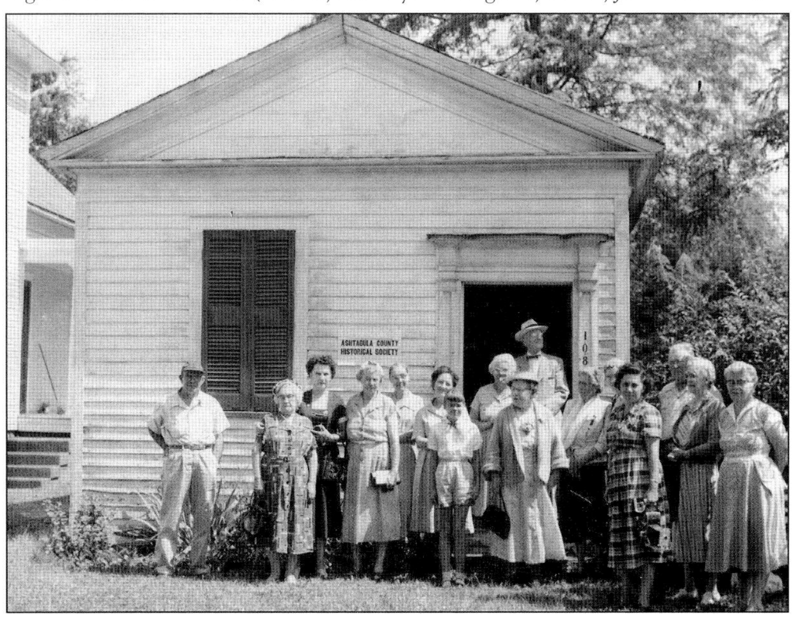

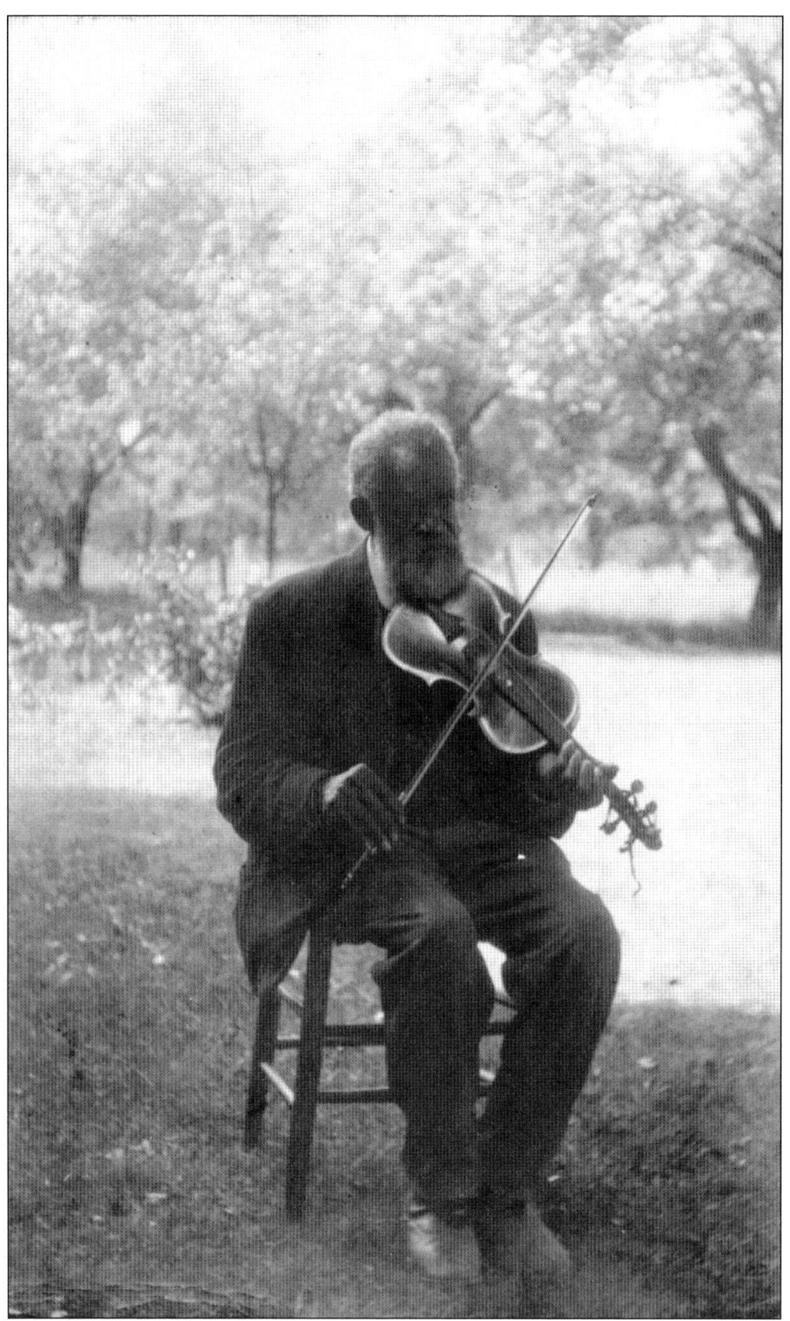

Charley Garlick. Charley A. Garlick, born Abel Bogguess, was a former slave who traveled through Ashtabula County from Virginia and liked the area so well that he decided to stay. Although uneducated when he arrived, Garlick quickly sailed through the local public schools and graduated from Oberlin College, one of the first colleges to admit black students. Garlick fought in the Civil War as a part of the 3rd Regiment, US Colored Heavy Artillery; worked as a lumberjack in Canada; and returned to Jefferson in his later years. He became good friends with Joshua R. Giddings and lived with Giddings's family and, later, in the back room of the Giddings Law Office. Garlick died at age 95 and is buried in Jefferson's Oakdale Cemetery. (Ashtabula County District Library.)

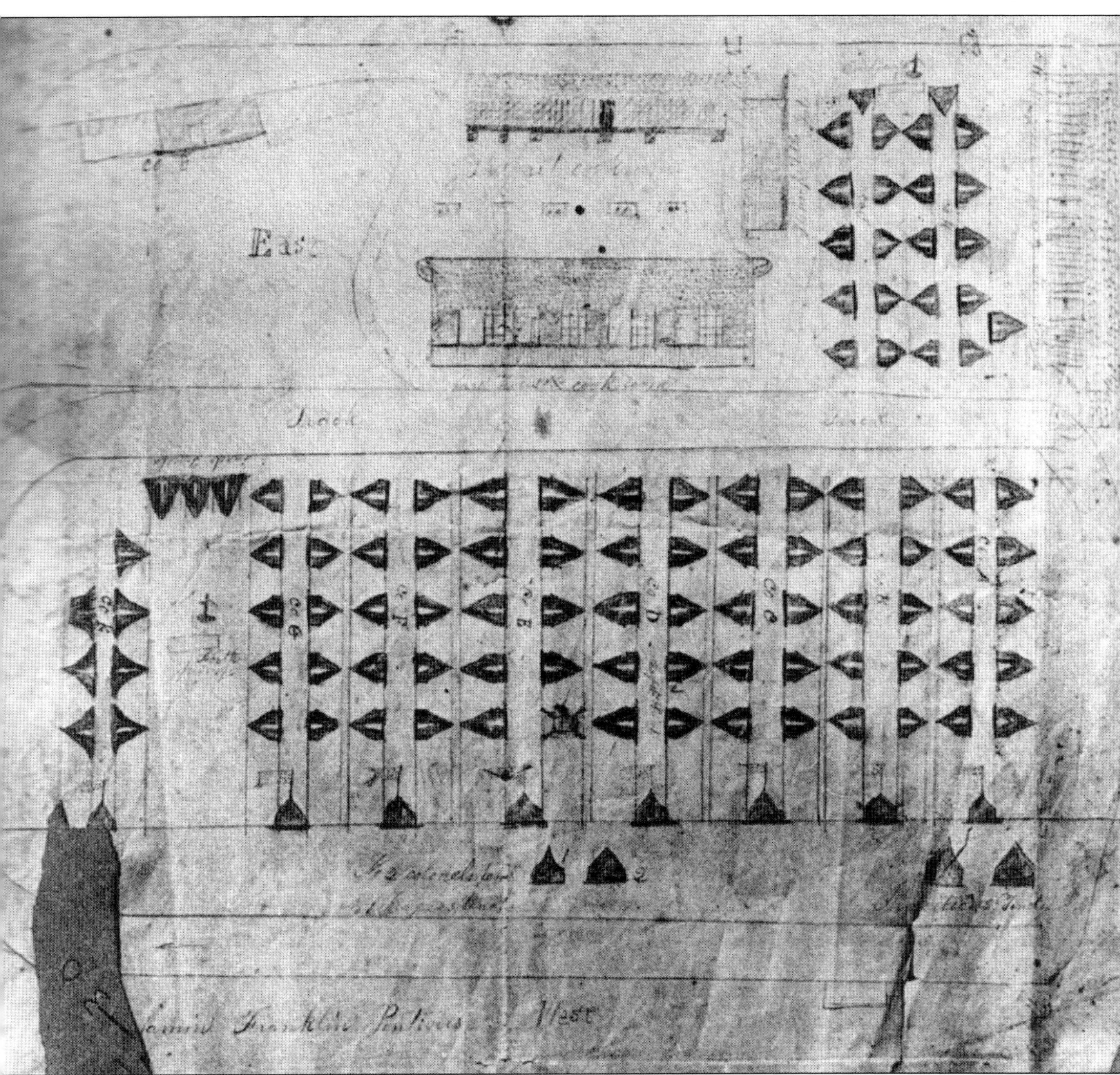

Camp Giddings. Camp Giddings, named for Joshua R. Giddings, was located on the site of the current Ashtabula County Fairgrounds. The camp served as a training and mustering facility for Union soldiers during the Civil War. The 29th Regiment, Ohio Volunteer Infantry (OVI) was organized at Camp Giddings in August 1861. A member of the regiment was so impressed by the layout of the camp that he sketched this drawing of Camp Giddings to take home and show his mother. The regiment had 1,529 members and saw action at Antietam, Chancellorsville, and Gettysburg. They lost 120 members to fighting and 151 to disease and illness before the conflict was over. The company's last battle was at Goldsboro, North Carolina, on March 23, 1865. The 29th Regiment, OVI disbanded on July 22, 1865, at Cleveland. (Ashtabula County District Library.)

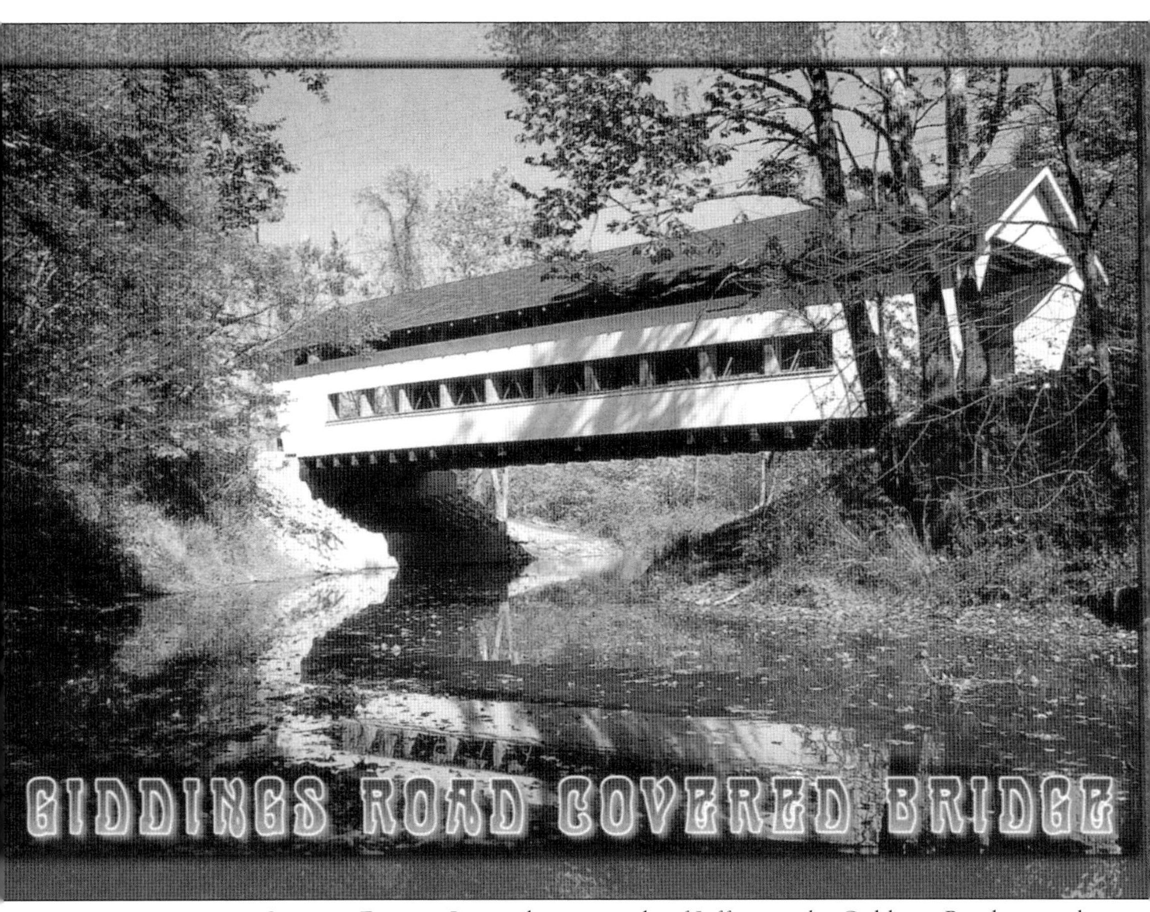

Giddings Road Covered Bridge. Located just outside of Jefferson, the Giddings Road covered bridge is one of 19 covered bridges in Ashtabula County. This one, constructed in 1995 using a traditional Pratt truss design, spans Mill Creek and measures 107 feet long, 22 feet wide, and 14 feet high. (Author's collection.)

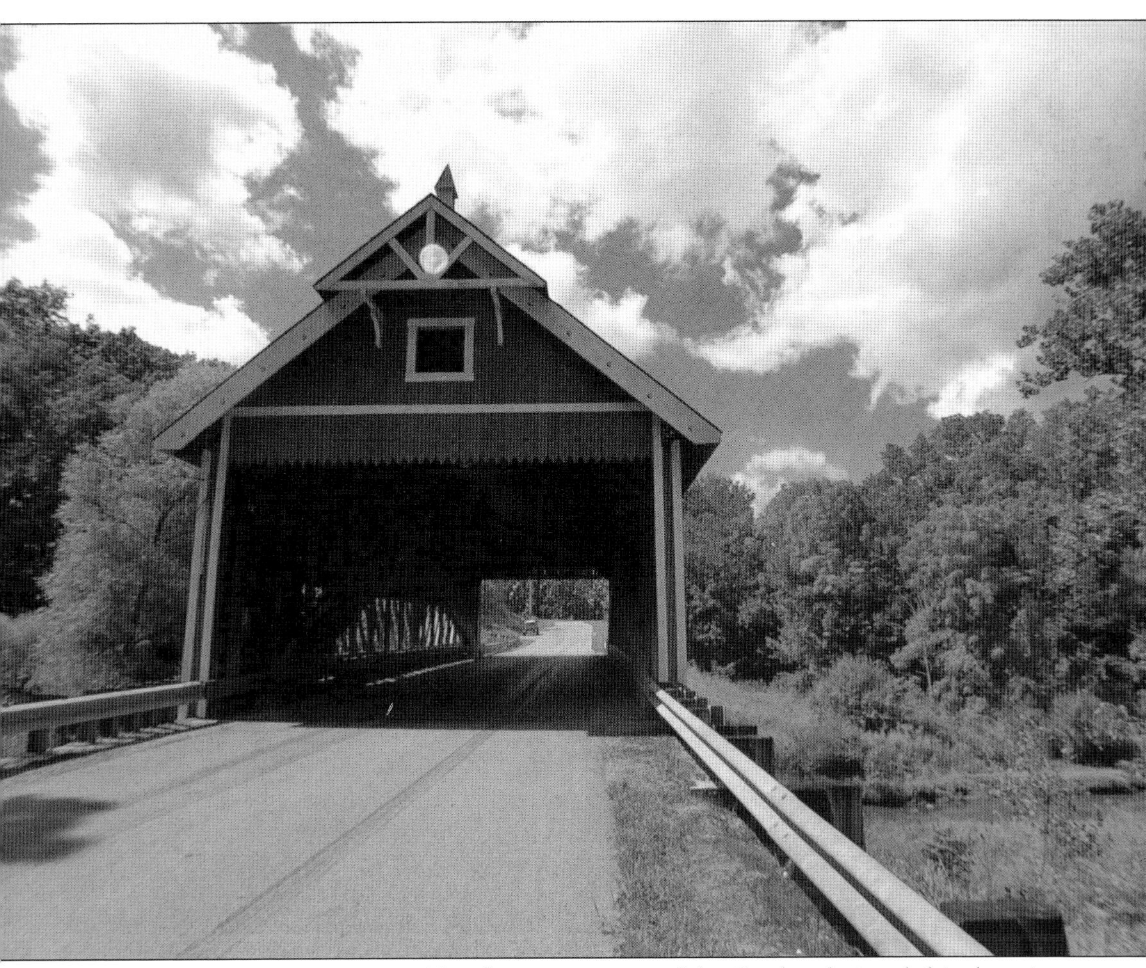

Netcher Road Covered Bridge. Noted county engineer John Smolen designed this charming covered bridge in Sheffield Township, just east of Jefferson, in 1998. The 110-foot-long, single-span bridge is designed using a timber arch construction with inverted Haupt walls. Ashtabula County celebrates all its 19 covered bridges the second full weekend of October for the annual Covered Bridge Festival. (Author's collection.)

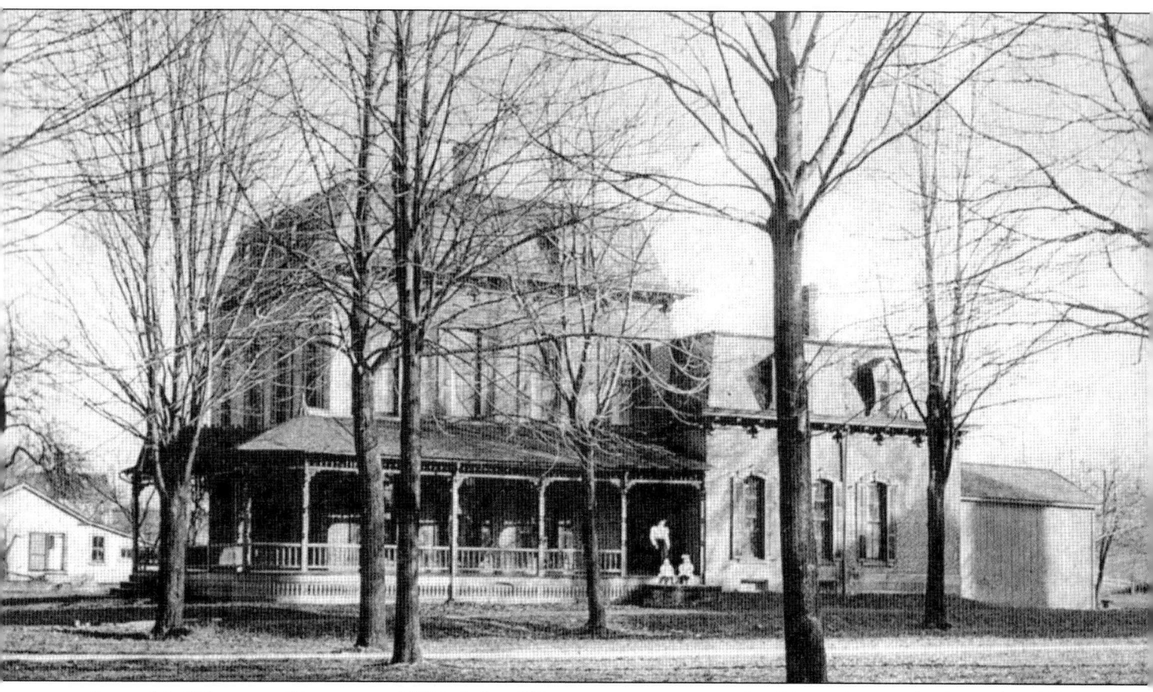

JOHN M. WATTERS HOUSE, C. 1908. John Watters was a master builder who worked on the 1870 Jefferson Educational Institute as well as the Beckwith House and the Benjamin Wade House. The Second Empire–style Watters home, constructed of brick with a mansard roof, was located just east of the old Jefferson High School building. (Jefferson Historical Society.)

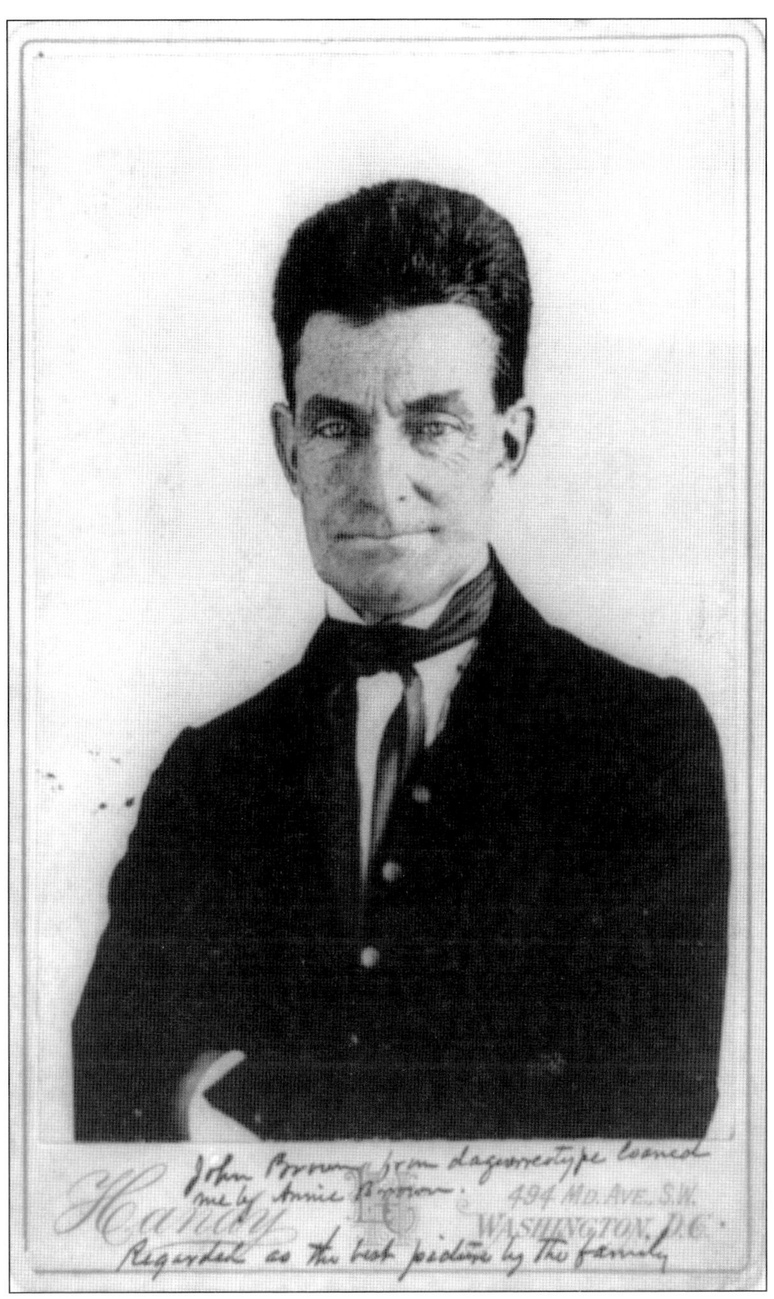

John Brown. John Brown, the abolitionist who led the raid on the arsenal at Harpers Ferry, Maryland, on October 16–18, 1859, had strong ties to Jefferson and Ashtabula County. He preached at the Jefferson Congregational Church, which took up a collection to help Brown with his work against slavery. Brown also met with Congressman Giddings to discuss the abolitionist cause. The weapons used at the raid on Harpers Ferry were stored for a time in a barn in Wayne Township that belonged to Brown's son's wife's sister and her husband. Thirteen of Brown's 21 recruits for the Harpers Ferry raid hailed from Ashtabula County. Brown was tried and found guilty of treason for his role in the raid. He became the first person to be executed for treason in the United States. (Library of Congress.)

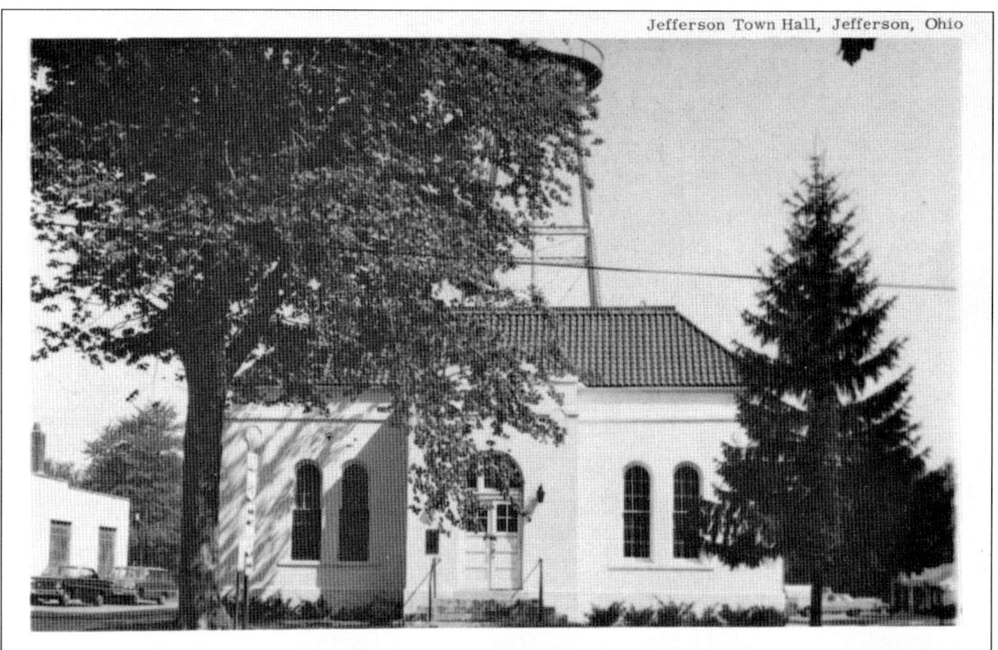

JEFFERSON TOWN HALL. Jefferson Town Hall, located just east of the courthouse on Market Street, was built between 1877 and 1880 at a cost of $12,000. The building was originally a three-story, Victorian-style structure. The second floor housed an auditorium/opera house that was used for concerts and other public functions. The top two floors were destroyed by fire in 1927 and were never rebuilt. It is barely recognizable as the same building that stands there today. (Ashtabula District Library Archives.)

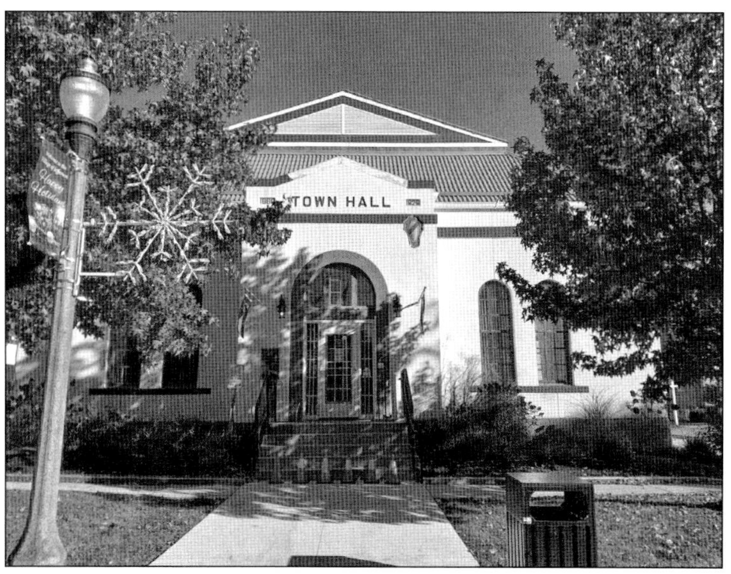

JEFFERSON TOWN HALL TODAY. There used to be a large water tower located directly behind the Jefferson Town Hall. It was erected in 1908 and taken down in 1968. Today, the Jefferson Town Hall houses the mayor's office, city council chambers, and other city administrative offices. The building was added to the National Register of Historic Places in 1981. (Author's collection.)

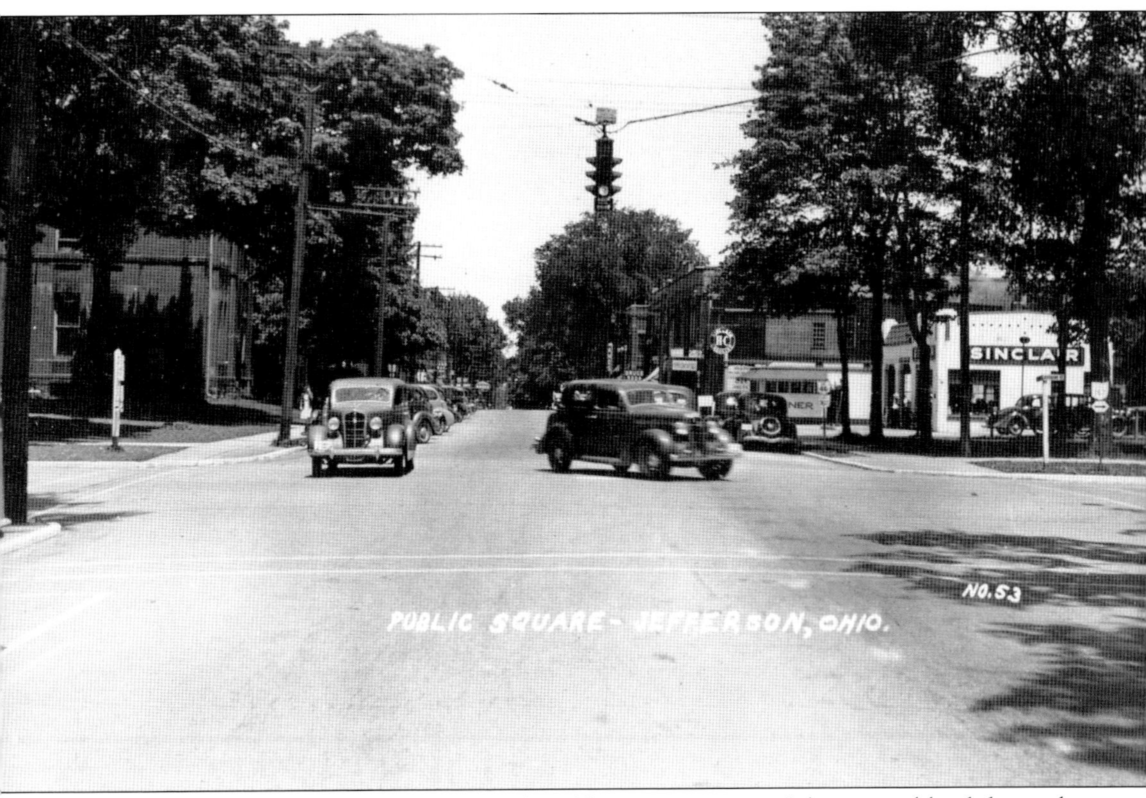

JEFFERSON PUBLIC SQUARE, 1930S. Jefferson's public square is part of the original land donated by Gideon Granger in 1811. Today, the square, at the corner of Chestnut and Jefferson Streets, is home to a gazebo and the village's electronic billboard. (Ashtabula County Historical Society.)

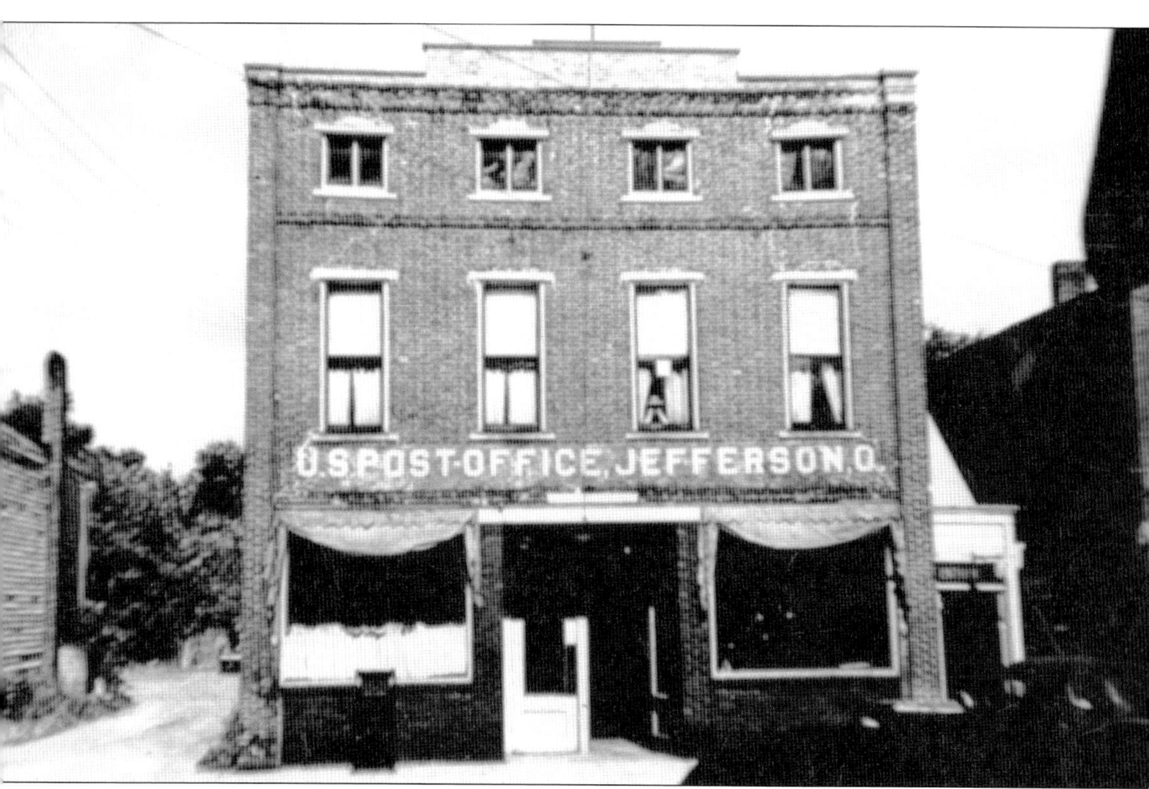

JEFFERSON POST OFFICE, 1950s. The first Jefferson Post Office was established in 1808, with mail carriers traveling twice a week from Jefferson to Unionville and back and once a week between Jefferson and Meadville, Pennsylvania. The office, pictured here, dates to the early 1920s and was located at 42 South Chestnut Street. The Jefferson Post Office moved to its current location on West Jefferson Street in 1959. (Ashtabula District Library Archives.)

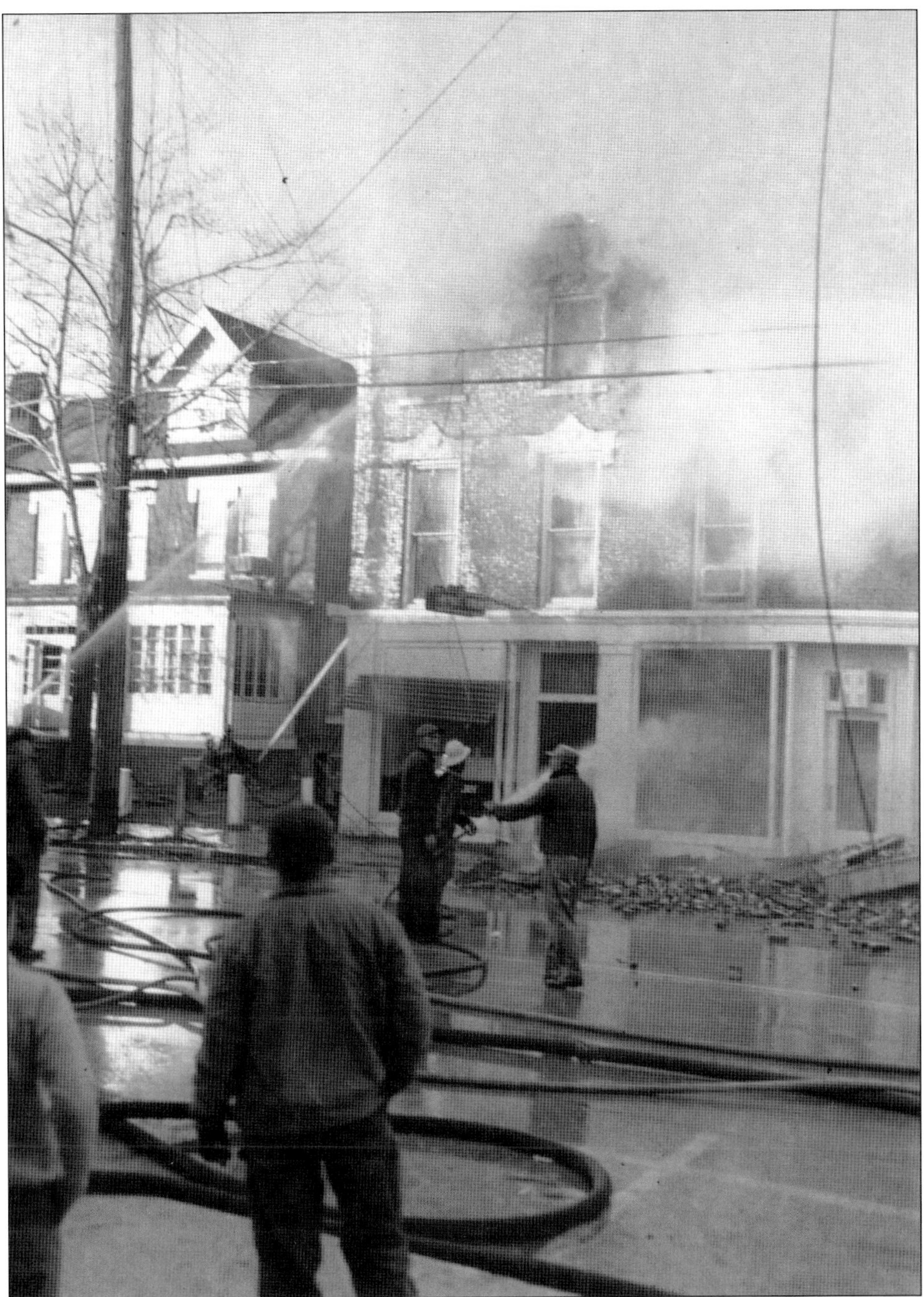

Fighting Fire in Jefferson. The Jefferson Fire Department was established in 1837 as the Phoenix Hose Company. It was renamed the Wade Hose Company in 1880 and is now known as the Jefferson Volunteer Fire Department. A new library and fire hall complex was constructed in 1909. The village of Jefferson suffered two major downtown fires: one in 1906 that destroyed much of the Warner-Wolcott block, Cornwall block, Jefferson Banking Company, and *Jefferson Gazette* buildings, and one in 1960 (pictured here) that destroyed much of the retail blocks on North Chestnut Street, just north of the courthouse. (Ashtabula County District Library Archives.)

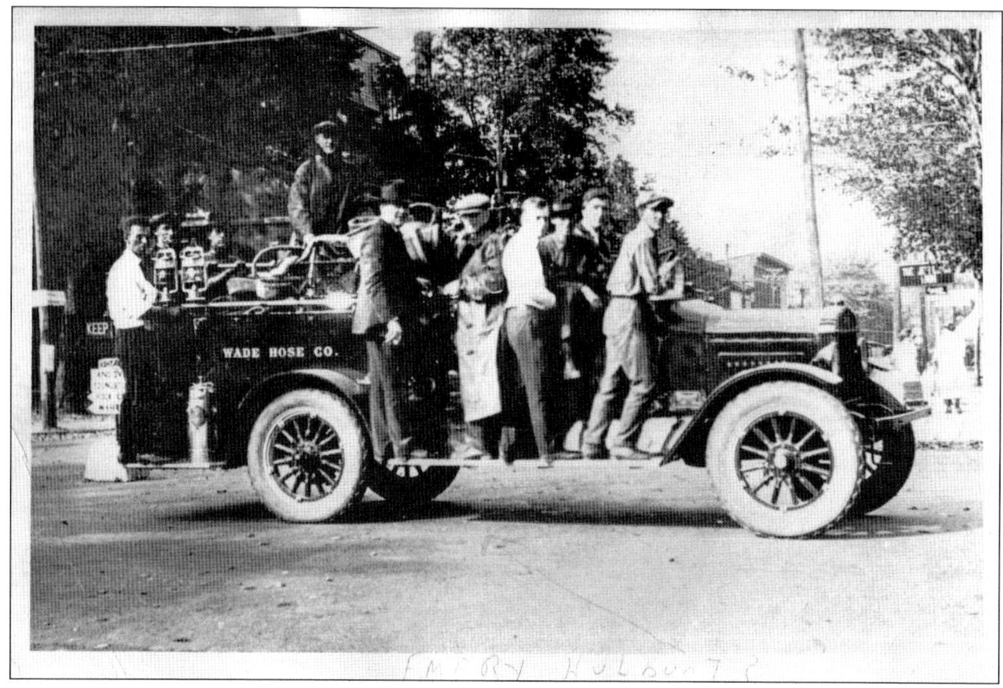

WADE HOSE FIRE COMPANY. The Jefferson Fire Department used the Wade Hose name (after the senator) until the 1990s. Equipment was limited to a single hand pumper until 1906, which took 10 men to operate. The company bought its first motorized truck in 1921, and in 1936, the city raised $4,150 to purchase a Ward LaFrance truck with a 500-gallon water tank and a rotary pump to increase water pressure. (Jefferson Historical Society.)

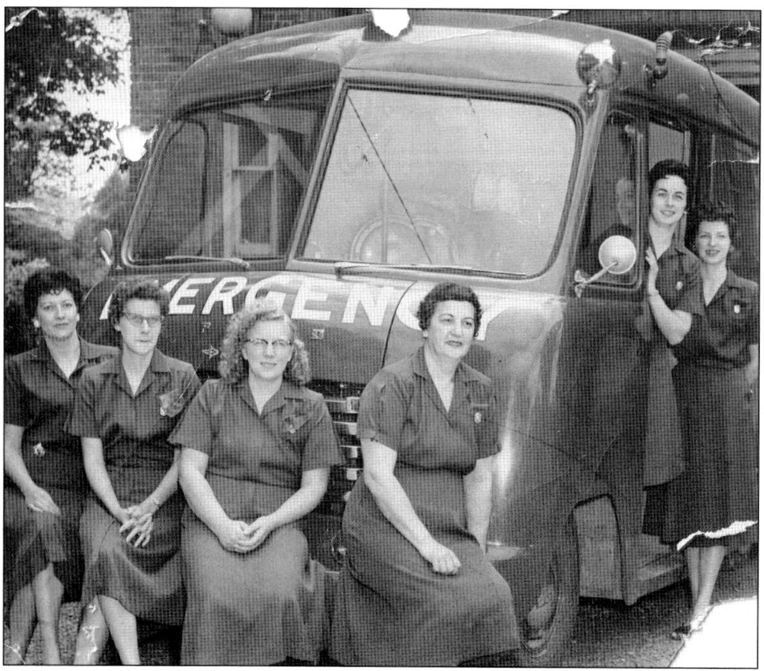

"FIRE JETS." Members of the women's auxiliary of the Wade Hose Fire Company were known as the Fire Jets. Pictured are, from left to right, Betty Brinninger, Shirley Case, Sophie Rieshka, Gladys Fink, Jane Vesey, and Adeline Bailey. (Jefferson Historical Society.)

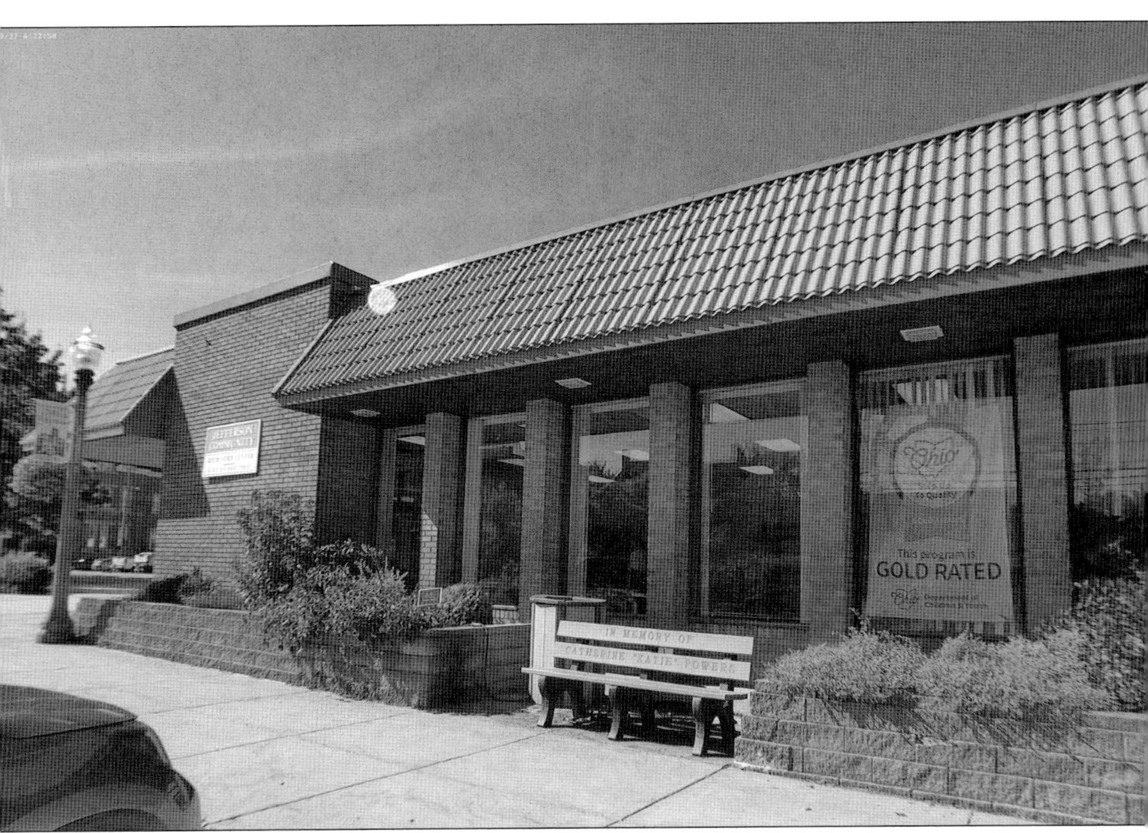

Jefferson Community Center. The Jefferson Community Center, located on East Jefferson Street across from the courthouse, was constructed in 1977. The building, located just east of the courthouse on Jefferson Street, houses the Jefferson Senior Center and is used for a full calendar of community events. (Author's collection.)

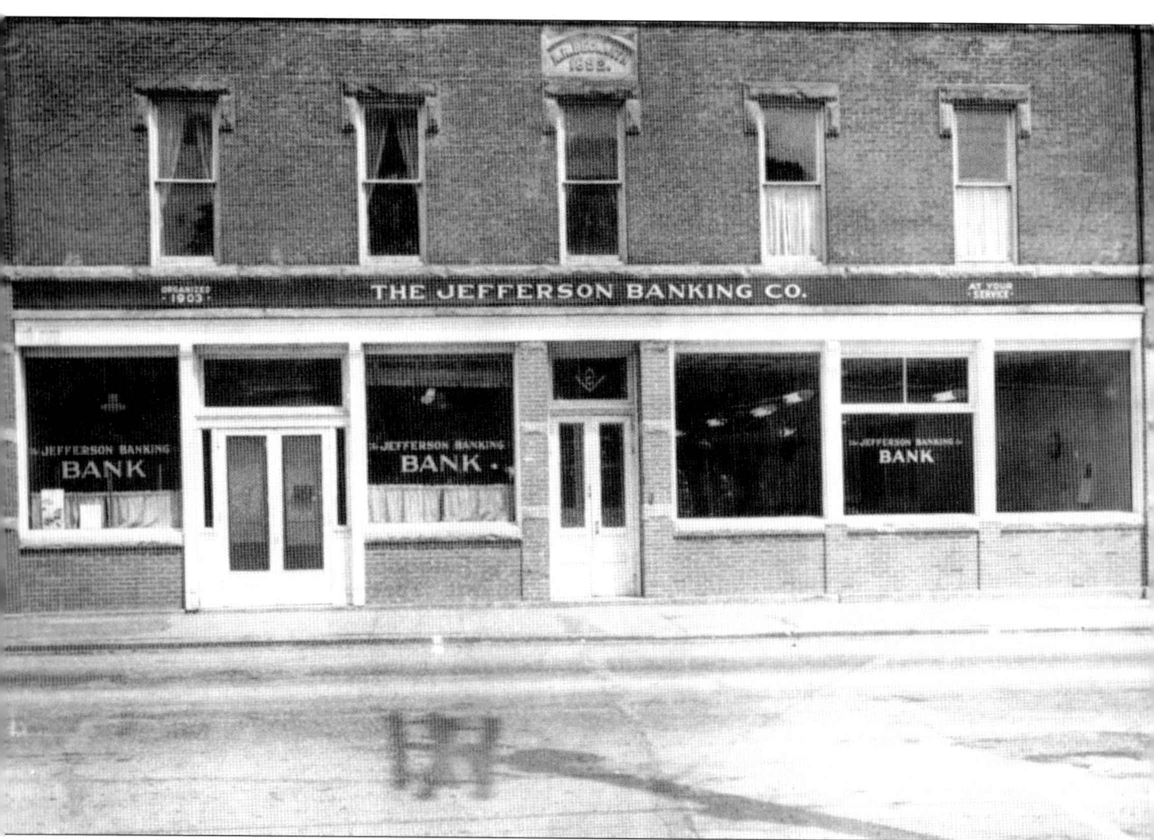

Jefferson Banking Company, 1955. The Jefferson Banking Company was founded in 1903 and was first located in the Cornwall block on the east side of North Chestnut Street. That building burned to the ground in the big fire of 1906, but the bank's safe and its contents survived. The company quickly rebuilt at the same location. Jefferson Banking Company merged with First National Bank in 1926 and moved to the Masonic building at 14 South Chestnut Street. They moved to a new building in 1964. (Ashtabula County Historical Society.)

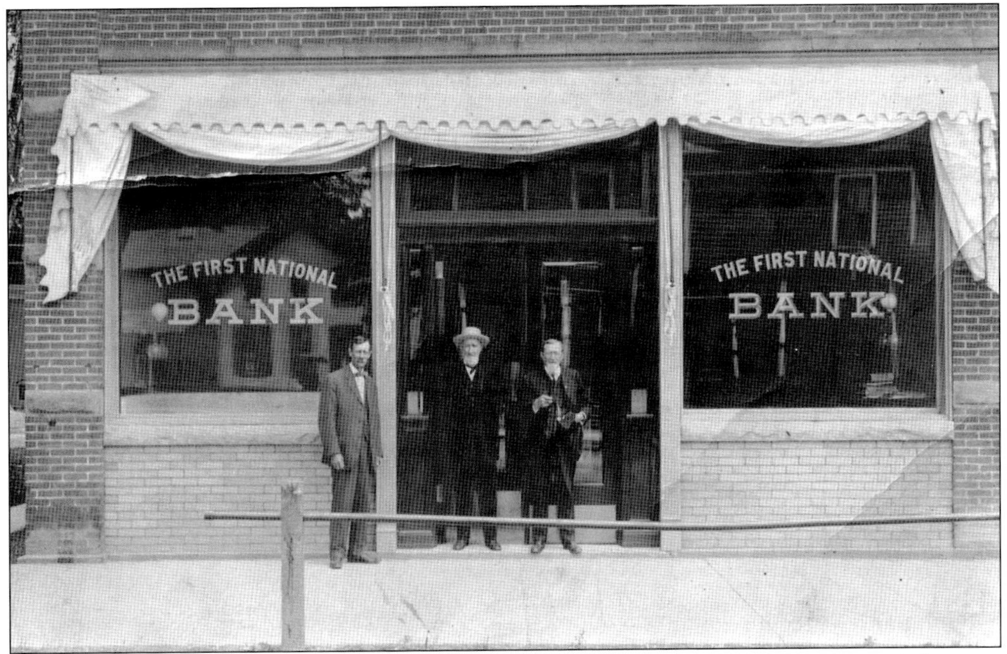

First National Bank. The First National Bank in Jefferson was established in 1864 with $70,000 in funds. Henry Talcott became the director in 1869. (Ashtabula County Historical Society.)

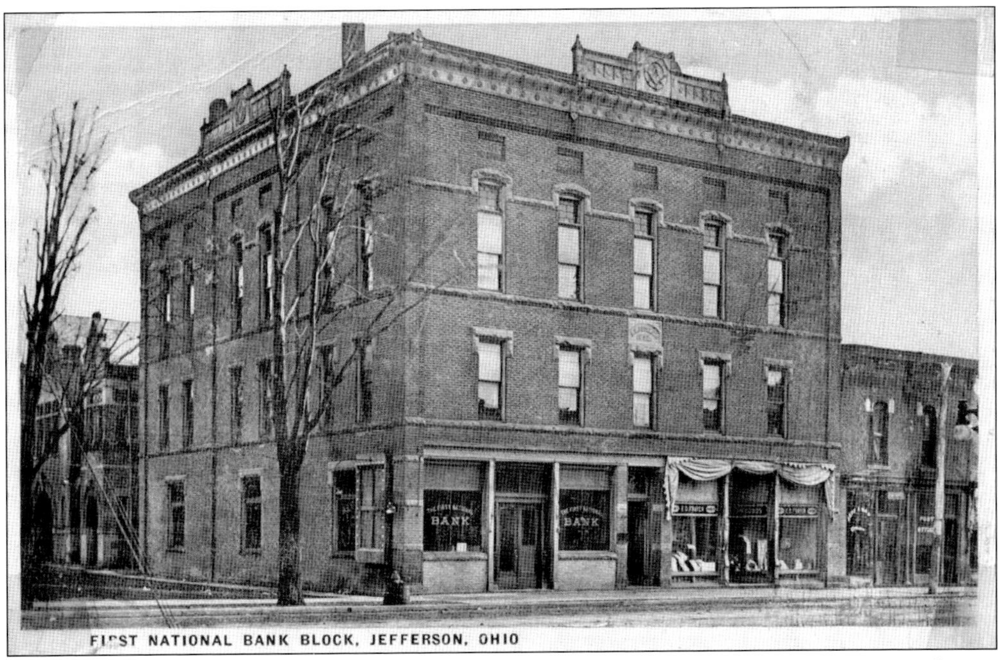

First National Bank Block, c. 1922. The brick bank building was located on West Jefferson Street, just east of the Wade family mansion. (Jefferson Historical Society.)

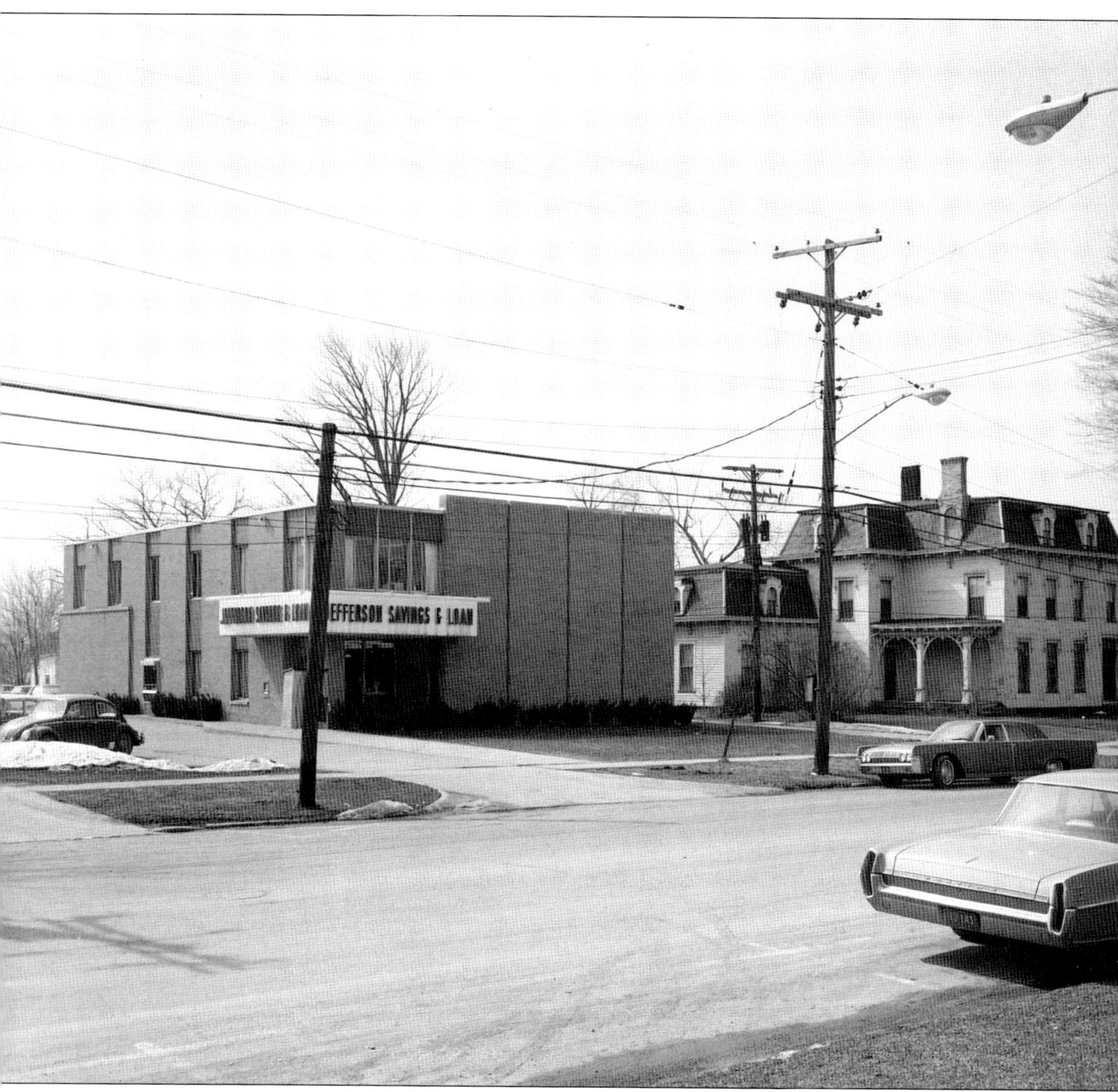

JEFFERSON SAVINGS AND LOAN. The original Jefferson Savings and Loan Association was established in 1869, also by Henry Talcott and other local businessmen, with initial funding of $50,000. He changed the name to the Second National Bank in 1872 and appointed local attorney S.A. Northway as president. The bank closed unexpectedly in 1882. Northway was indicted on several counts of misappropriating funds in relation to the bank closing. The case was in the courts for five years, but Northway was eventually acquitted on all charges. The company that bore the same name in the 1950s (pictured) is no relation to the original Jefferson Savings and Loan. (Library of Congress.)

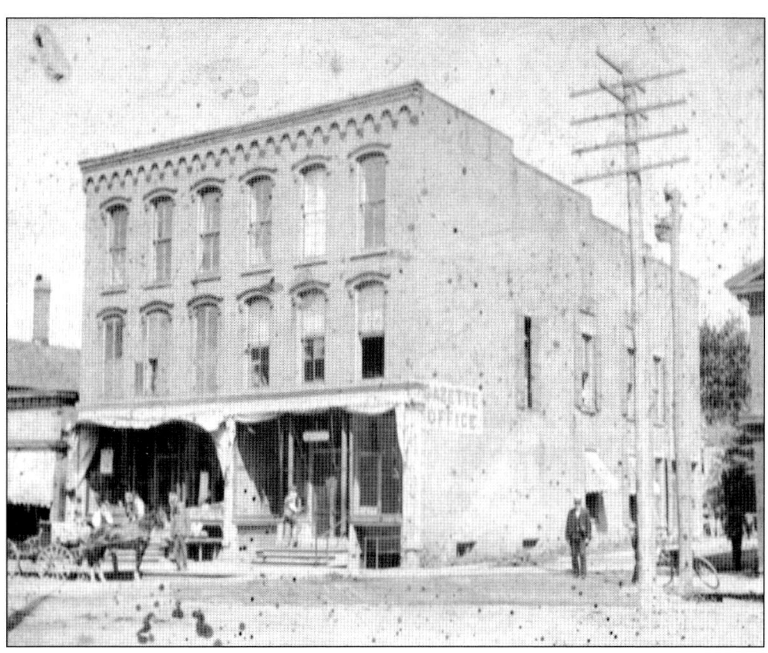

JEFFERSON GAZETTE. The *Jefferson Gazette* was founded in 1876 by D. Lee & Son and continued by E.L. Lampson, who purchased the paper in 1883. The company is still run by the Lampson family, now in the fifth generation, and today includes four weekly newspapers, a monthly paper, and a printing business. (Ashtabula County Historical Society.)

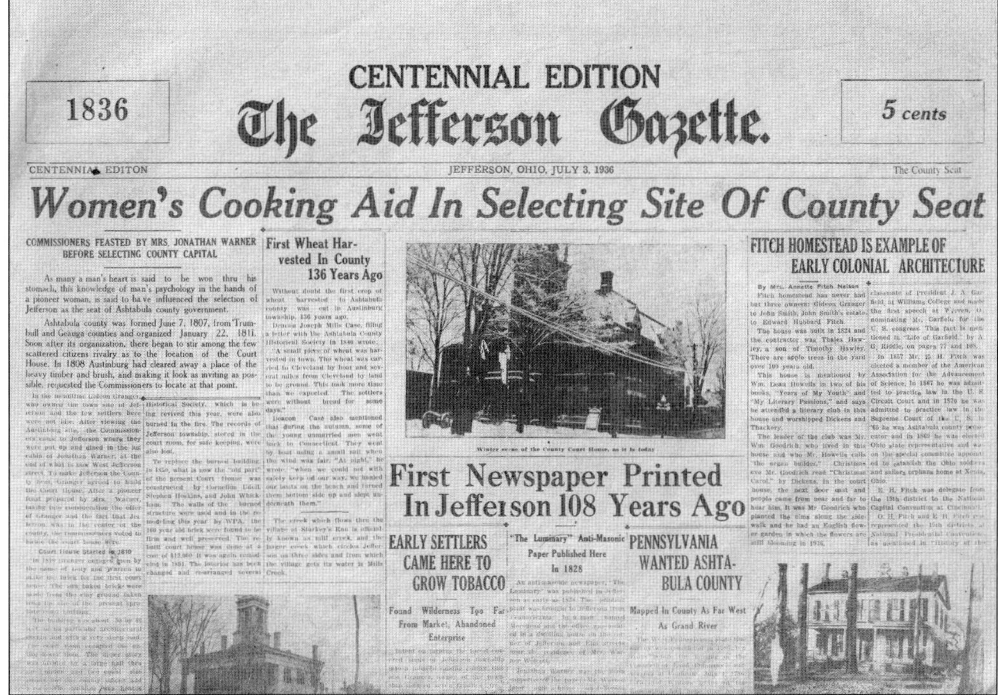

CENTENNIAL EDITION

1836 — The Jefferson Gazette. — 5 cents

CENTENNIAL EDITON — JEFFERSON, OHIO, JULY 3, 1936 — The County Seat

Women's Cooking Aid In Selecting Site Of County Seat

COMMISSIONERS FEASTED BY MRS. JONATHAN WARNER BEFORE SELECTING COUNTY CAPITAL

As many a man's heart is said to be won thru his stomach, this knowledge of man's psychology in the hands of a pioneer woman, is said to have influenced the selection of Jefferson as the seat of Ashtabula county government.

Ashtabula county was formed June 7, 1807, from Trumbull and Geauga counties and organized January 22, 1811. Soon after its organization, there began to stir among the few scattered citizens rivalry as to the location of the Court House. In 1808 Austinburg had cleared away a place of the heavy timber and brush, and making it look as inviting as possible, requested the Commissioners to locate at that point.

First Wheat Harvested In County 136 Years Ago

FITCH HOMESTEAD IS EXAMPLE OF EARLY COLONIAL ARCHITECTURE

By Mrs. Annette Fitch Nelson

First Newspaper Printed In Jefferson 108 Years Ago

EARLY SETTLERS CAME HERE TO GROW TOBACCO

Found Wilderness Too Far From Market, Abandoned Enterprise

"The Luminary" Anti-Masonic Paper Published Here In 1828

PENNSYLVANIA WANTED ASHTABULA COUNTY

Mapped In County As Far West As Grand River

JEFFERSON GAZETTE MASTHEAD. The Lee family moved the *Gazette* to Jefferson in 1876. After Lampson purchased the company, he constructed a three-story brick building on the corner of Chestnut and Wall Streets as the company headquarters. The post office occupied the ground floor, the paper's business offices were on the second floor, the print shop on the third, and the newspaper press was in the basement. (Judy Pallutch.)

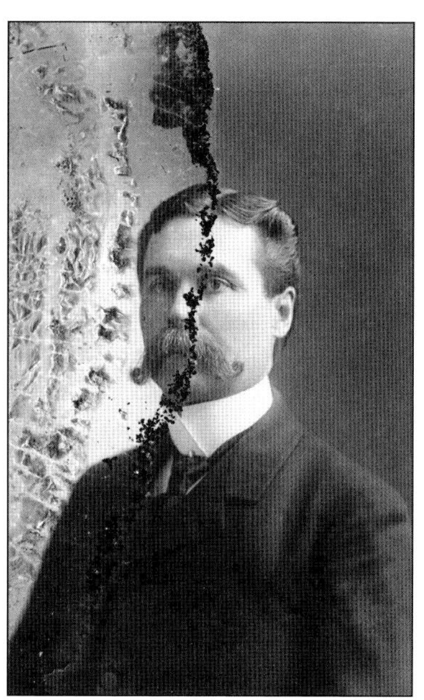

E.L. Lampson. Elbert L. Lampson, the eldest of seven children, grew up on a farm in Windsor Township in the extreme southwestern corner of Ashtabula County. His grandfather, a Revolutionary War veteran, settled there in 1809. Lampson attended the Grand River Institute in Austinburg and briefly taught school in Trumbull County before reading law in Jefferson in 1875 in the office of the Honorable S.A. Northway, a prominent Ashtabula County lawyer and later a member of the US Congress. Lampson was briefly the lieutenant governor of Ohio and a US congressman. His family lived in a grand home at the corner of North Chestnut and East Ashtabula Streets. (Library of Congress.)

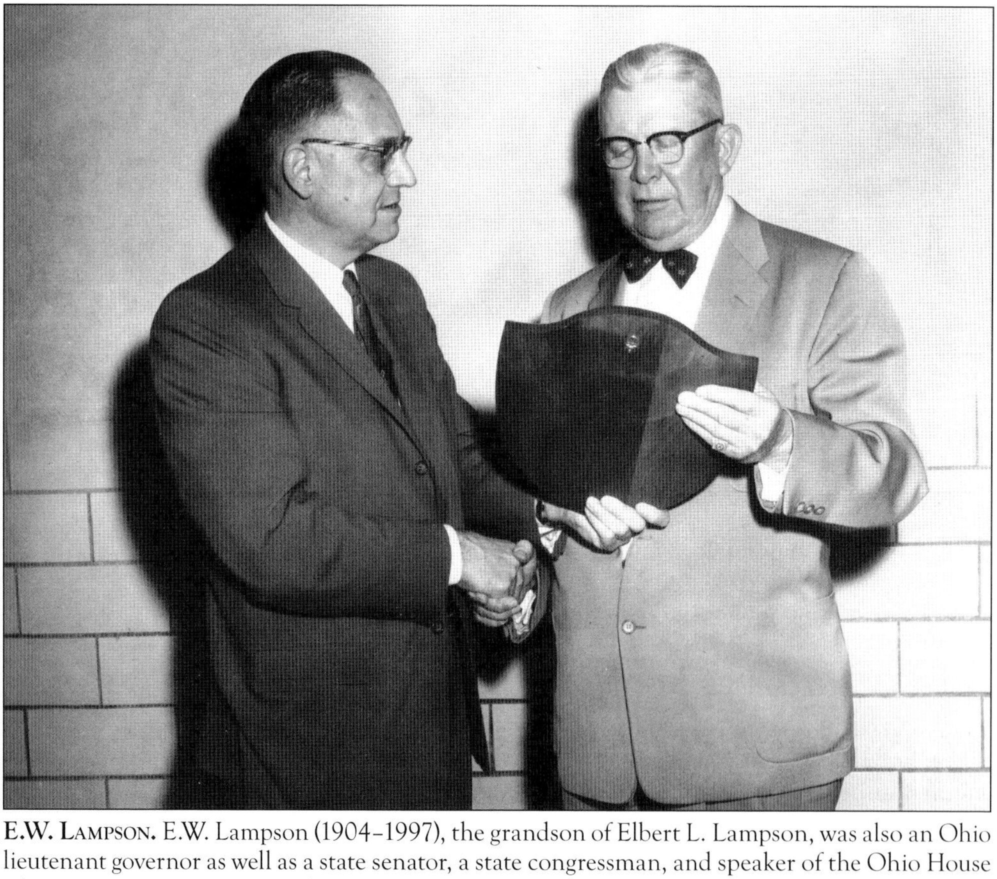

E.W. Lampson. E.W. Lampson (1904–1997), the grandson of Elbert L. Lampson, was also an Ohio lieutenant governor as well as a state senator, a state congressman, and speaker of the Ohio House of Representatives. However, he is best known as the owner and editor of the *Jefferson Gazette*. (Ashtabula District Library Archives.)

Platt Rogers Spencer. Platt R. Spencer grew up in Jefferson in the early 19th century, arriving there when he was 10 years old. He is the father of Spencerian penmanship, a distinctive and elegant style of cursive writing popular in the late 19th and early 20th century. He claims in his diary that, since paper was scarce in the early Ashtabula County settlements, he practiced his writing on birch bark, the fly leaves of the family Bible, and even in the snow. (Ashtabula District Library Archives.)

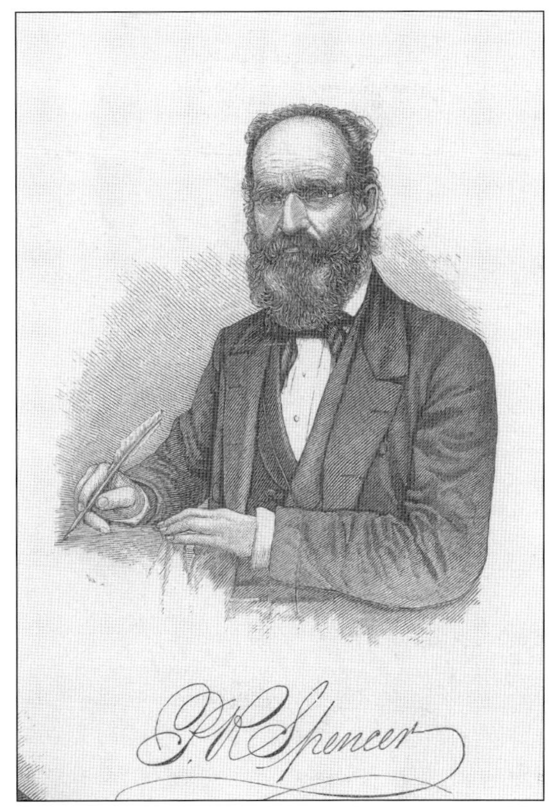

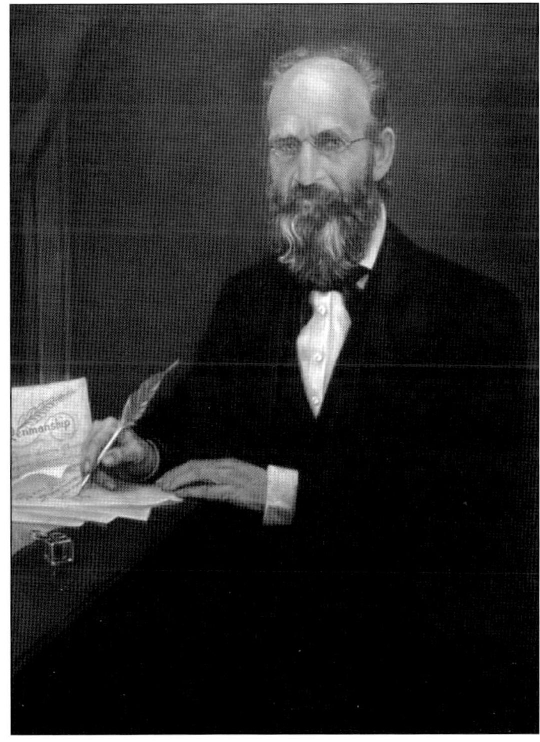

Platt R. Spencer. Spencer served as the Ashtabula County treasurer from 1842 to 1852 as well as an officer of the Ashtabula County Historical and Philosophical Society and the Ashtabula Agricultural Society. He and his family lived on North Myers Road outside of Geneva. The trip to his office in Jefferson would take a full day, so he maintained a second home in Jefferson during his term as treasurer. (Platt R. Spencer Society.)

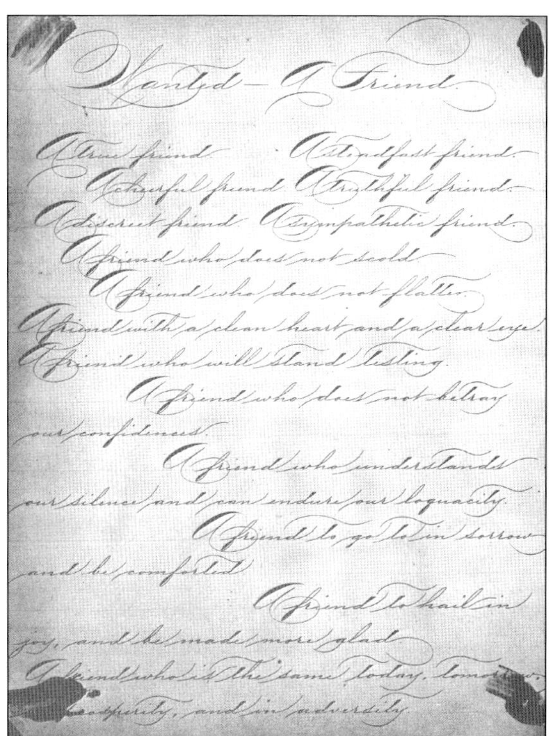

Wanted — A Friend.

A true friend. A steadfast friend.
A cheerful friend A truthful friend.
A discreet friend A sympathetic friend.
A friend who does not scold.
A friend who does not flatter.
A friend with a clean heart and a clear eye.
A friend who will stand testing.
A friend who does not betray
our confidences.
A friend who understands
our silence and can endure our loquacity.
A friend to go to in sorrow
and be comforted.
A friend to hail in
joy, and be made more glad.
A friend who is the same today, tomorrow,
in prosperity, and in adversity.

SPENCERIAN PENMANSHIP. Spencerian script, developed by Spencer in 1840, was the standard for cursive writing in the United States between 1850 and 1925. Pres. James A. Garfield called the Spencerian script "the pride of our country and the model of our schools." It was eventually replaced by the simpler Palmer method. (Ashtabula District Library Archives.)

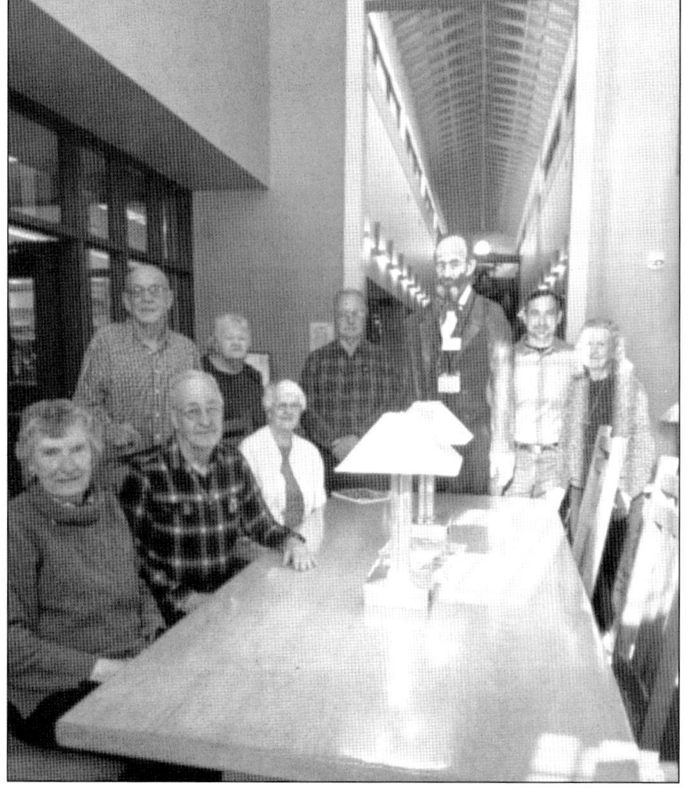

PLATT R. SPENCER HISTORICAL SOCIETY. The Platt R. Spencer Historical Society strives to keep interest in Spencerian penmanship and Platt R. Spencer alive. The group of around a dozen members is restoring the Spencer homestead outside of Geneva and meets monthly at the Geneva branch of the Ashtabula County District Library. Pictured are, from left to right, (first row) Cathie Schmidt, Phil Schmidt, and Barbara Rand; (second row) Dan Smith, Lois Bosely, Bill Peters, "Platt Spencer," Tom Norman III, and Beth Stillwell, president. (Members of the society not shown are Jim Frenelle, Sally Fisher, and Roger Williams.) (Author's collection.)

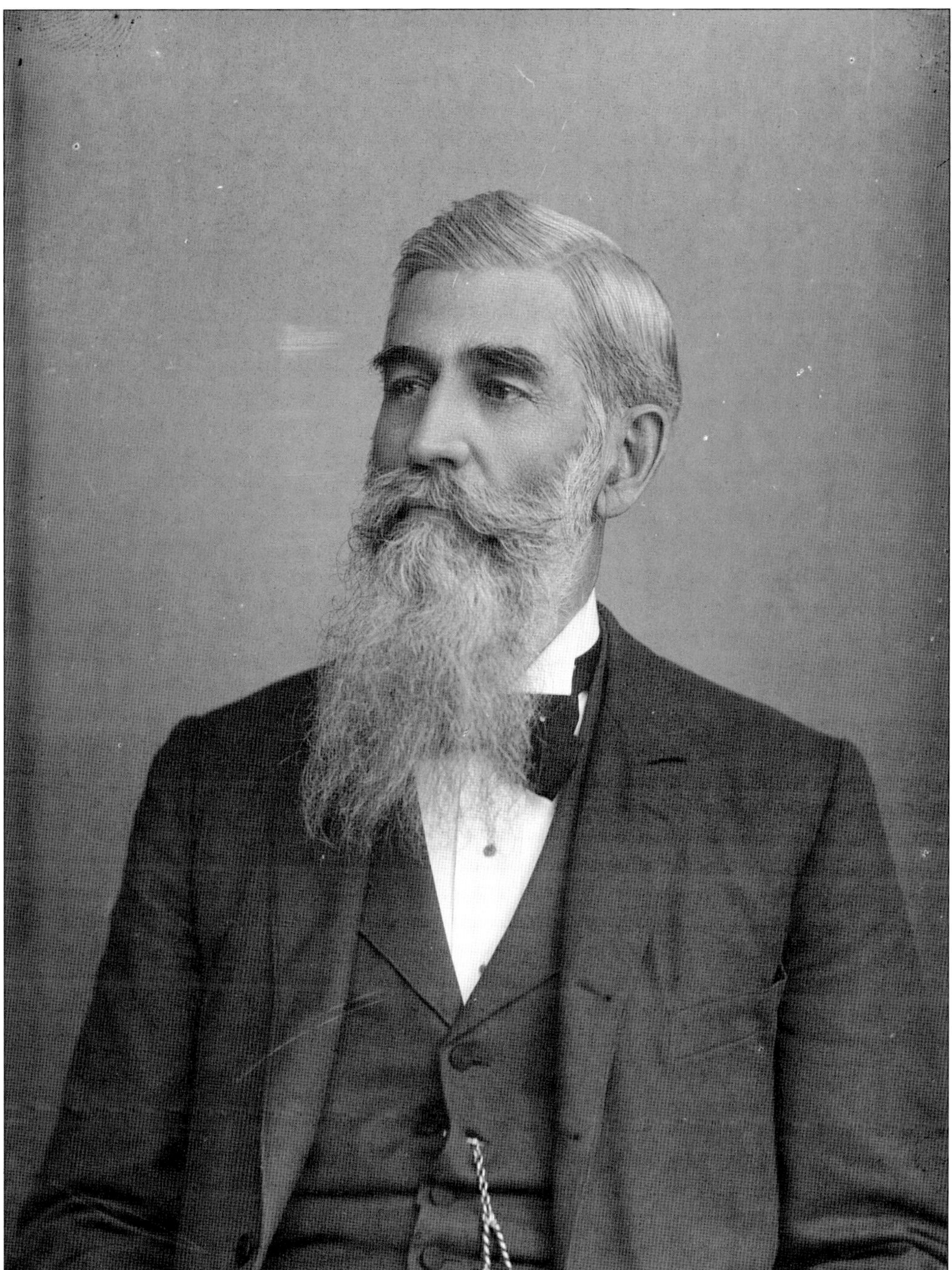

S.A. Northway. Stephen Asa Northway represented Ashtabula County as a US representative to Congress between 1893 and 1899. Born in New York in 1833, Northway spent most of his childhood in Orwell, Ohio. He became a prominent lawyer in Jefferson and later the prosecuting attorney for Ashtabula County before being elected to Congress. He later served as the controversial president of the Second National Bank, which closed unexpectedly in 1882. He and his wife, Lydia, had two children, one of whom died in childhood. Northway died in 1898 and is buried in Jefferson's Oakdale Cemetery. (Library of Congress.)

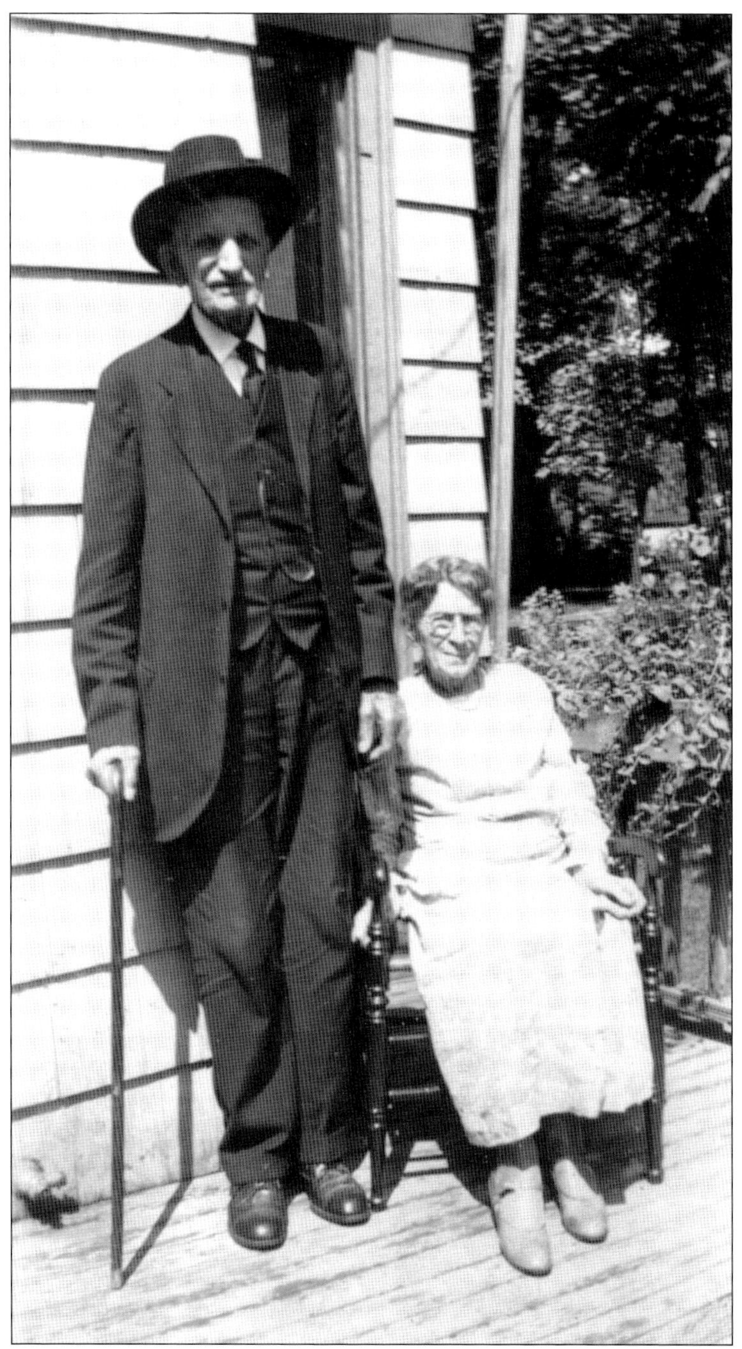

Rufus Ranney, 1924. Another Jefferson lawyer and judge was Rufus Ranney. Born in Massachusetts in 1913, Ranney moved with his parents to a farm in Fairport Harbor in 1822. He studied briefly at Western Reserve College in Hudson before reading law with the Jefferson firm of Giddings and Wade. He became a partner in the firm in 1839. Ranney ran unsuccessfully for Congress before being elected to the Ohio Supreme Court in 1851. He was considered one of the premier jurists of his day and was the first president of the Ohio Bar Association. Ranney died in Cleveland in 1891 and is buried in Cleveland's Lakeview Cemetery. (Judy Pallutch.)

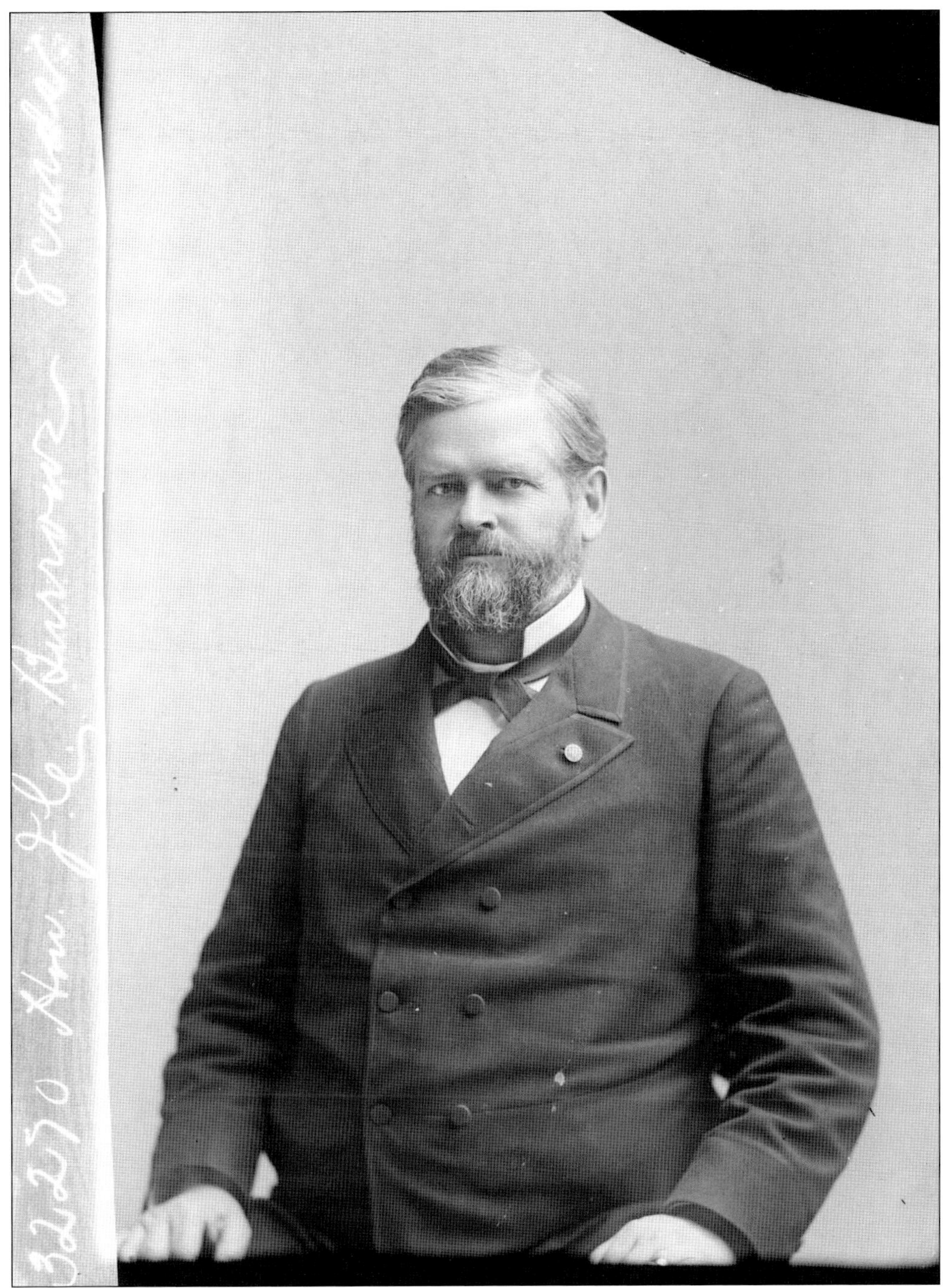

Hon. Julius C. Burrows. Julius Burrows, born in 1837, was a Jefferson lawyer who later moved to Michigan and was elected to the US House of Representatives and later the US Senate. Burrows moved to Jefferson with his parents when he was a child and went to school at Grand River Institute (now Academy) in Austinburg. (Library of Congress.)

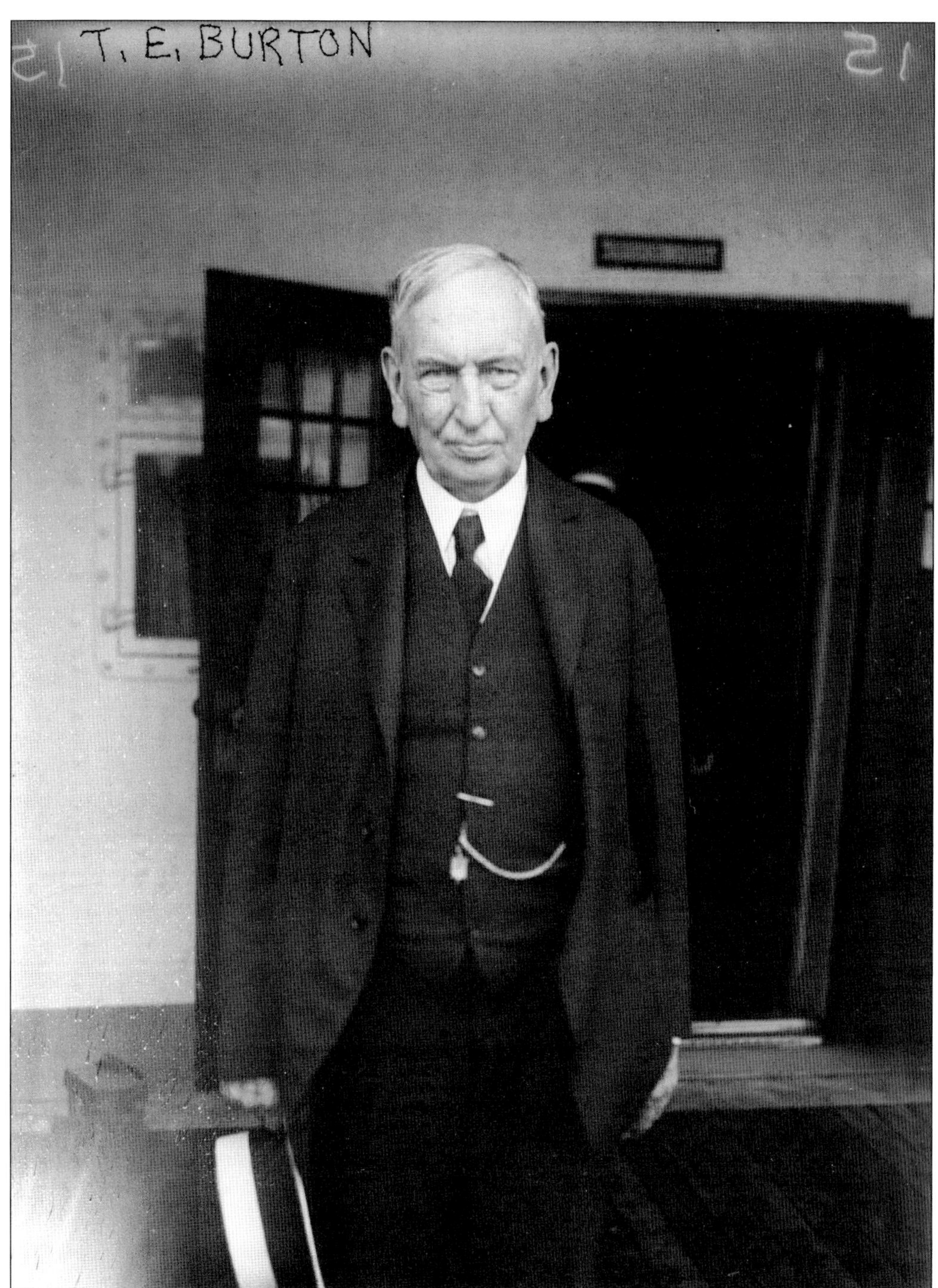

THEODORE ELIJAH BURTON. Theodore Burton (1851–1929), an Ohio congressman, US senator, 1916 GOP candidate for president, and *Time* magazine cover person, was also a Jefferson native. Burton, a lawyer with a degree from Oberlin College, served 12 years in Congress before being picked to serve out the Senate term of Frank B. Willis, who died in office. Burton, too, would die while a senator, a little more than 10 months after taking office. He is buried in Cleveland's Lakeview Cemetery. (Library of Congress.)

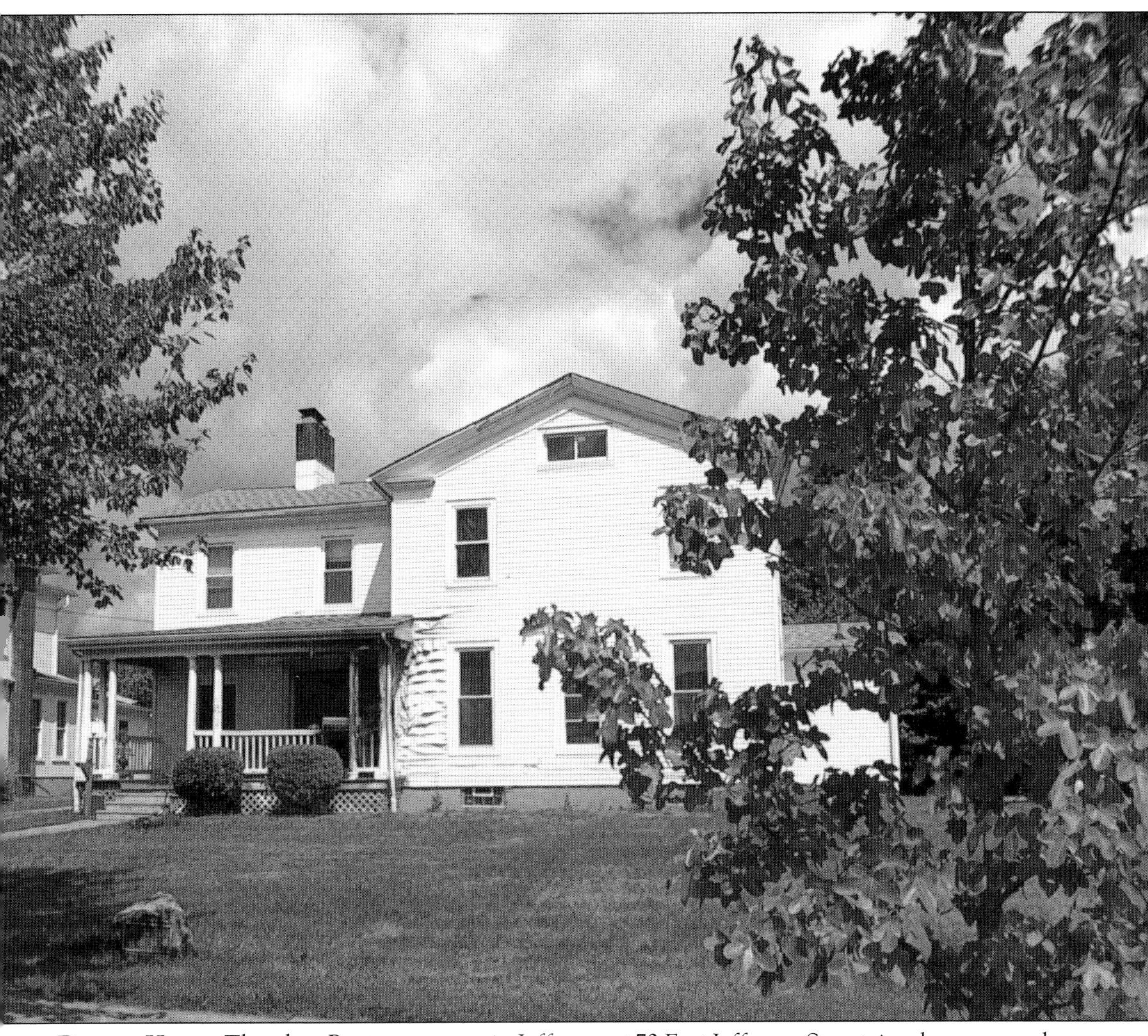

Burton House. Theodore Burton grew up in Jefferson at 73 East Jefferson Street, in a home owned by his father, Rev. William Burton, a pastor at the Congregational Church in Jefferson. Burton's boyhood home is still standing. (Author's collection.)

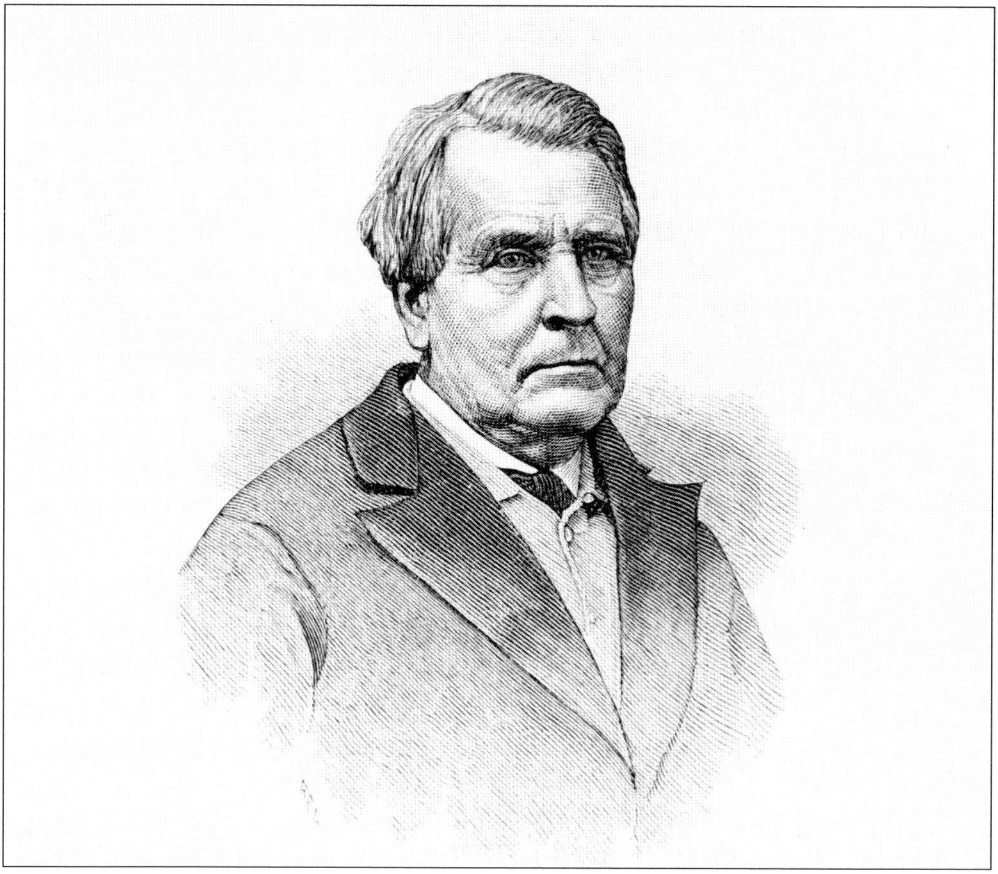

William C. Howells. William C. Howells, the father of the novelist William Dean Howells, was the co-owner and publisher of the *Ashtabula Sentinel*. He purchased the paper in 1853 and moved the plant and paper to Jefferson. William C. Howells's autobiography, *Recollections on Life in Ohio: 1813–1840*, details his time in the Western Reserve. (Ashtabula County District Library.)

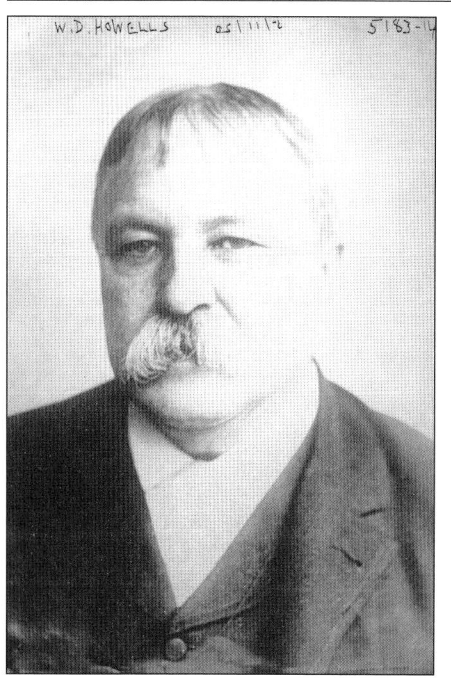

William Dean Howells. W.C. Howells younger son, William Dean Howells, grew up working at his father's newspaper. He was a popular novelist and playwright in the late 19th and early 20th centuries and earned the nickname "Dean of American Writers." Howells is best known for writing the 1855 novel *The Rise of Silas Lapham* and for being the editor of *Harper's* and *Atlantic Monthly* (now *The Atlantic*) from 1871 to 1881. (Library of Congress.)

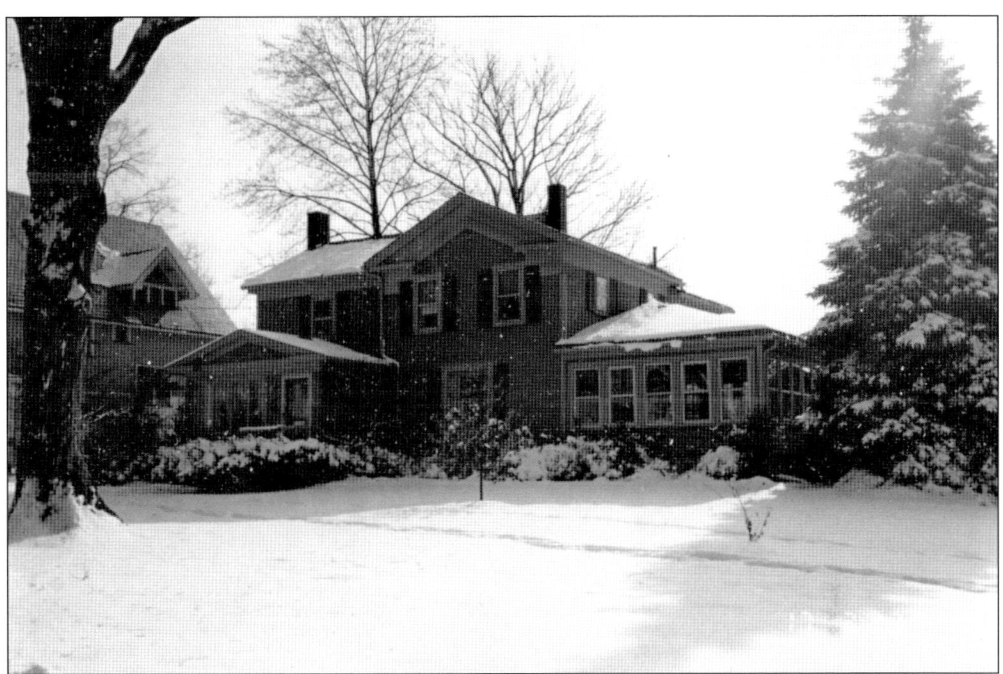

The Howells House. William Dean Howells began his career as a statehouse correspondent for a Cincinnati newspaper. He was later appointed vice consul to Venice by President Lincoln, who was impressed by a campaign biography written by Howells. The Howells family lived at 110 West Jefferson Street. Built in the late 1850s, the home was also once owned by Joshua A. Giddings (the son of the congressman). (Judy Pallutch.)

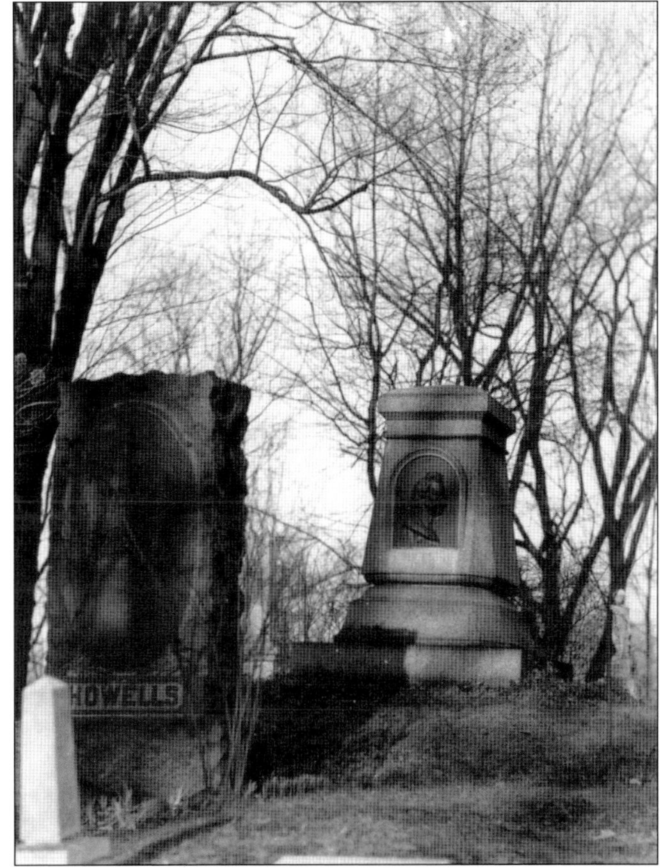

Howells Monument, Oakdale Cemetery. W.C. Howells died in 1894 in Jefferson at the age of 87 and is buried along with other members of the Howells family in Oakdale Cemetery. William Dean Howells died in 1920 at the age of 83 and is buried in Cambridge, Massachusetts. (Ashtabula District Library Archives.)

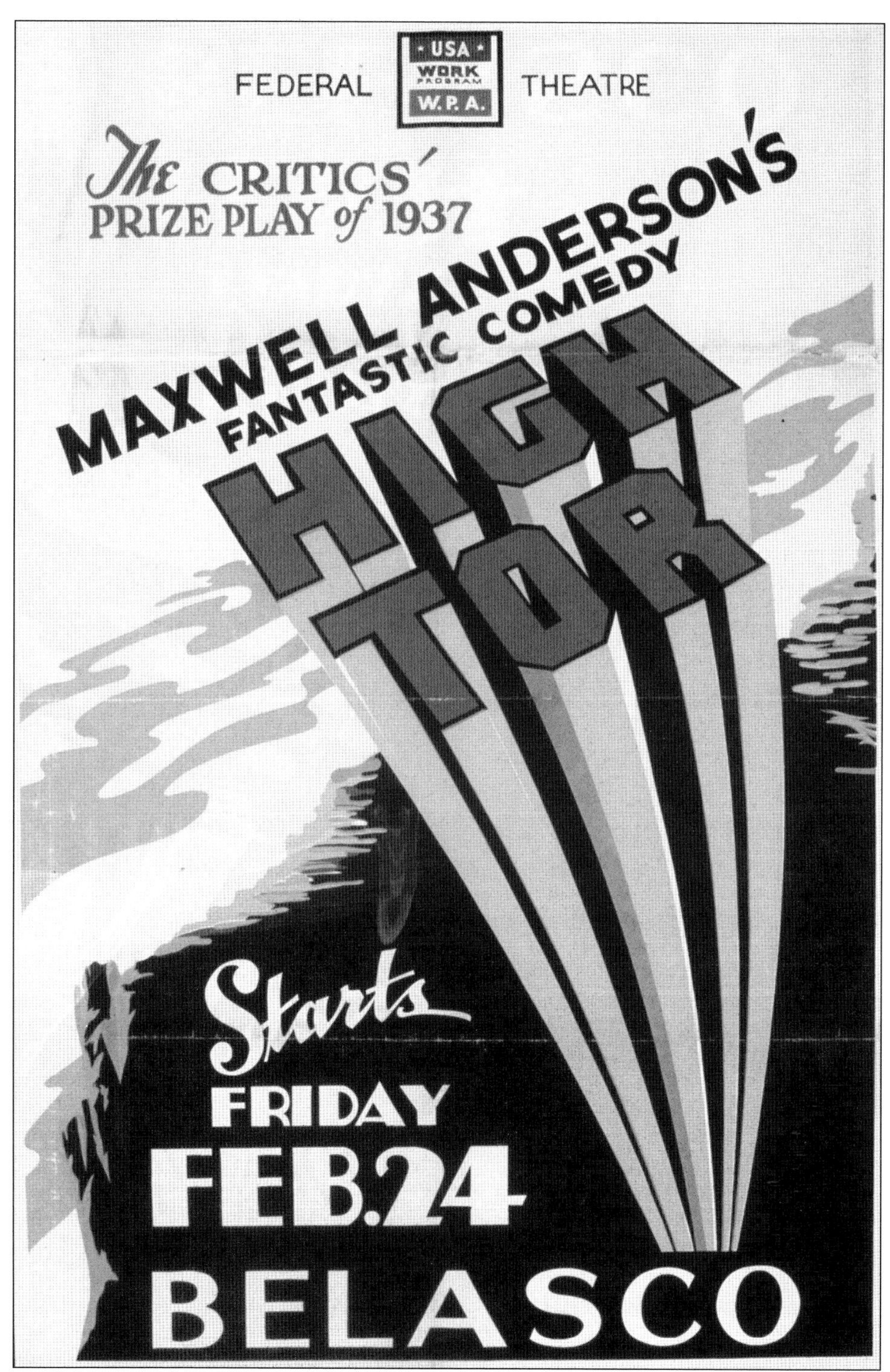

Maxwell Anderson. Maxwell Anderson was a mid-20th-century playwright and author who spent a portion of his childhood just outside Jefferson, Ohio. Anderson penned more than two dozen plays and even more screenplays. Anderson was awarded the gold medal in drama from the National Institute of Arts and Letters in 1954. (Library of Congress.)

Clarence Darrow. Clarence Darrow, the late-19th-century, early-20th-century lawyer most famous as the defense attorney in the 1925 Scopes Monkey Trial, spent a portion of his law career in Jefferson and Ashtabula County. Born in Farmdale, Ohio (in Trumbull County), Darrow was admitted to the Ohio bar in 1878 and had law offices in Andover and Ashtabula. He often appeared in courtrooms in Jefferson before taking his practice to Illinois in 1884. A famous letter (pictured below) from Darrow to attorney (later mayor) H.J. Redmond is part of the Jefferson Historical Society collection. In the letter, dated May 21, 1923, Darrow advises Redmond that "as much exact information as possible should be gathered about each prospective juror, as to his religion, habits, business, etc., and what he has said. This is more important than anything else, except the verdict." (Left, Library of Congress; below, Jefferson Historical Society.)

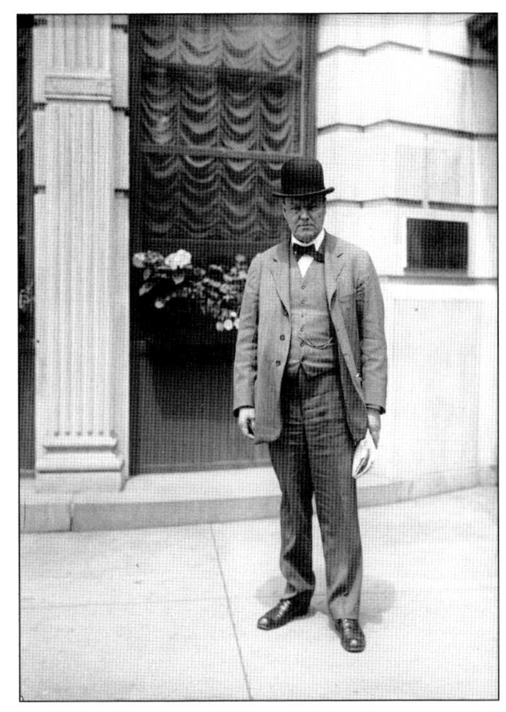

CLARENCE DARROW

May 21, 1923 .

To Mr. H. J. Redmond, Attourney;
Jefferson, Ohio.

Dear Mr. Redmond ,

I will be on hand on June second, or, possibly before.

As much exact information as possible should be gathered about each prospective juror; as to his religion, habits, business, etc., and what he has said, if it can be found out. This is more important than any thing else, except the verdict.

Yours very sincerely,

Clarence Darrow

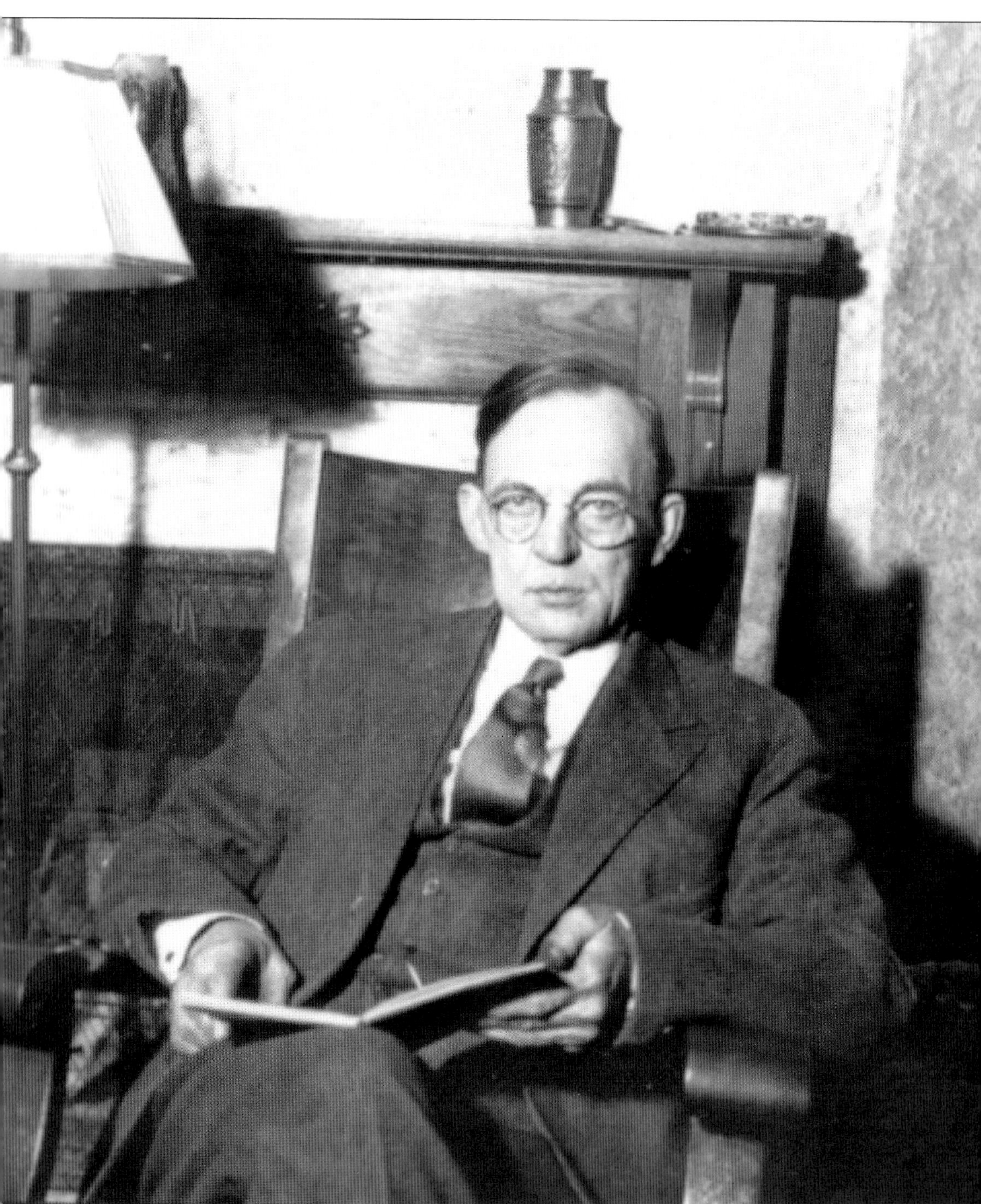

E.T. Fetch. E.T. "Tom" Fetch was born in Jefferson, where his father had a machine shop. He is best known as the first person to drive an automobile coast-to-coast. In 1903, Fetch piloted a 4.5-horsepower Packard Model F from San Francisco to New York City. The journey took 63 days. Fetch went on to work for the Packard Motor Car Company before he returned to Jefferson and opened an automobile dealership. (Ashtabula District Library Archives.)

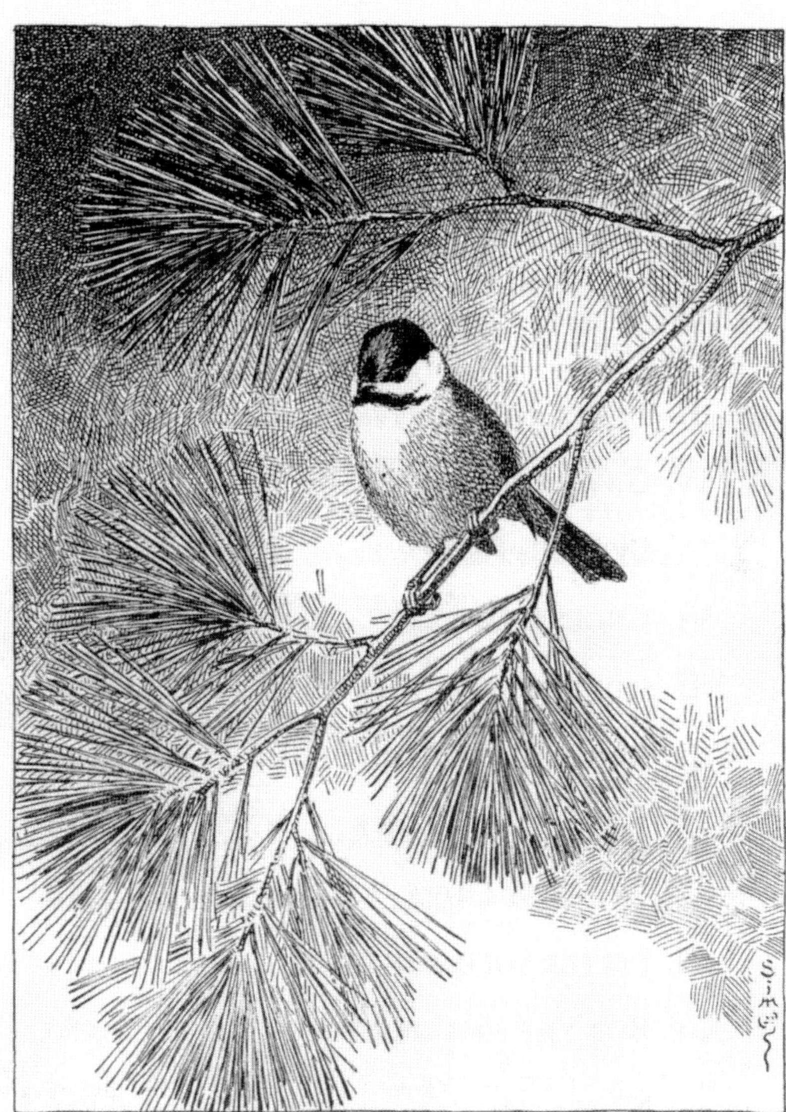

Chick, D. D. in his pulpit.

Robert J. Sim. Robert J. Sim, an 1899 graduate of the Jefferson Educational Institute, was a prominent early-20th-century illustrator, well-known for his nature and wildlife drawings (such as the one pictured above). He was born in New York before moving with his family to Jefferson. He later graduated from the Cleveland Institute of Art. (Author's collection.)

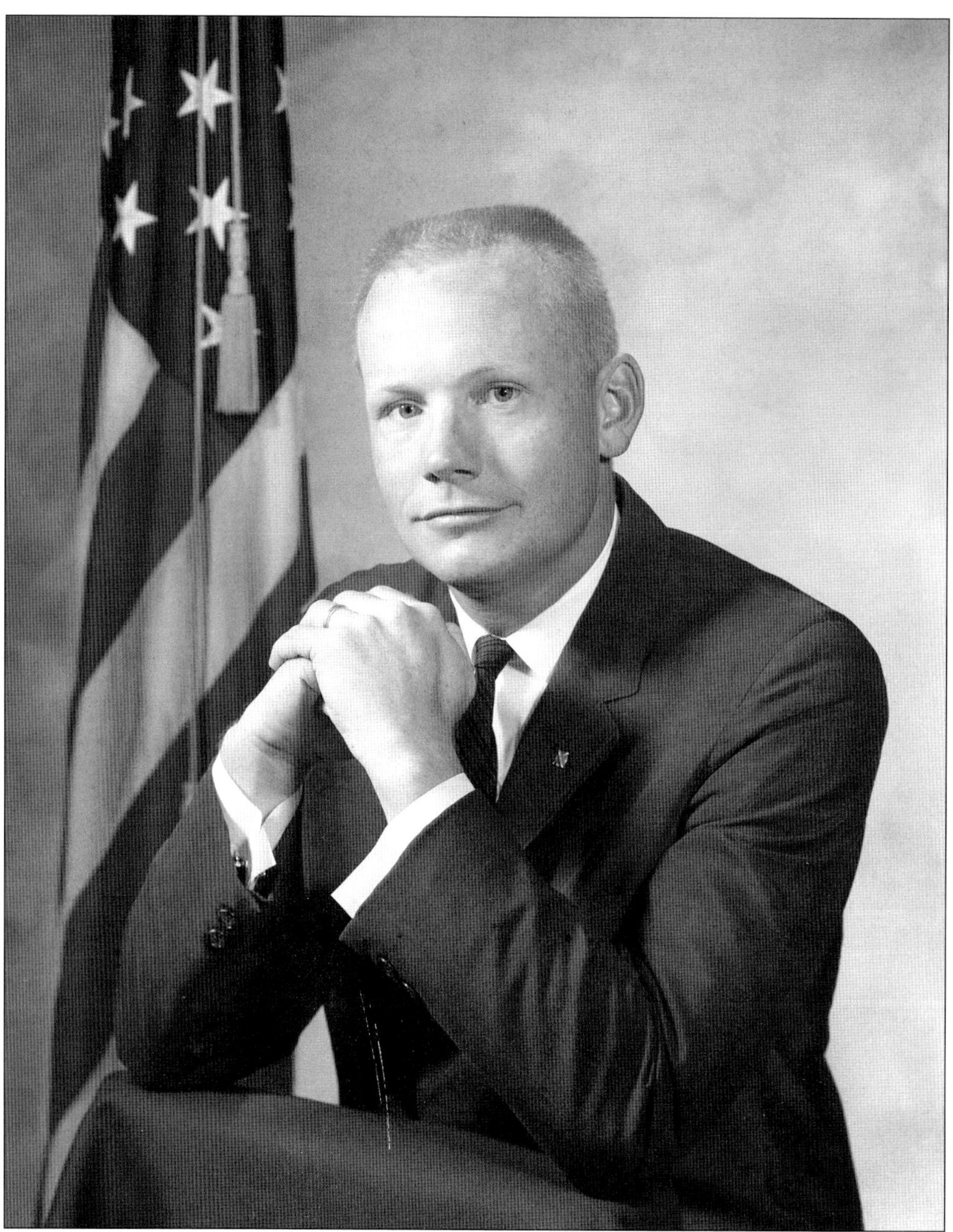

Neil Armstrong. Neil Armstrong is best remembered as the first person to set foot on the moon on July 27, 1969. However, long before he was an astronaut, Armstrong spent part of his childhood in Jefferson and attended Jefferson Elementary School. His father worked for the Ohio Auditor's Office, and the family moved there in 1931. His brother and sister were born in Jefferson. All three children were baptized at First Congregational Church. His family lived in what is now the dental office house next to Circle K on North Chestnut Street. (NASA.)

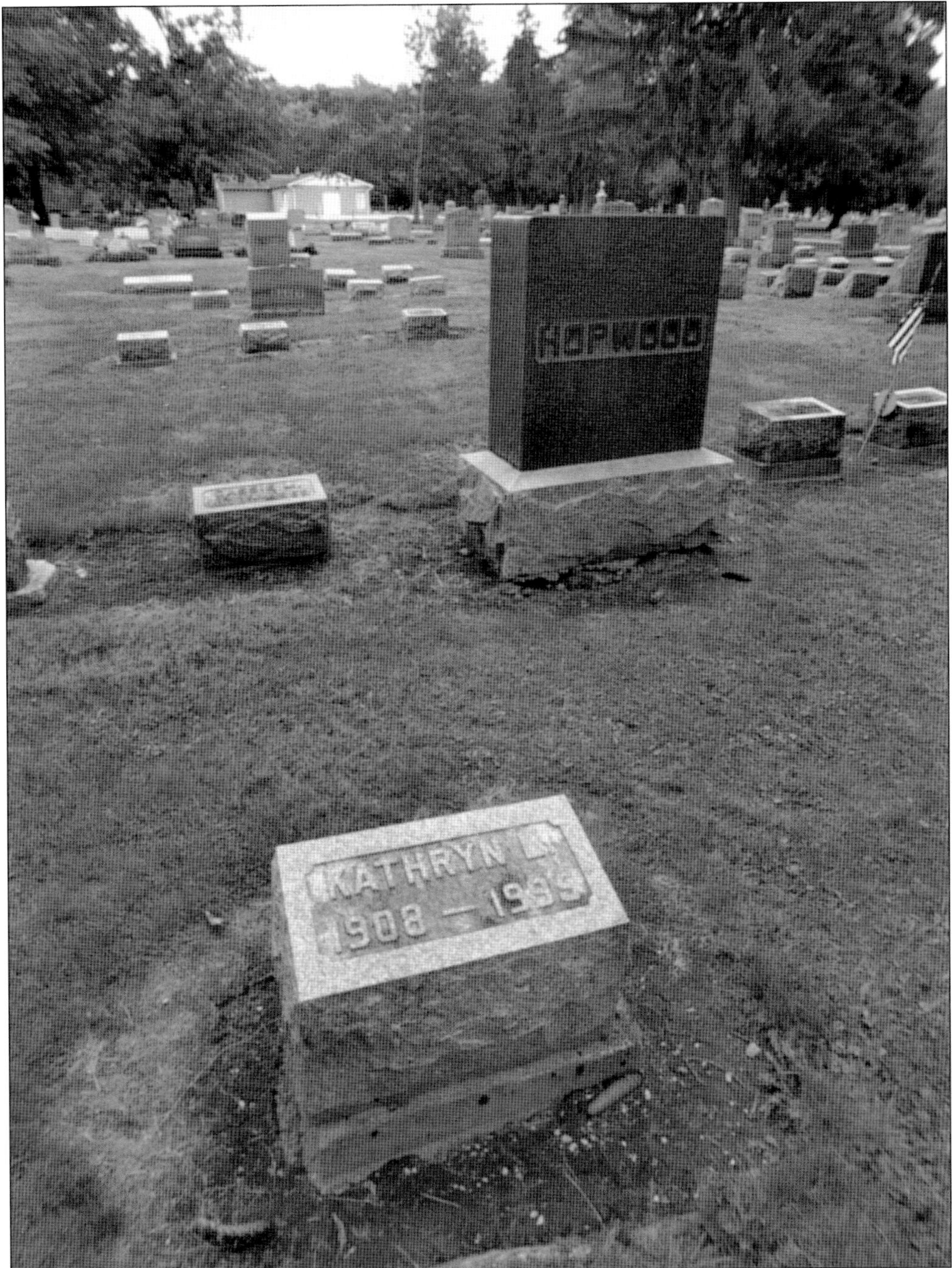

Kathryn Louise Hopwood. Born in Lenox Township, Kathryn Louise Hopwood spent her childhood in Jefferson and graduated from Jefferson High School in 1926. She and her family lived in a large Victorian home that still stands on the east side of North Market Street between Walnut and Ashtabula Streets. She graduated from Oberlin College and taught at several Ohio high schools and later at the Ohio State University. She was dean of women at Hunter College in New York City from 1955 to 1974. Hopwood is buried alongside her parents in Jefferson's Oakdale Cemetery. (Author's collection.)

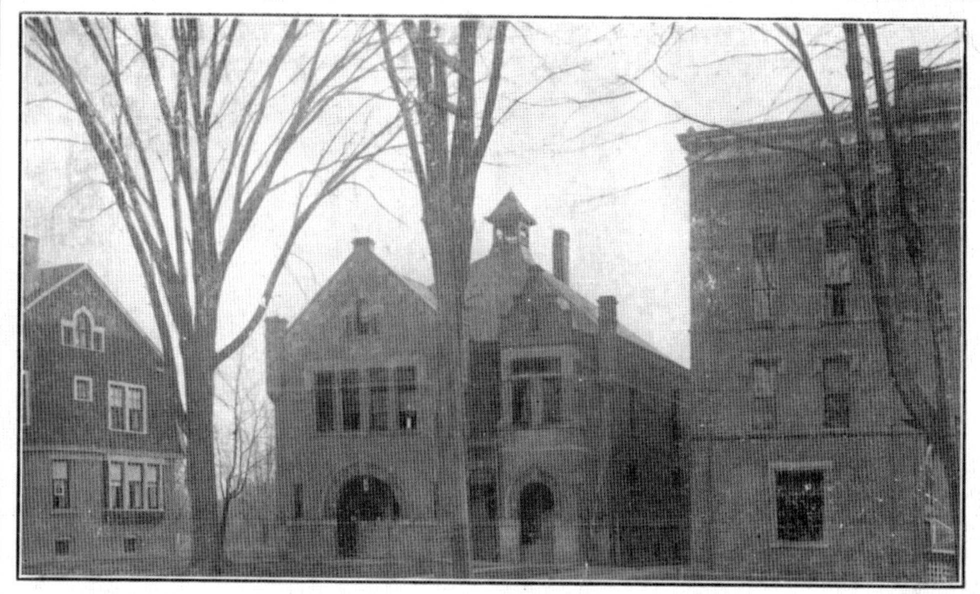

JEFFERSON PUBLIC LIBRARY. The first written mention of a Jefferson library is from a document dated August 2, 1817. That first library, located in a room in the town hall, was known as the Jefferson Public Library. Later, the books from this library were turned over to the Citizen's Library. The Citizen's Library of Jefferson was established in 1883 by the Women's Christian Temperance Union. A new library and fire hall complex (pictured) was constructed in 1909. The current Henderson Memorial Public Library dates from 1972. (Ashtabula County Historical Society.)

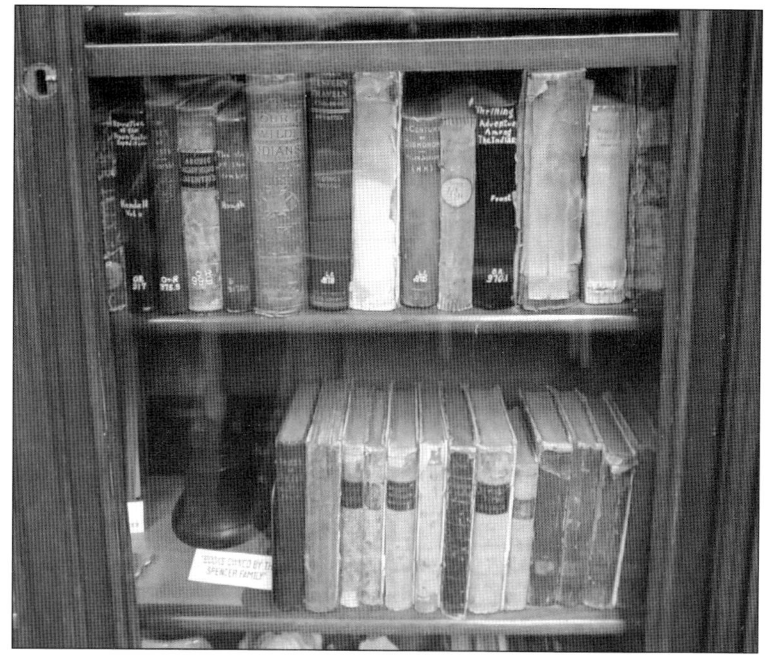

JEFFERSON PUBLIC LIBRARY ARCHIVES. The archives and historical books from the Jefferson Public Library have been moved next door to the Jefferson Historical Society. The collection includes several volumes owned by the Platt R. Spencer family (pictured). (Author's collection.)

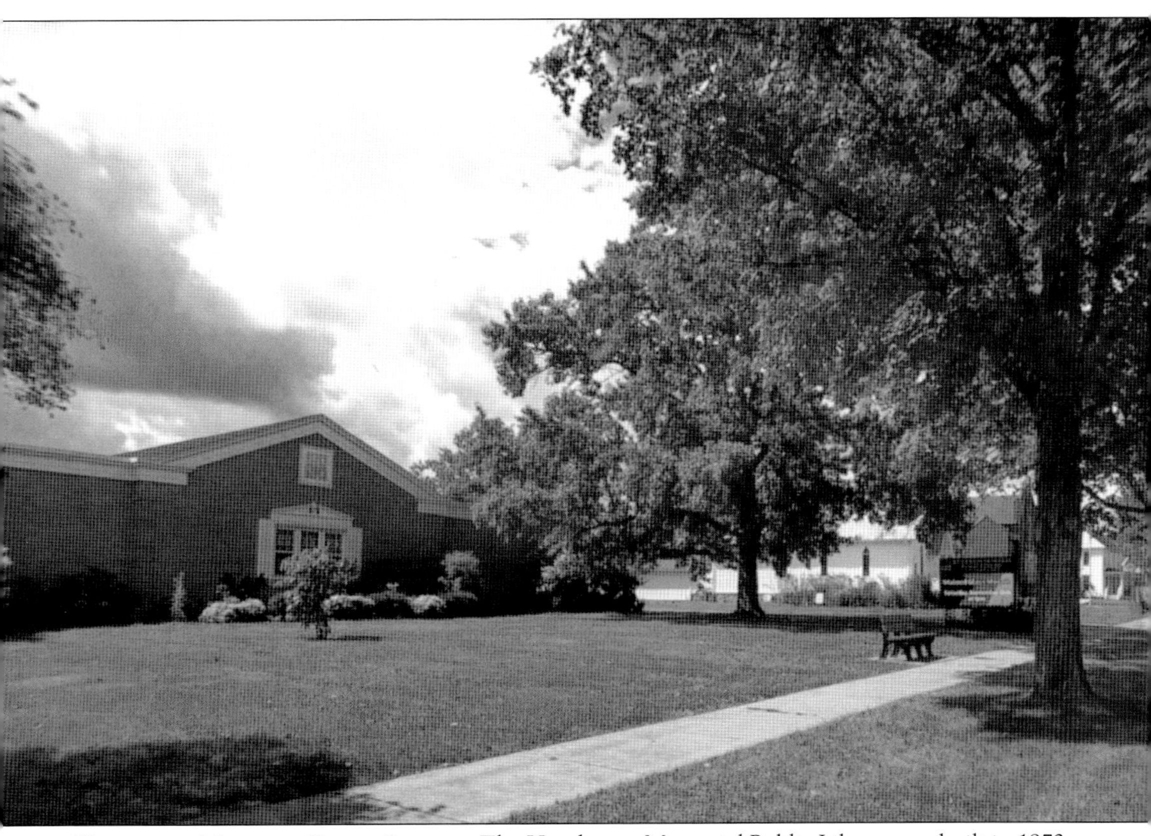

Henderson Memorial Public Library. The Henderson Memorial Public Library was built in 1972 and named for Ora Henderson, who donated the funds for its construction. The library houses more than 50,000 books and hosts a variety of special programs and author events. (Author's collection.)

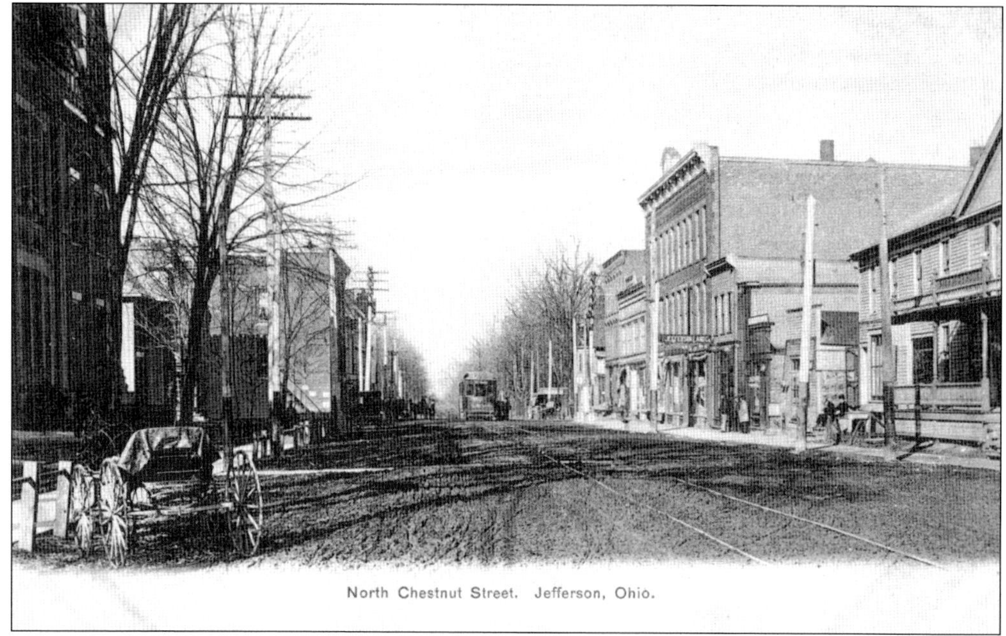

NORTH CHESTNUT STREET, 1909. North Chestnut Street used to be lined with magnificent chestnut trees and elegant homes. Joshua Giddings lived there (near where McDonald's is today), as did Platt R. Spencer and his family. The first paved road in Jefferson was added in 1910, shortly after this picture was taken. (Author's collection.)

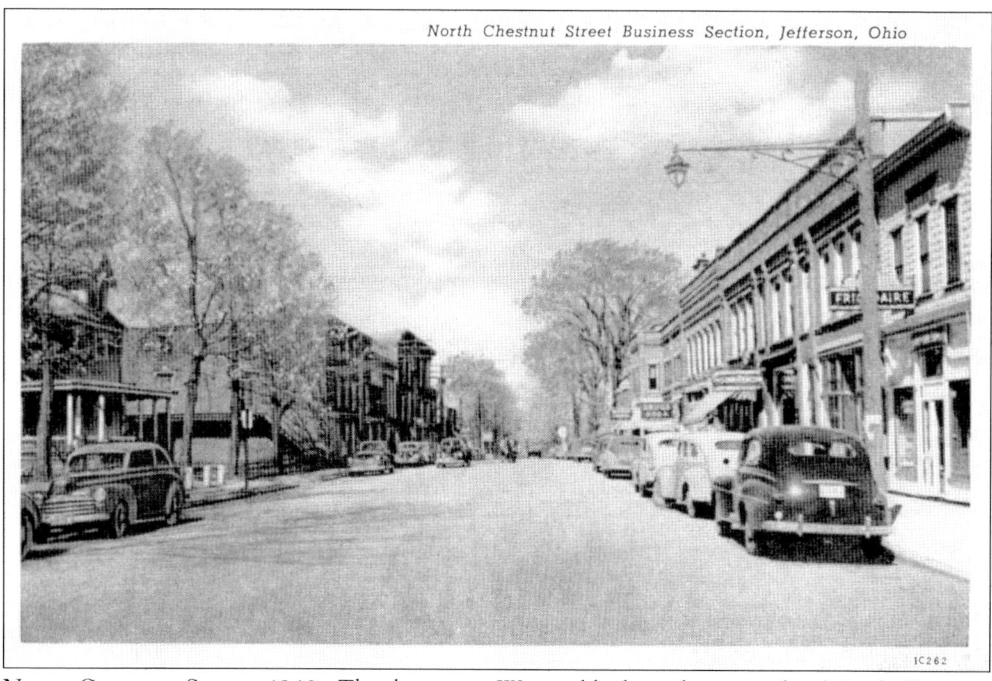

NORTH CHESTNUT STREET, 1940S. The three-story Warner block on the west side of North Chestnut Street was built just after the Civil War. It was destroyed by fire in 1960. Pictured here are the Second National Bank, Dr. F.A. Tuttle's Drug Store, and Wolcott's Grocery. (Ashtabula County Historical Society.)

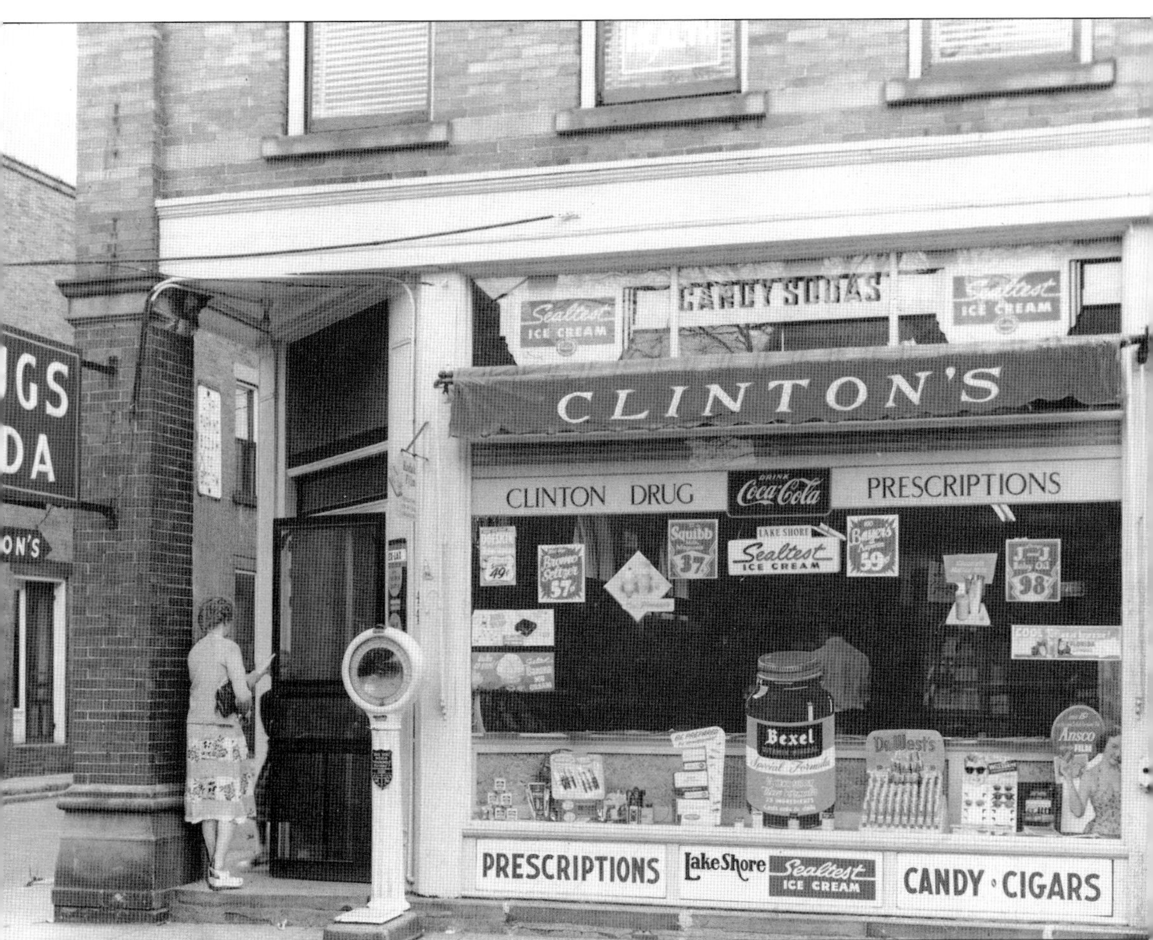

CLINTON'S DRUG STORE. Located at 44 North Chestnut Street, Clinton's Drug Store was originally Jones Pharmacy and later Jefferson Pharmacy. Clinton's in the 1950s is fondly remembered for its soda fountain and the nickel Cokes served there. (Ashtabula County Historical Society.)

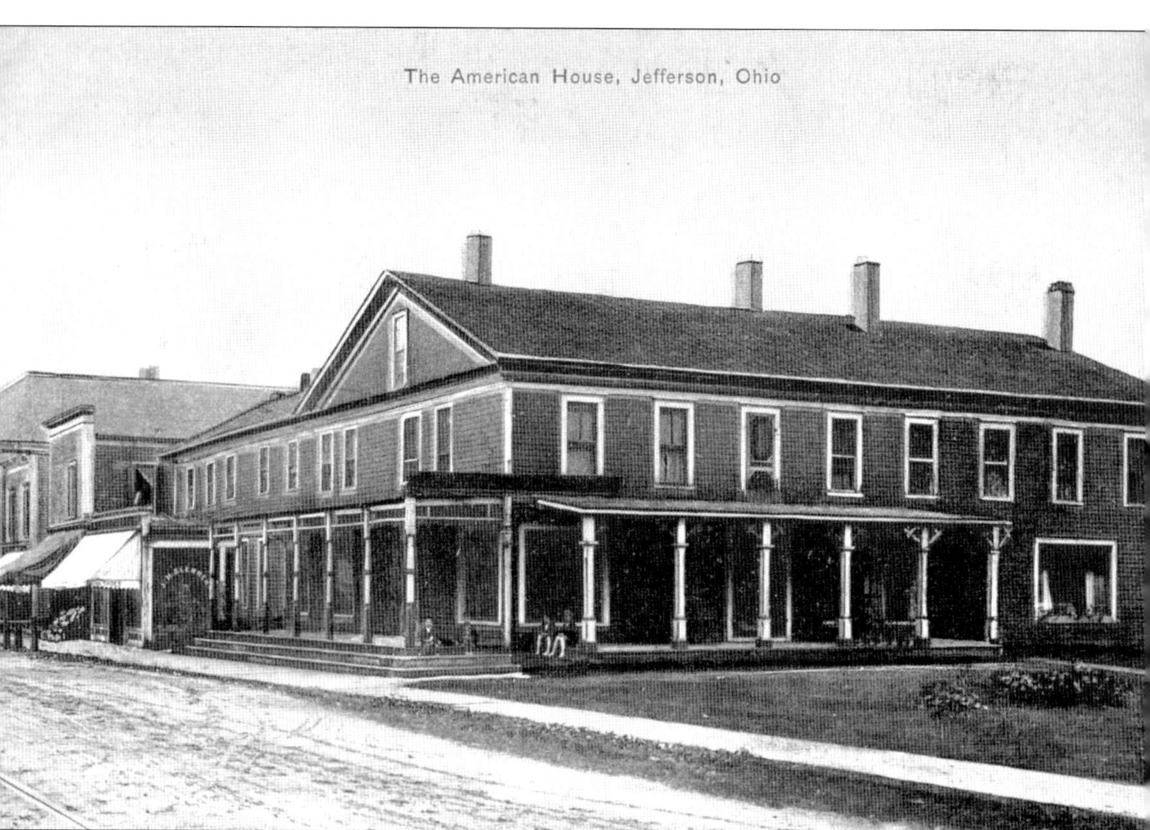

The American House. Located at the corner of Jefferson and Chestnut Streets, the American House was a popular hotel, tavern, and restaurant in Jefferson. It first appeared in the plat maps of 1874. The American House was noted for its Sunday chicken dinner, which included all the trimmings plus homemade pie for 50¢. (Jefferson Historical Society.)

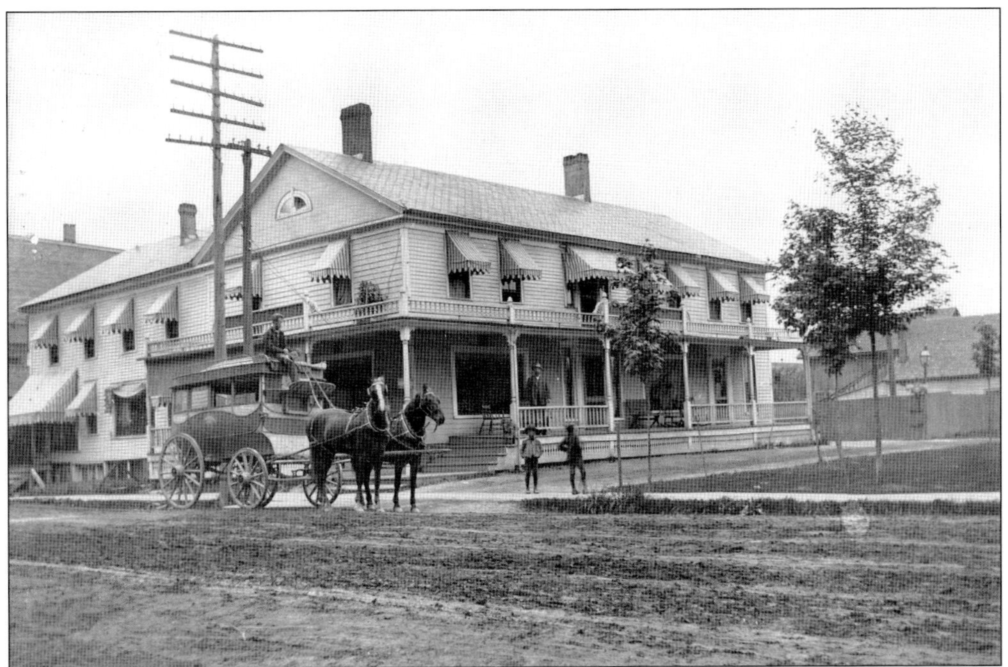

Beckwith House. The Beckwith House, located at the northeast corner of Jefferson and Chestnut Streets, was one of three hotels in Jefferson in the late 19th century. It burned in the 1906 fire. The hotel was rebuilt and, beginning in 1910, was called the Jefferson House Hotel. It is rumored to have had connections to the Underground Railroad in the pre–Civil War years. (Jefferson Historical Society.)

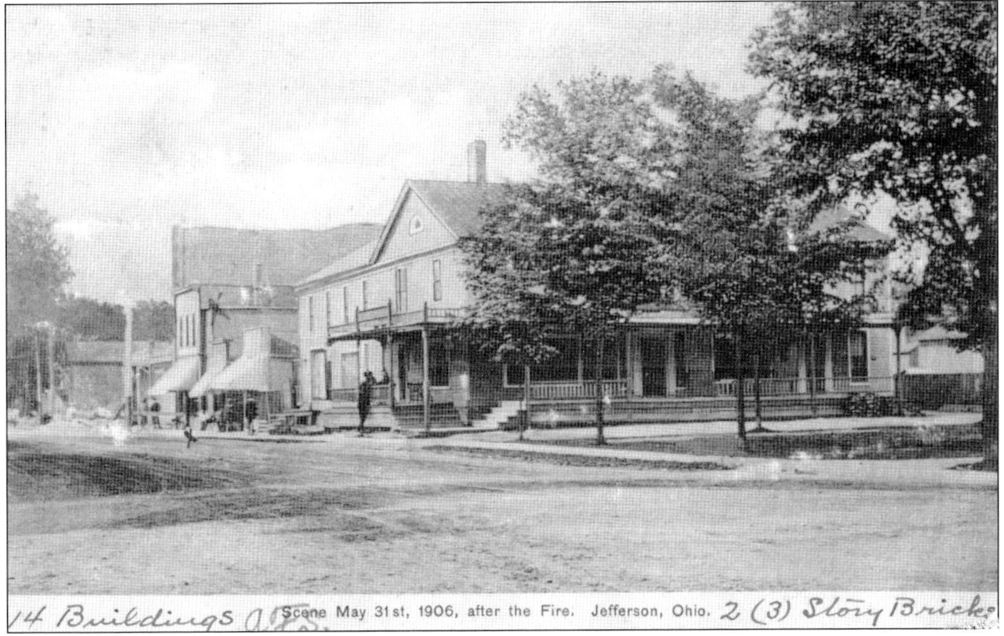

Beckwith House after the 1906 Fire. Beckwith House was one of several Jefferson businesses destroyed in the 1906 downtown fire. The hotel quickly rebuilt and continued until 1930, when it closed and the structure was razed. (Jefferson Historical Society.)

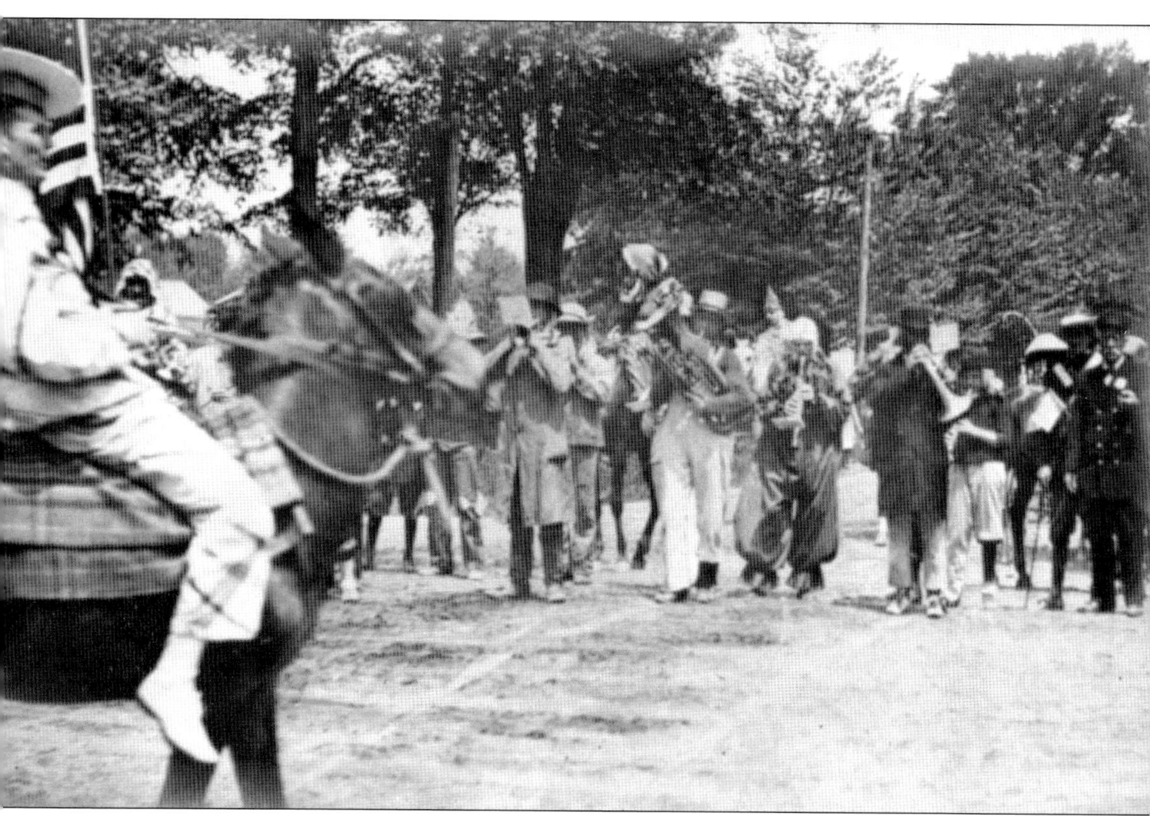

Bond Rally Parade in Jefferson, 1918. More than 256,000 draftees, volunteers, and Ohio National Guardsmen from Ashtabula County served in World War I. A total of 6,777 troops from the county died as a result of the war, either in combat or from disease. Those at home in Ashtabula County enthusiastically supported the war effort, as this 1918 bond rally indicates. (Jefferson Historical Society.)

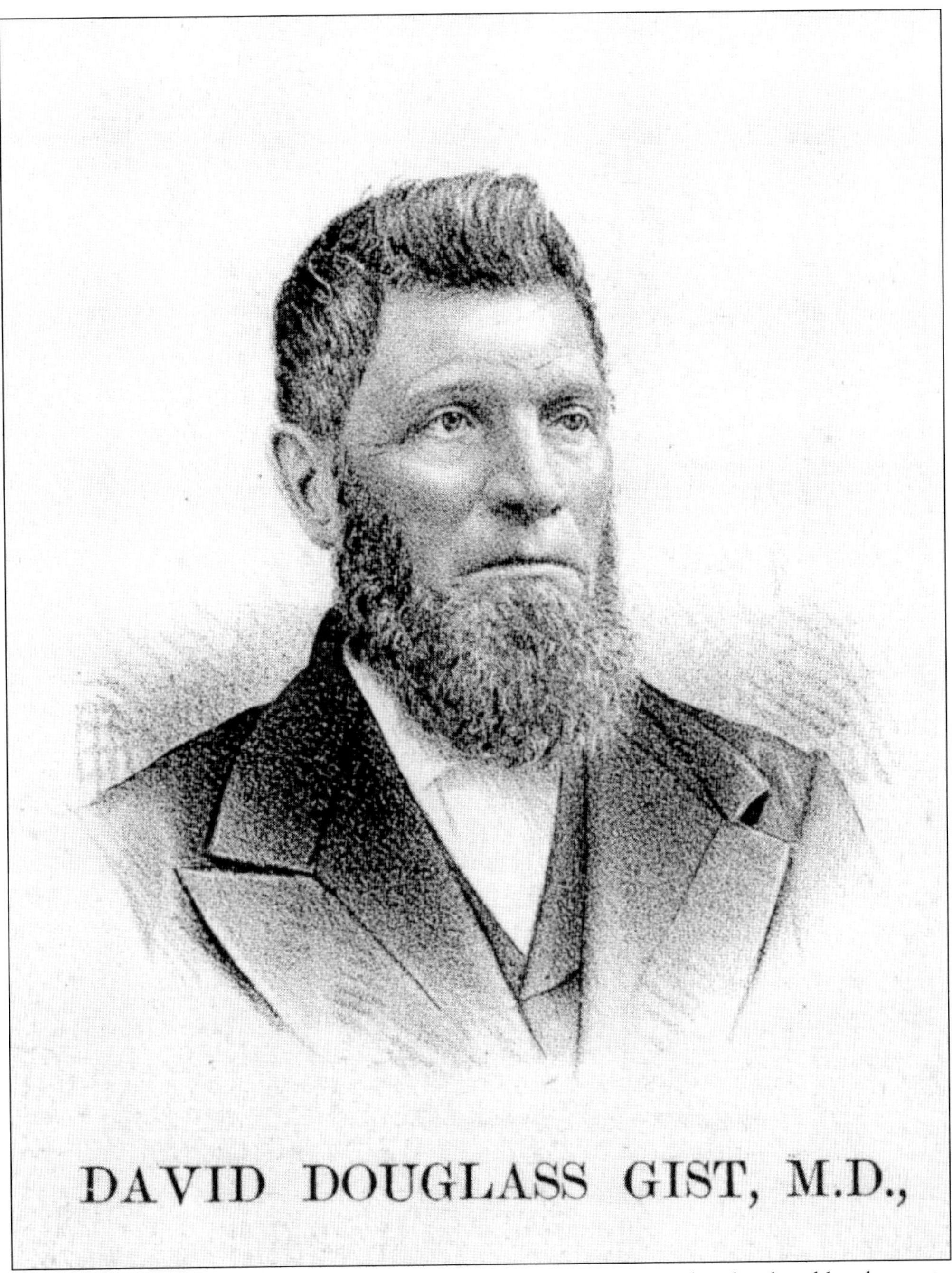

The Gist House. The Gist House, constructed in 1823 and reputed to be the oldest house in Jefferson, was the home of Dr. David Douglas Gist, a doctor who specialized in treating people with cancer from 1840 until his death in 1892. Dr. Gist married twice. His first wife died in 1836 after one child and three years of marriage. He had three additional children with his second wife, Sarah. Dr. Gist is buried in Jefferson's Oakdale Cemetery. (Ashtabula County District Library.)

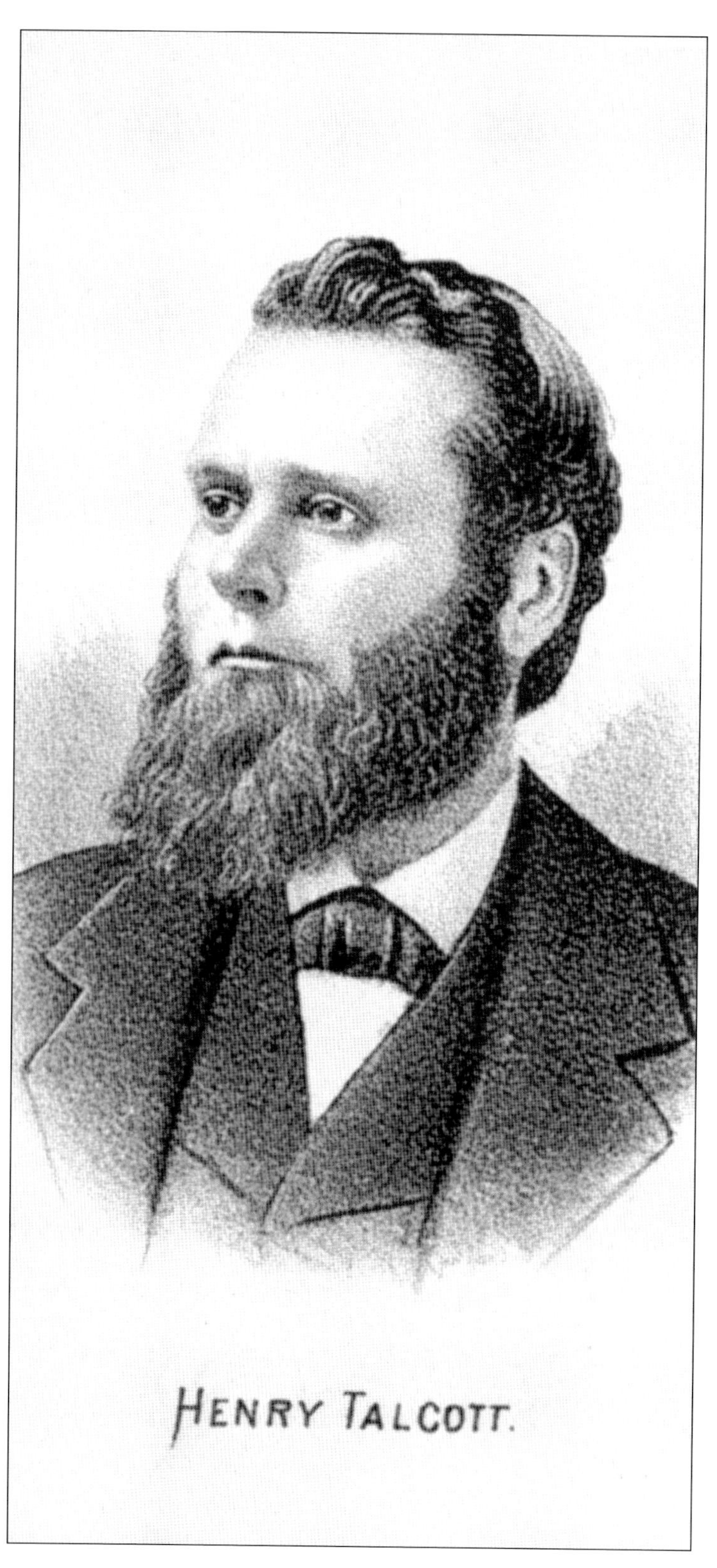

HENRY TALCOTT. Henry Talcott was, for a time, the wealthiest man in Jefferson. He arrived in the Western Reserve in the early 1860s and opened a three-story hardware store on North Chestnut Street, just north of the courthouse. Talcott would go on to own a gristmill and sawmill (located at what is now the fairgrounds parking lot). He was also the prime benefactor for the Jefferson Educational Institute, built in 1870. Talcott died in 1894 and is buried at Oakdale Cemetery. (Ashtabula County District Library.)

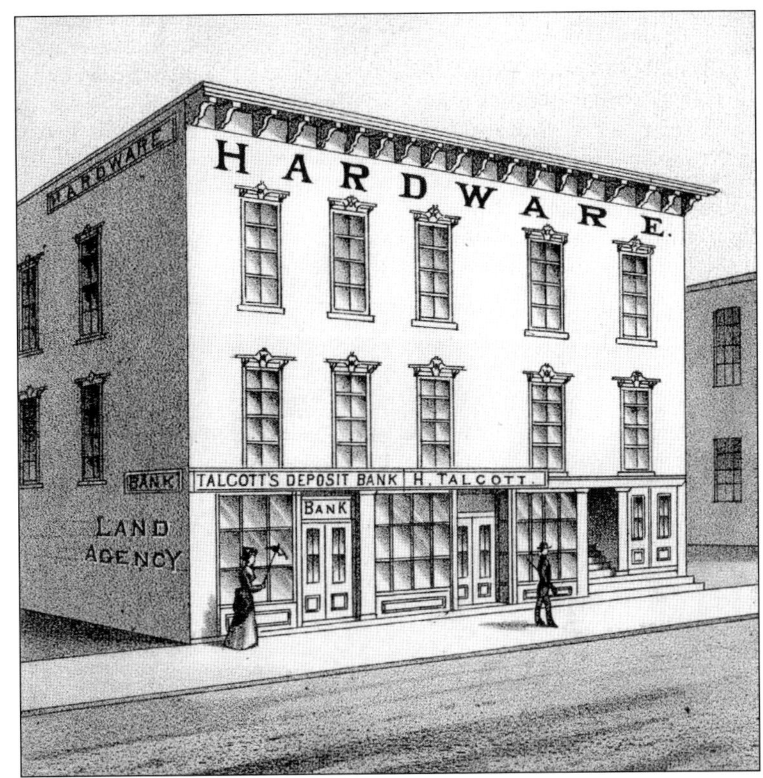

Talcott Hardware Store. One of Henry Talcott's first businesses was Talcott Tin and Stove Store. This grew into the hardware store. At one time, Talcott also had a bank in the back corner of the store. (Ashtabula County District Library.)

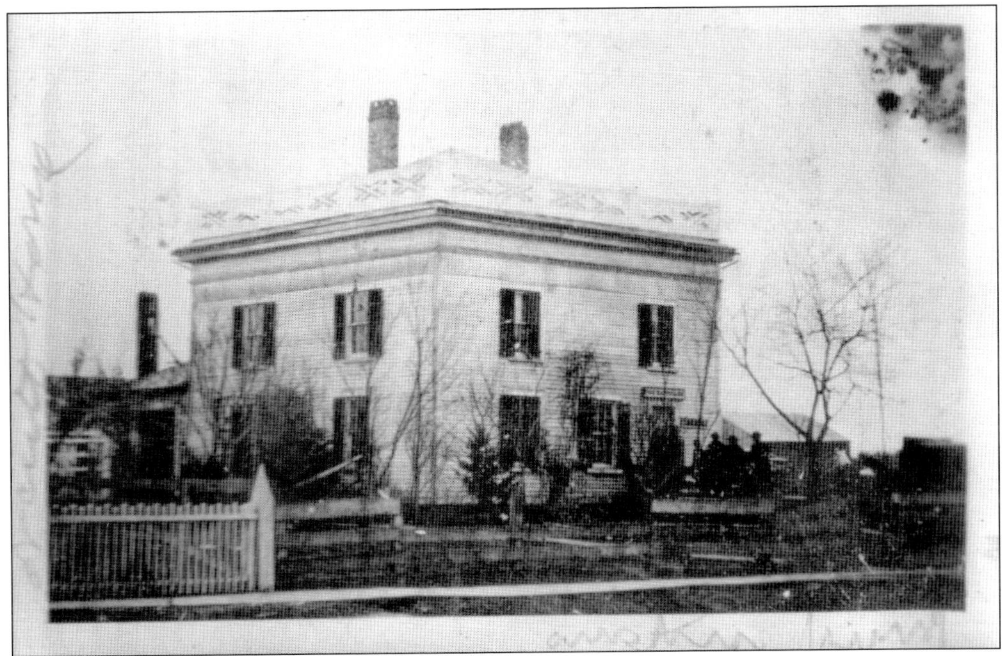

The Talcott House. Located at 175 West Jefferson Street, this Italianate, four-story brick house was built in 1867 for $5,000 by John Watters, who also constructed the Wade mansion. The elegant house still stands. It is noted for its cupola atop the roof, accessible from the fourth floor. (Judy Pallutch.)

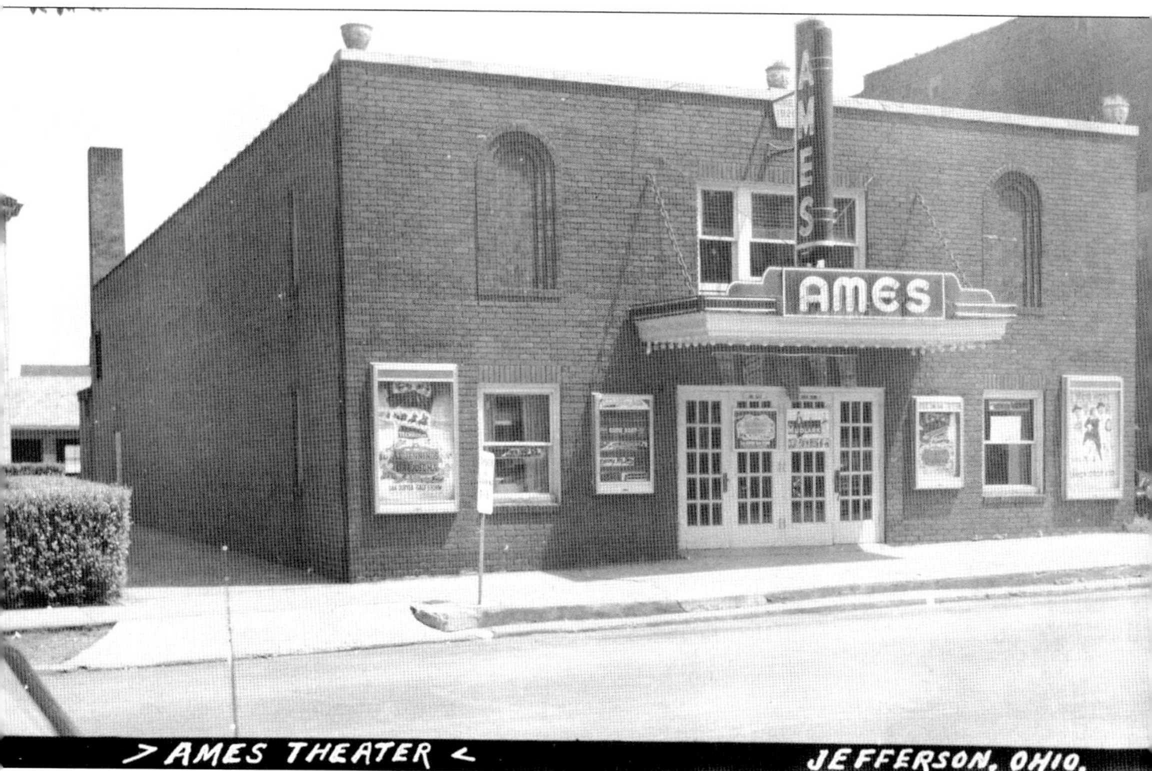

AMES THEATER, 1951. Located at 66 North Chestnut Street in downtown Jefferson, the 414-seat Ames Theater was a favorite of generations of residents. In the 1940s, one could see a movie at the Ames for just a dime. In the 1950s, when this photograph was taken, the price had increased to 15¢. The theater closed in 1979, but the building is still standing. (Jefferson Historical Society.)

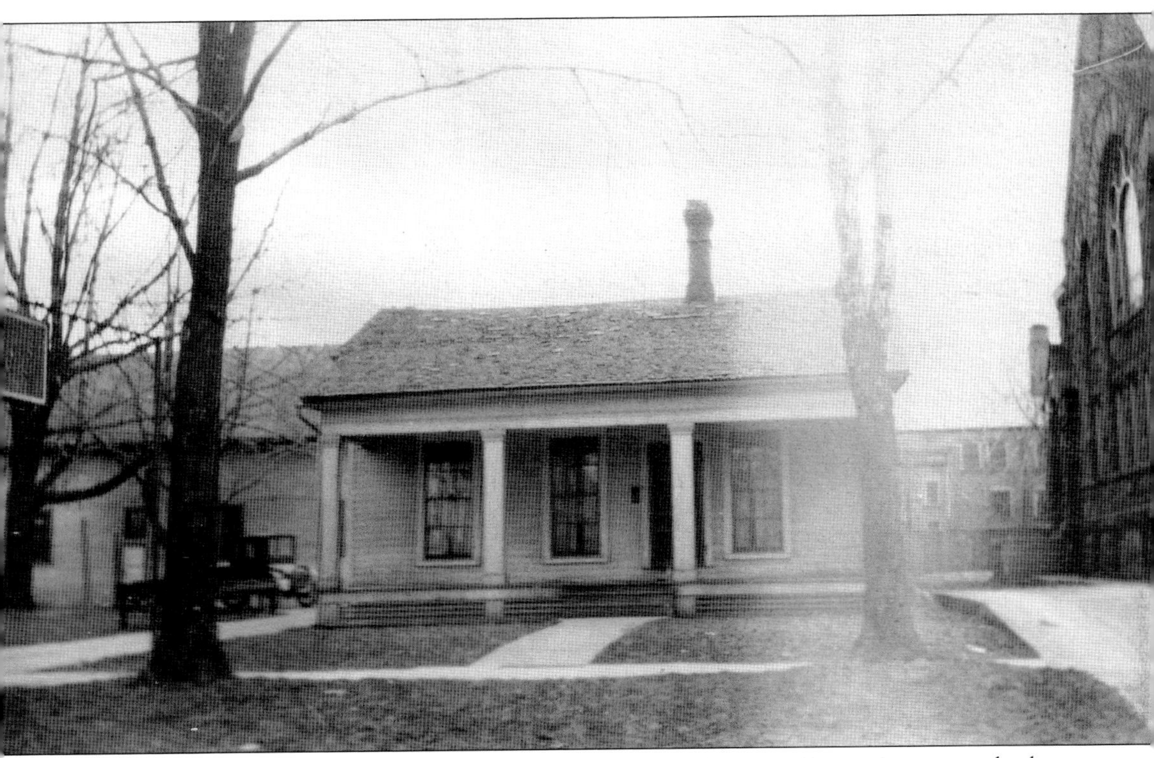

The Fitch Birthplace. The Fitch Homestead, located at 25 West Jefferson Street, was built in 1832. It was the home of Edward and Alta Fitch. The site is now part of the new Justice Center complex. (Judy Pallutch.)

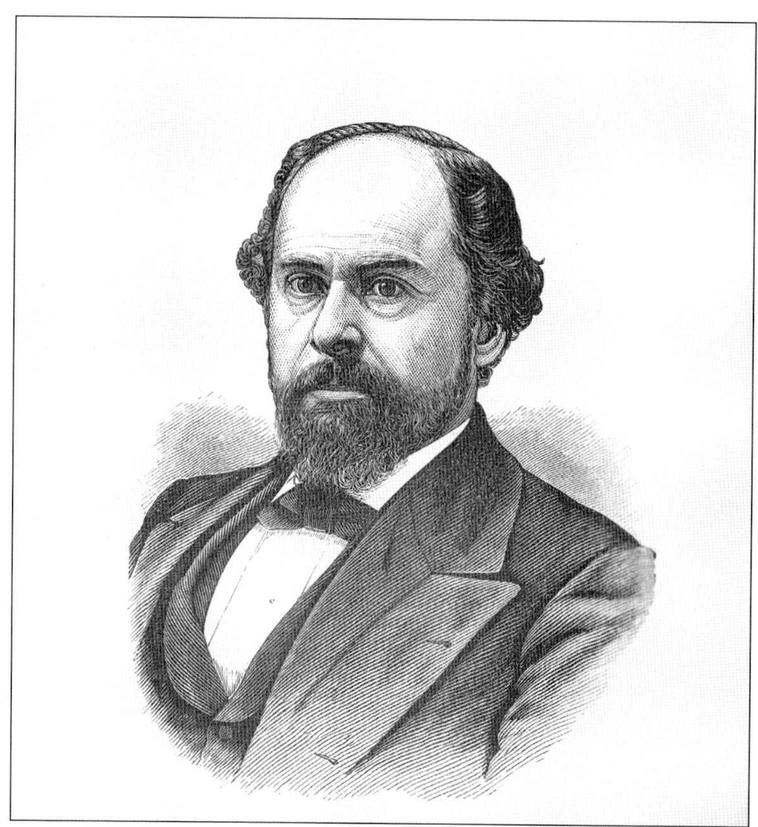

E.H. Fitch. Edward H. Fitch, born in Ashtabula on May 27, 1837, was a Jefferson lawyer, Ashtabula County prosecuting attorney, an Ohio state representative, and a close friend of James A. Garfield. A graduate of Smith College in Massachusetts, Fitch was admitted to the Ohio bar in 1860. He married the former Alta Winchester in 1863, and the couple had eight children, five of whom survived into adulthood. (Ashtabula County Historical Society.)

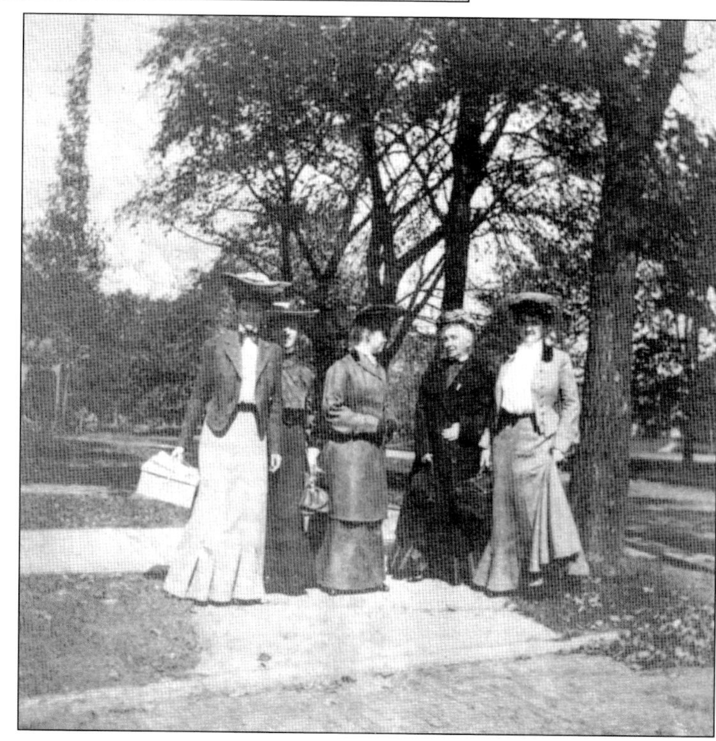

Alta Fitch, 1903. Pictured here is Alta Fitch, Edward's wife, with, from left to right, her daughters Bess and Flora, plus Nan and Laura McFarlane. (Judy Pallutch.)

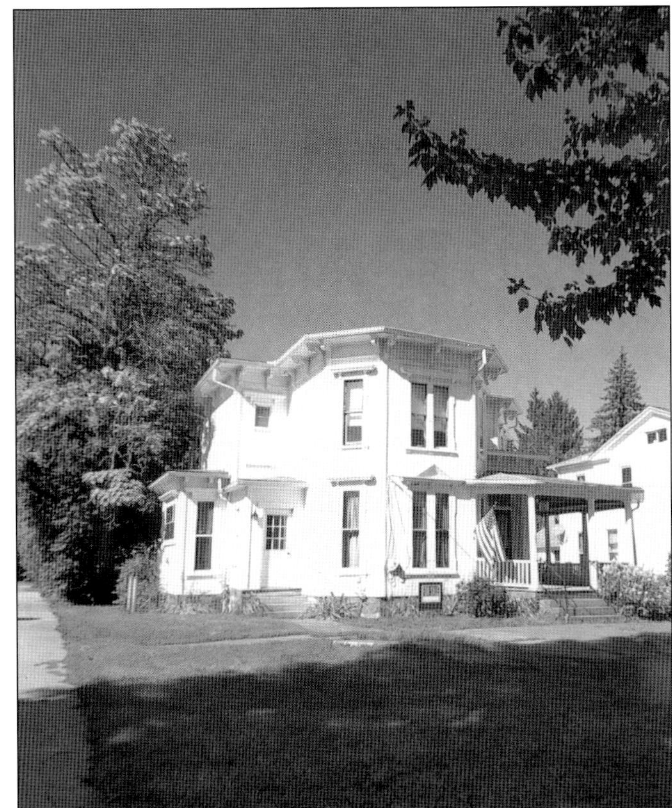

The Home at 67 East Jefferson Street. This home was originally the parsonage for the Congregational Church. Later, it was the office and home of Dr. William Campbell, an optometrist. It still stands. (Author's collection.)

The Home at 137 West Jefferson Street. Built in 1855, this two-story brick home is noted for its widow's walk, its high ceilings, and its original stained-glass windows. The home is still standing. (Author's collection.)

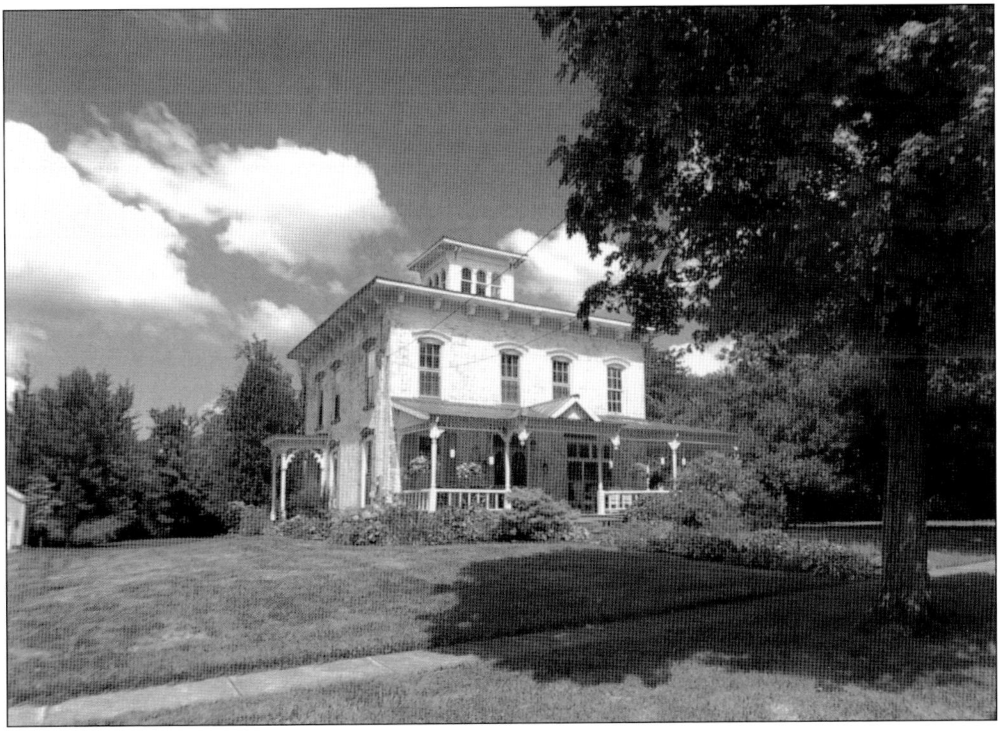

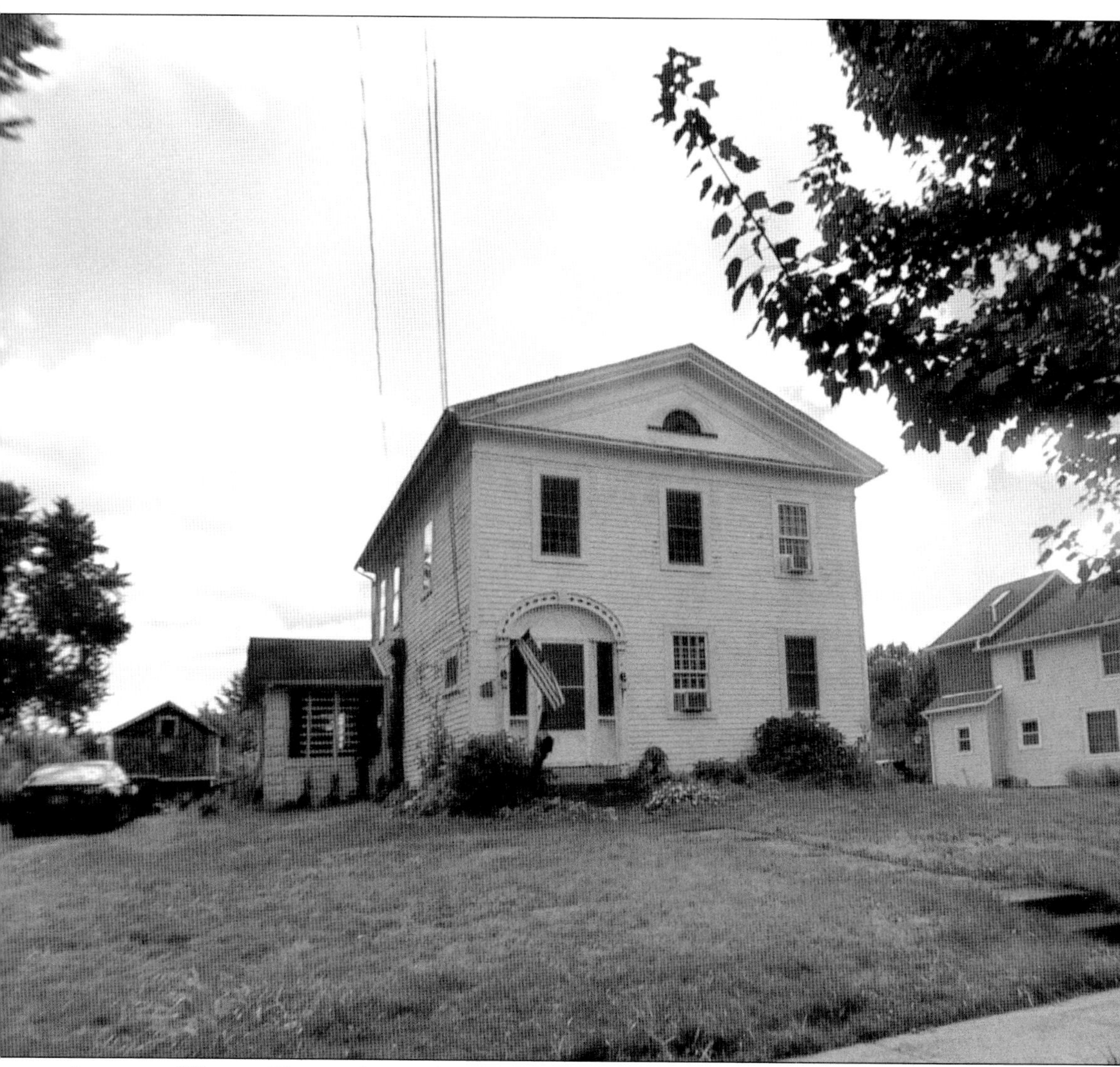

Jonathan Warner House. One of the oldest homes in Jefferson, the Jonathan Warner home at 192 West Jefferson Street, was built in 1832. Warner, the first mayor of Jefferson, lived there with his wife, Nancy Frithy, and their 11 children. Warner was a tavern owner and served as mayor from 1836 to 1838. Their marriage in 1807 was the first performed in Jefferson. All 15 village residents attended the ceremony. (Author's collection.)

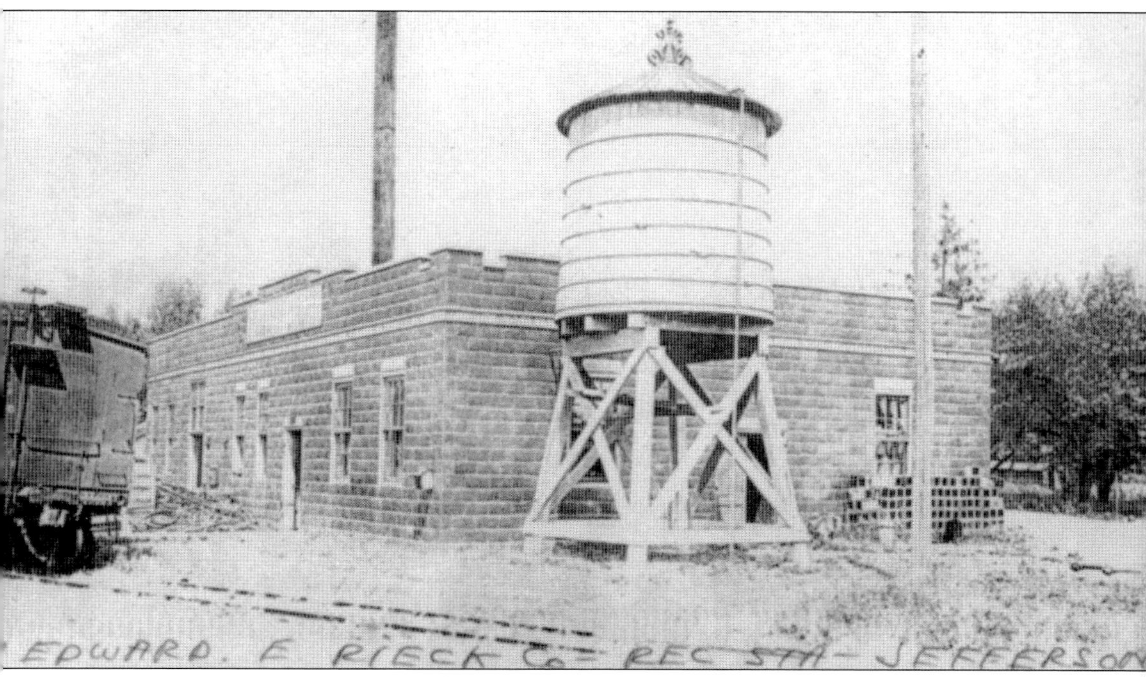

RIECK-MCJUNKIN PLANT, JEFFERSON. The Rieck-McJunkin plant was located adjacent to the railroad tracks, next to the Jefferson Milling Company. The plant, which processed milk from local dairy farms, was built around 1910 and operated until after World War II. Rieck was a large Western Pennsylvania dairy firm that was alternatively known as Rieck-McJunkin and subsequently as National Dairy. Later, National Dairy acquired Sealtest, Kraft Foods, Hydrox, and several other companies. The 1938 plat map of Jefferson lists the building as being owned by the Telling-Belle Vernon Dairy Company; earlier maps show it as the Rieck Company. (Jefferson Historical Society.)

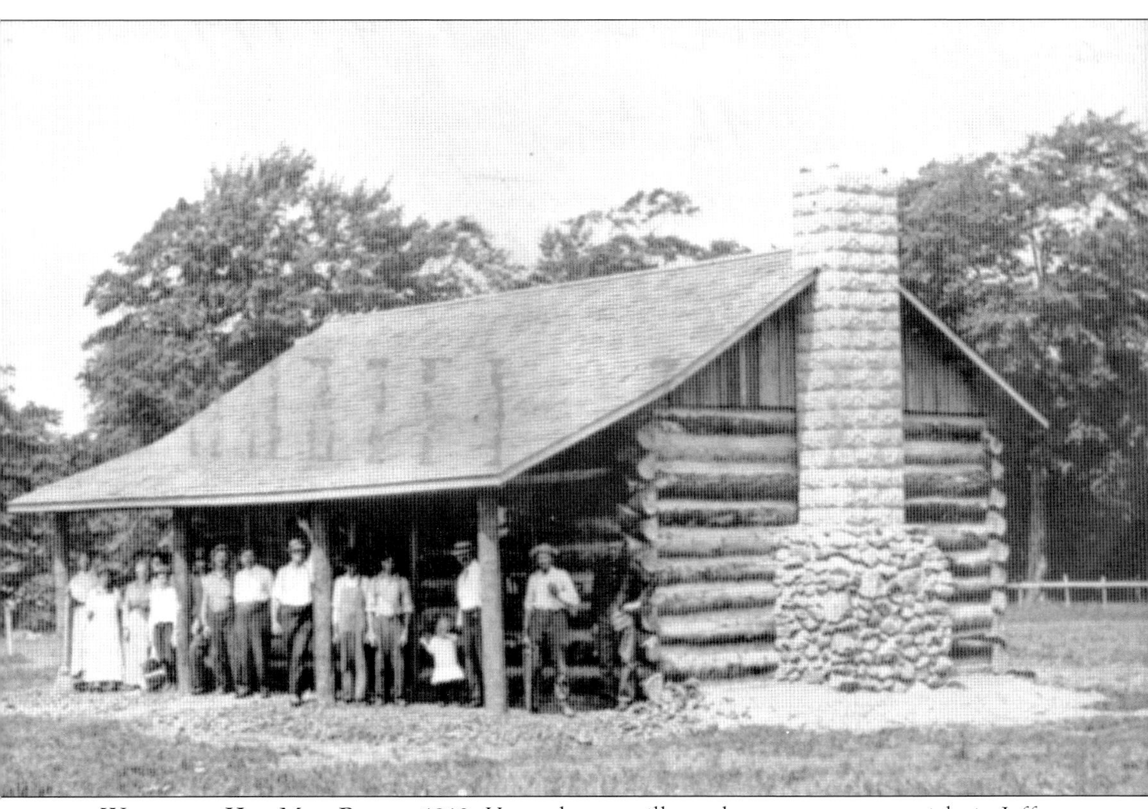

WEBBE AND HILL MILK ROUTE, 1912. Horse-drawn milk trucks were a common sight in Jefferson in the early 20th century. Families had fresh milk and other dairy products delivered to their doorstep. The products were put in metal-lined boxes, located outside the front door, to help keep them cold. (Jefferson Historical Society.)

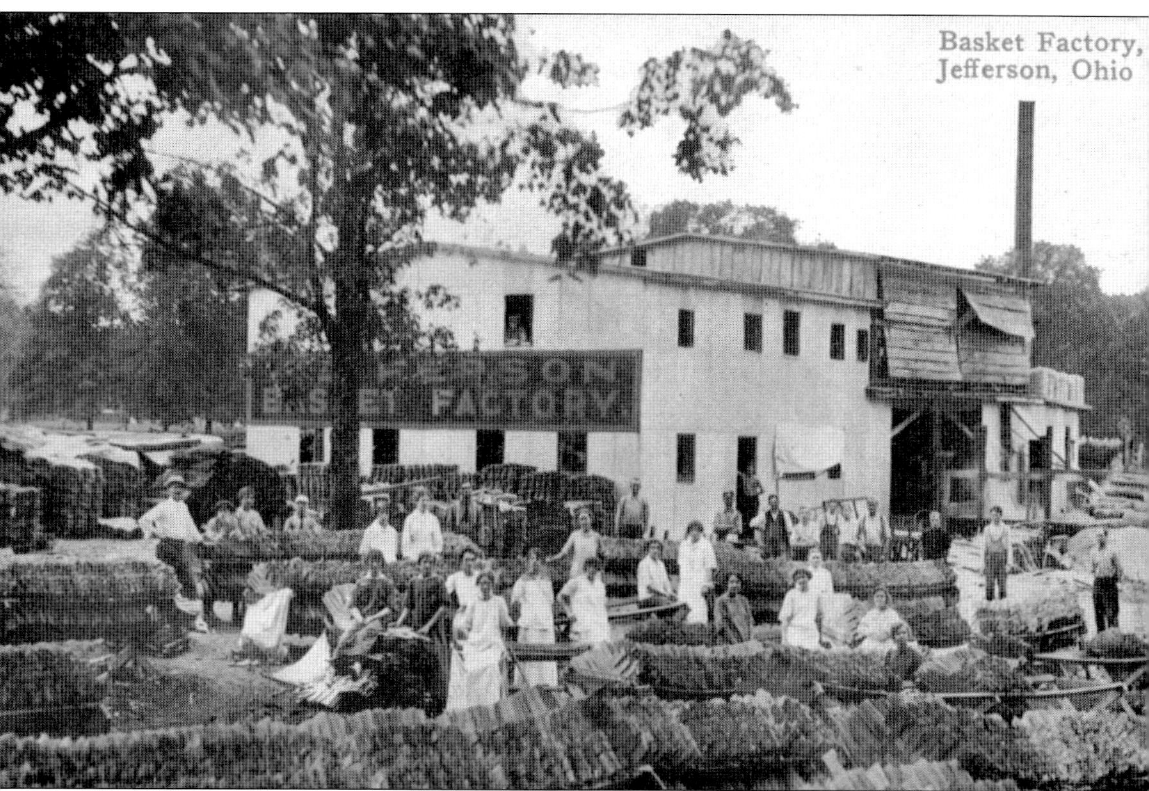

Jefferson Basket Factory. The Jefferson Basket Factory opened in 1911 and was owned by G.F. Wolcott and M.W. Chapin. The factory, located on East Walnut Street near the railroad tracks, produced quality half-bushel baskets. In its heyday, the factory employed 35 workers, most of them women. The Jefferson Basket Factory was acquired by a Pennsylvania company in 1920 and closed in 1935. (Ashtabula County Historical Society.)

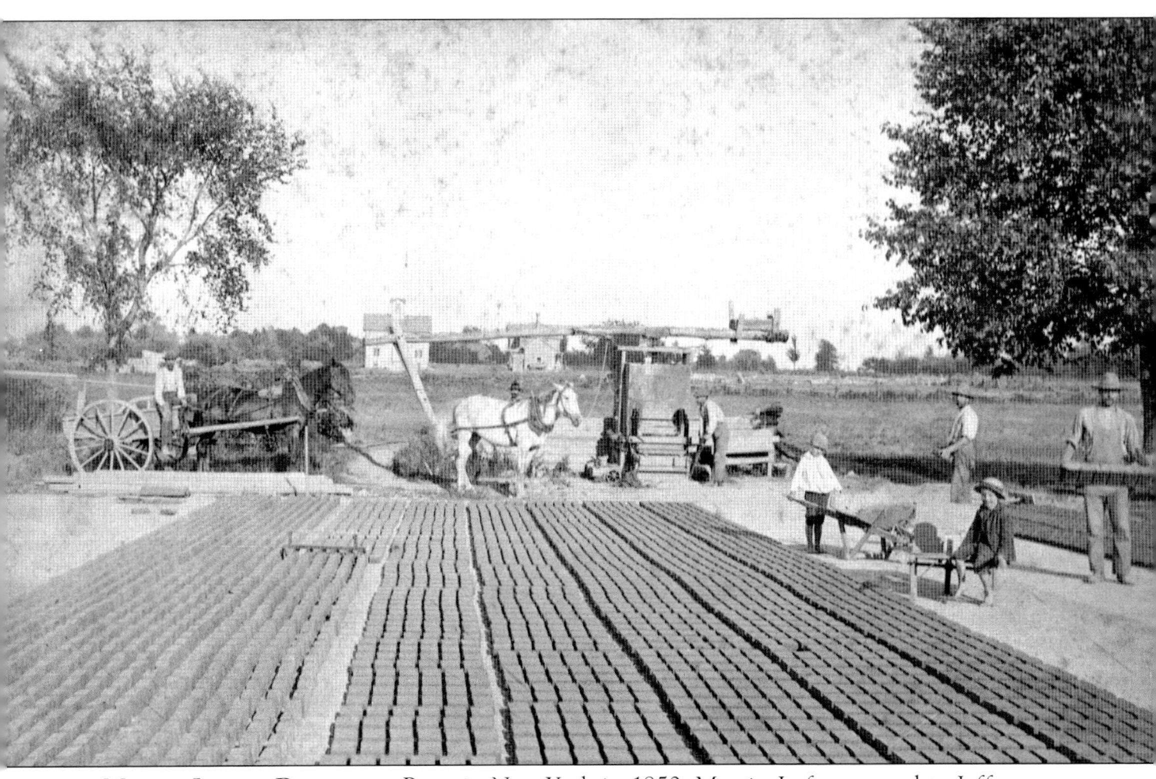

MARTIN LOFTUS BRICKYARD. Born in New York in 1850, Martin Loftus moved to Jefferson as a child. He spent his adult life as the owner of a brick company in town, located on South Chestnut Street near Mulberry Street. Loftus married Susan Hall, and the couple had seven children. Loftus died in 1918 and is buried at Oakdale Cemetery. (Ashtabula County Historical Society.)

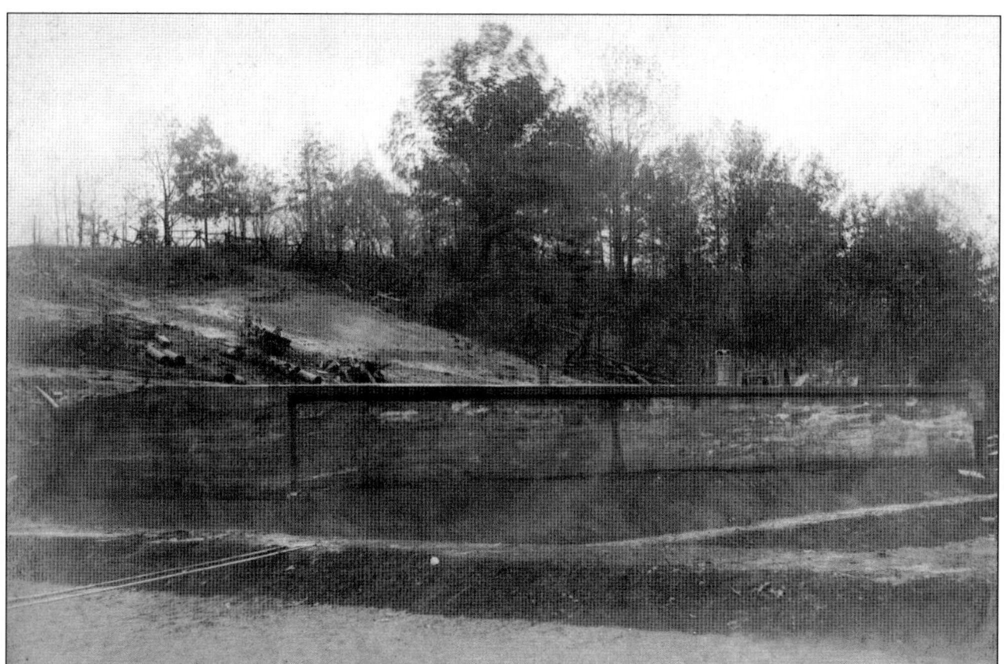

Jefferson Water Works. The Jefferson Water Works was created in 1906 as the water source for the village of Jefferson. Located just east of the village, the area is now Lampson Reservoir, part of the Ashtabula County Metroparks. (Jefferson Historical Society.)

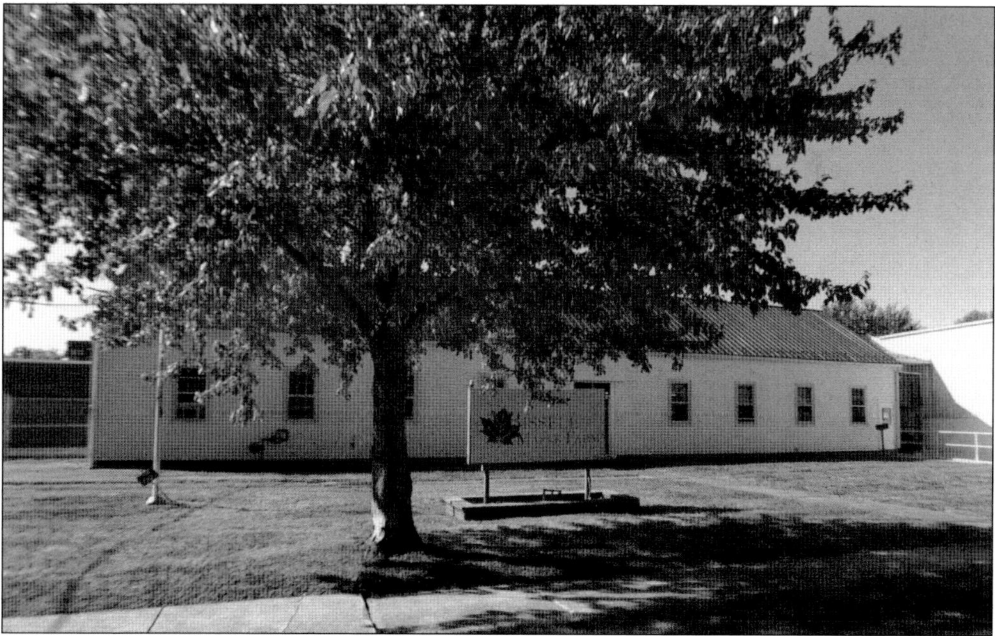

Bissell Maple Farm. Bissell Maple Farm has been crafting quality maple syrup and other maple products for more than 100 years. Now owned and managed by Nate Bissell, the sixth generation in his family to run the business, Bissell Maple Farm has expanded to occupy a 40,000-square-foot facility on the west side of Jefferson. Bissell Maple Farm is the largest maple producer in Ohio. (Author's collection.)

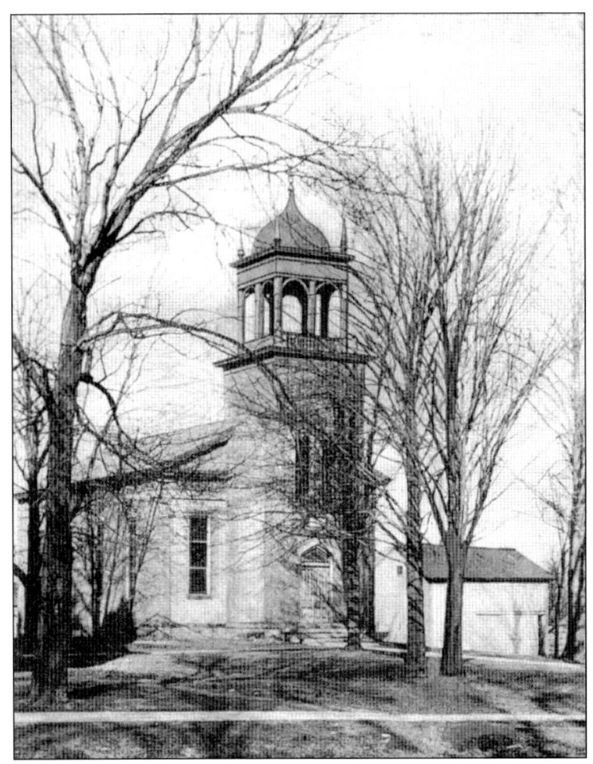

First Congregational Church, Jefferson. First Congregational Church, now UCC Jefferson, was organized in 1831, at a time when the entire village of Jefferson was surrounded by forest and had around 300 total residents. The current church building, made from Austinburg brick, was erected in 1835. Funds for the church were solicited from Connecticut and other East Coast donors. The church raised $4,000. One of these donors was Kentucky senator Henry Clay, who gave $10 with the condition that the church not be used to express "sentiments hostile to slavery." (His wish was ignored.) The abolitionist John Brown (of Harpers Ferry infamy) preached here in 1859. (Ashtabula County Historical Society.)

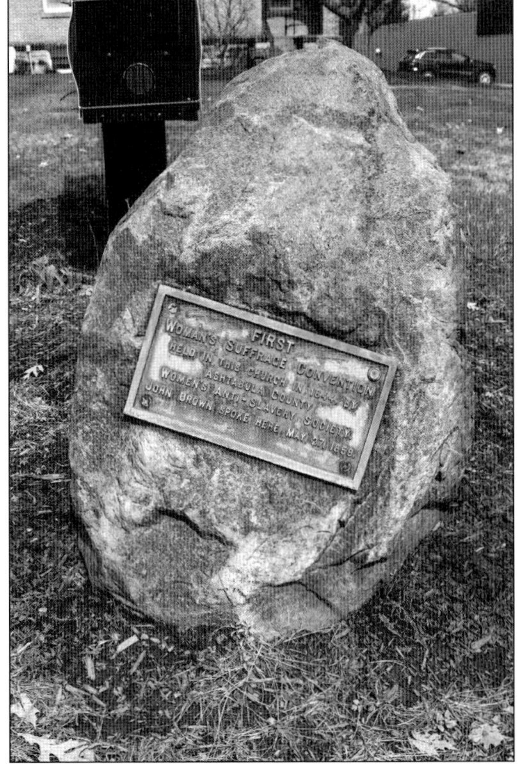

First Congregational Church and the Women's Suffrage Movement. According to a plaque on the side of the Jefferson Congregational Church, the first suffrage convention in the United States was held in Jefferson in 1844. This predates the convention held in Seneca Falls, New York, which is generally accepted as being the first such gathering. According to the plaque, the event was a combination antislavery and suffrage event. Austinburg native Betsy Mix Cowles spoke at the event. Researchers at Kent State University (which is home to the Betsy Cowles and Cowles family archives) believe that this event did happen, but it was held two years later than indicated on the church plaque. Cowles also organized and spoke at a suffrage event in Salem, Ohio, in 1850. Cowles was elected president of that convention and, as a result, founded the Female Anti-Slavery Society of Ashtabula County. (Andrew Holt Frazier.)

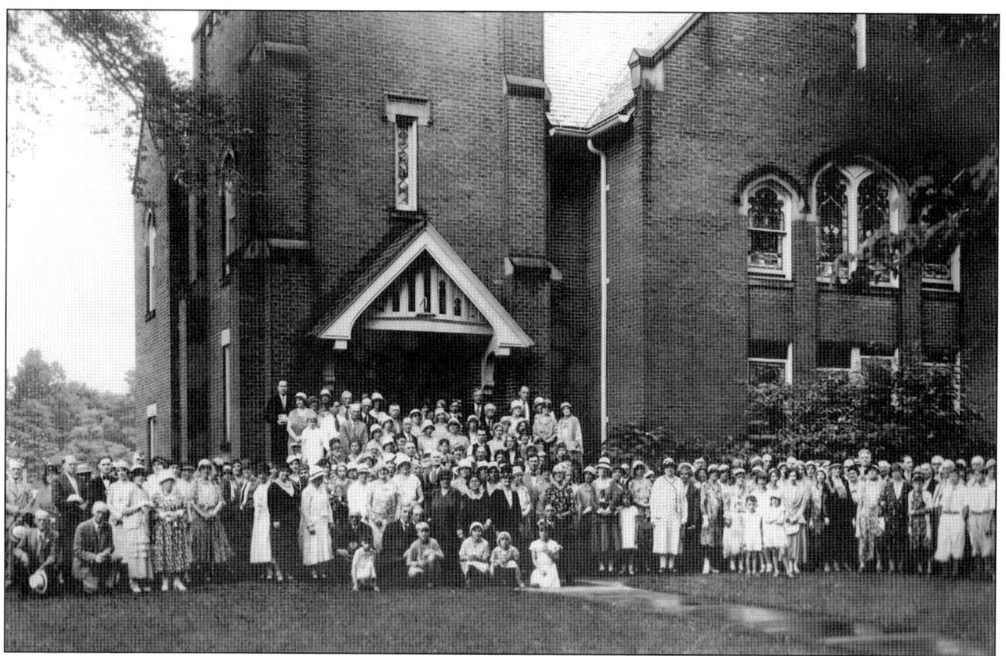

FIRST CONGREGATIONAL CHURCH IN JEFFERSON. The cornerstone for the 1835 church was brought from Windsor via oxen team, a two-day trip. The building also used sand from Ashtabula Harbor and timbers from trees on West Walnut Street in Jefferson. Pew boxes with doors were rented for $34 annually, a practice that was eventually dropped. The church was extensively remodeled in 1908, taking on its current appearance. (Jefferson Historical Society.)

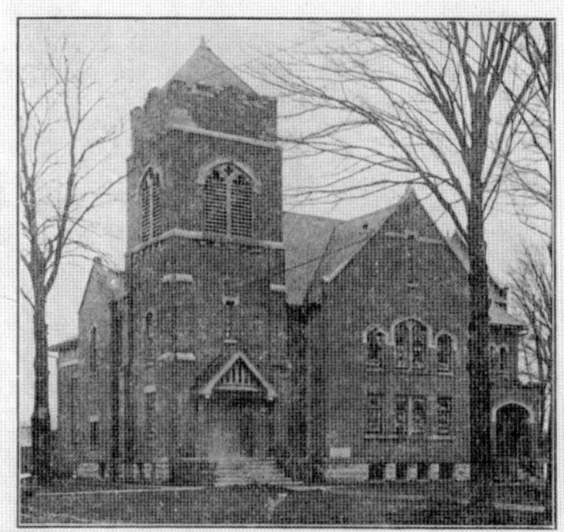

"Whosoever thou art that enterest this church leave it not without a prayer to God for thyself, for him who ministers and for those who worship here."

The First Congregational Church

JEFFERSON. OHIO.

Rev. J. A. Goodrich, Pastor.

Seek ye first His kingdom and His righteousness.

Strangers and all without a church home are cordially invited to unite with us. Seats are free.

UNITED CHURCH OF CHRIST, JEFFERSON. First Congregational Church has had several organs throughout its history. The current 628-pipe instrument was installed in 1957. It includes 21 tubular chimes. The church affiliated with the United Church of Christ when that denomination was created in the merger of the Congregational Church with the Evangelical and Reformed Churches in 1961. (Ashtabula County Historical Society.)

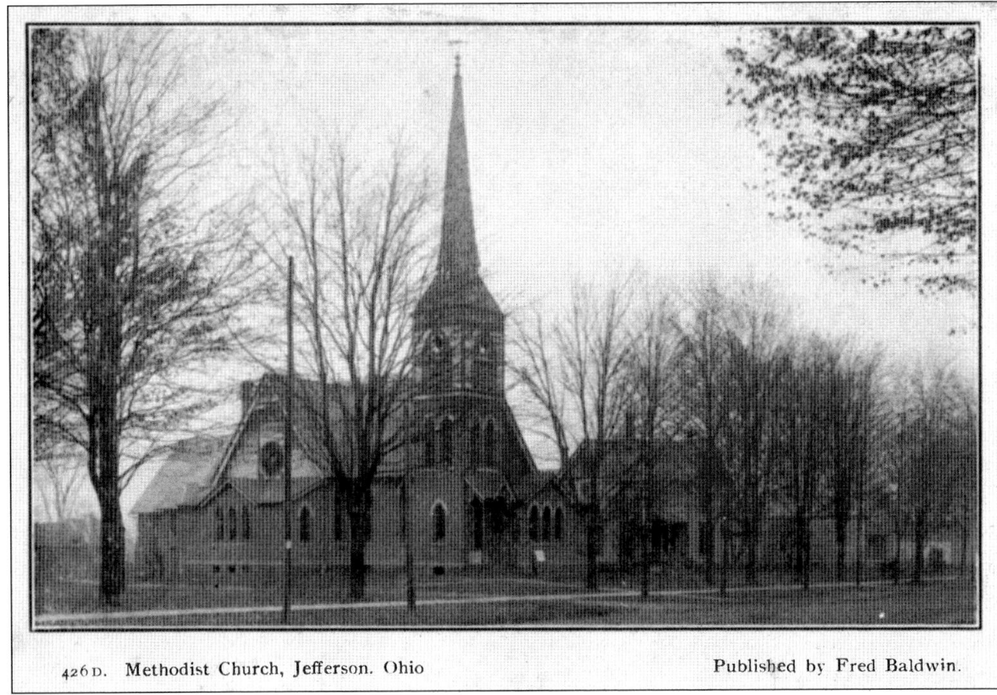

Jefferson United Methodist Church. The Methodist congregation is one of several churches that claim to be the oldest church in Jefferson. The Jefferson Methodists trace their roots back to 1807, when the first Methodist class met in a private home with services led by an occasional itinerant minister. The first Methodist church structure in Jefferson (pictured above) was dedicated on July 22, 1848. (Jefferson United Methodist Church.)

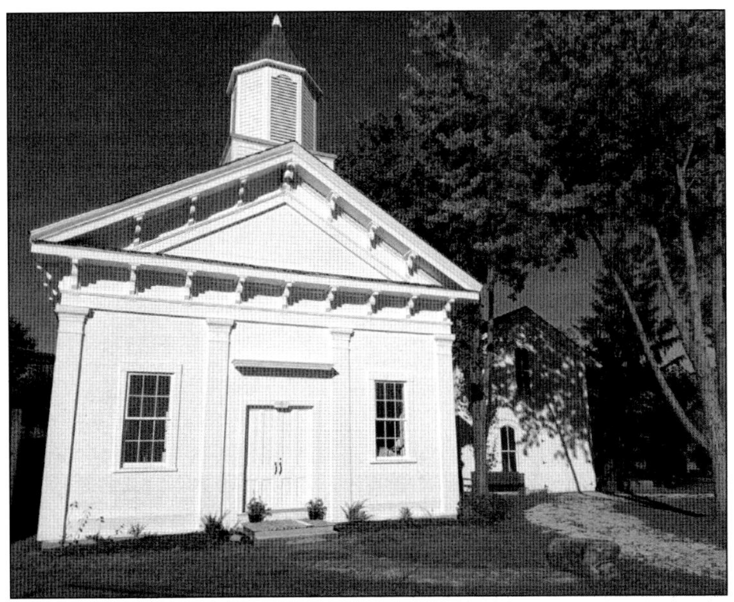

Original Methodist Church, Jefferson Depot Village. Two of the buildings at the Jefferson Depot Village, located next to the Methodist church, relate to the church. They are the original Jefferson Methodist Episcopal Church (the forerunner to Jefferson United Methodist Church), built in 1848 and dubbed "the Church in the Wildwood," and the church parsonage. (Author's collection.)

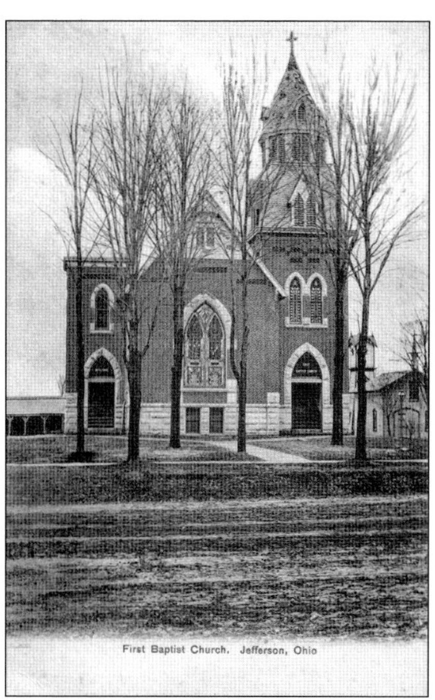

First Baptist Church, Jefferson. The First Baptist Church in Jefferson also lays claim to being the first church in the village. The church was organized in 1811 by 18 persons, most of whom lived in nearby Denmark Township. Their first pastor was Elder Judah Richmond, and the first services were held in log cabins and schoolhouses in Jefferson and Denmark. (Ashtabula County Historical Society.)

First Baptist Church. The congregation quickly outgrew this small church, and a new one was dedicated in 1892. The congregation added onto the original church by turning it 90 degrees, covering the original wood with brick veneer, and adding electric lights. It was at this time that the church's memorial stained-glass windows were added. This "new" Neo-Gothic church also featured a three-story bell tower and arched sandstone windows and doorways. (Jefferson Historical Society.)

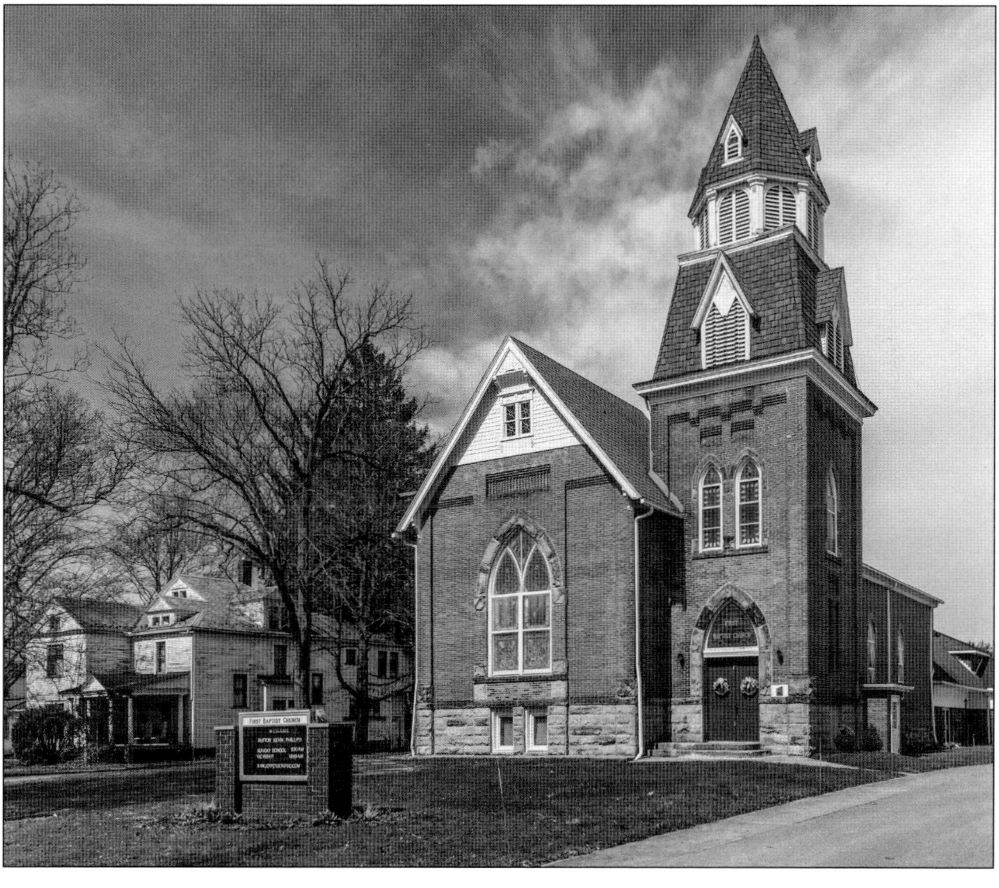

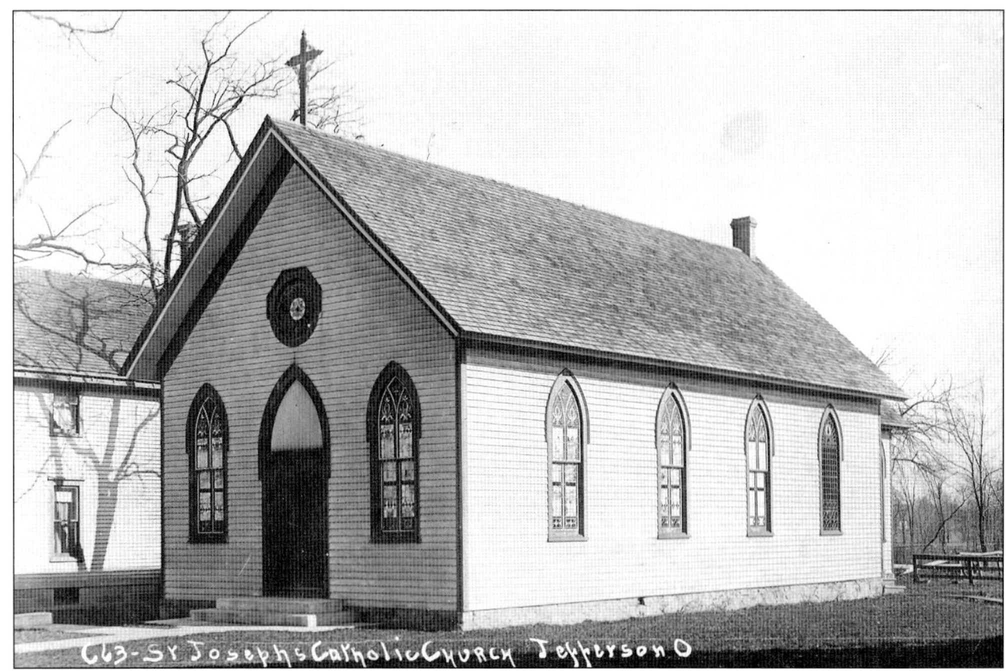

St. Joseph Calasanctius Church. St. Joseph Calasanctius Roman Catholic Church in Jefferson was organized in 1858 as a mission church affiliated with the Diocese of Erie, Pennsylvania. The congregation worshiped in various parishioners' homes until 1869, when a church building was constructed. Fire completely destroyed that structure (pictured above) one year later, but it was rebuilt in 1880. The current Spanish-Roman structure used today was completed in 1925 and features dark tapestry brick and Indiana limestone. (Above, Jefferson Historical Society; below, Ashtabula County District Library.)

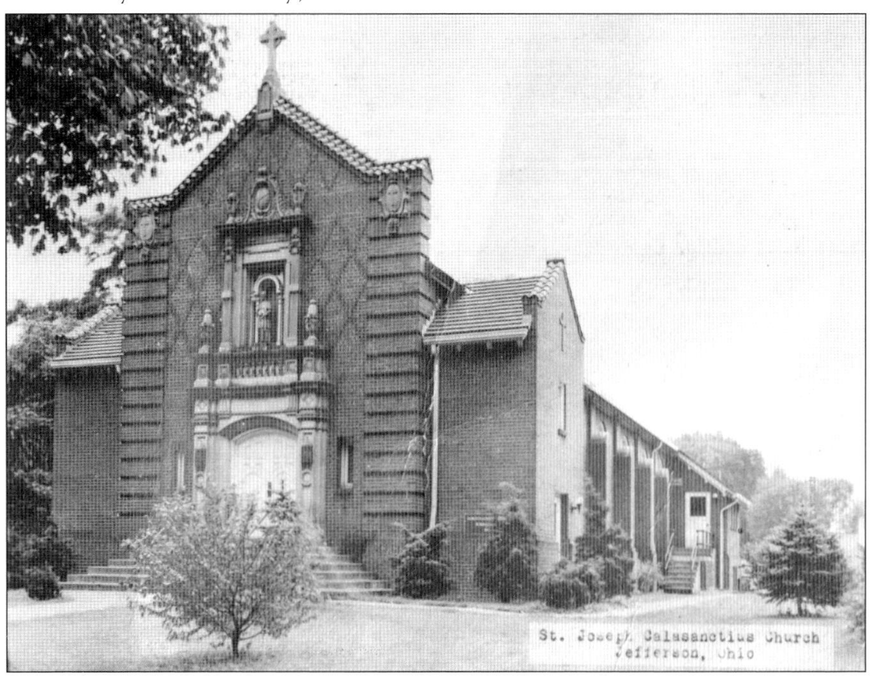

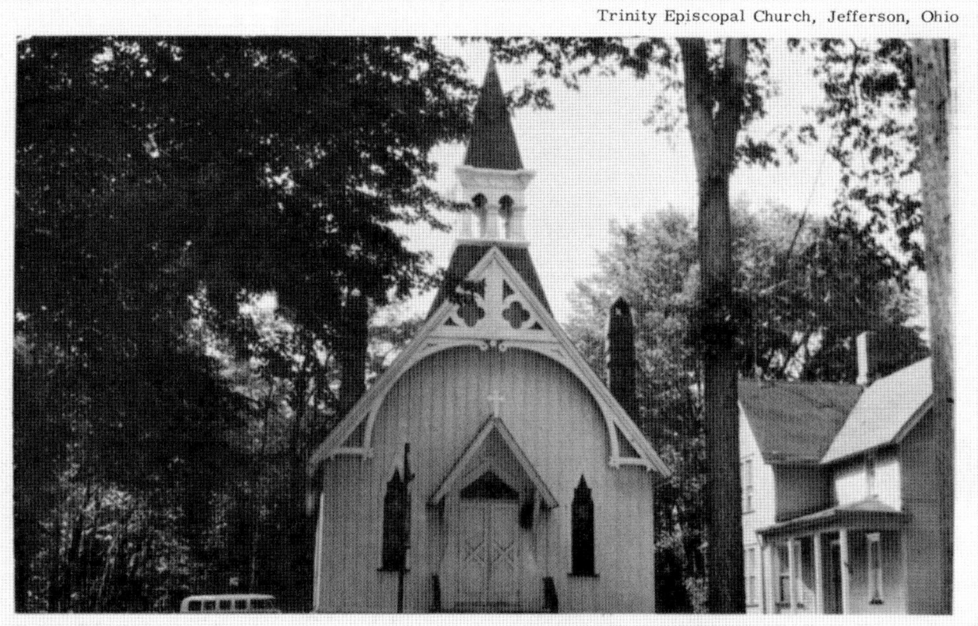

TRINITY EPISCOPAL CHURCH. Trinity Episcopal Church was founded in 1837 with four members from Austinburg, Ashtabula, and Jefferson. Services were held in a schoolhouse until a church building was constructed in 1846. The cornerstone for the present American Gothic–style church building was laid in 1876. The 19th-century author William Dean Howells (see page 58) was baptized in this church. Today, the former church is home to the Jefferson Historical Society. (Jefferson Historical Society.)

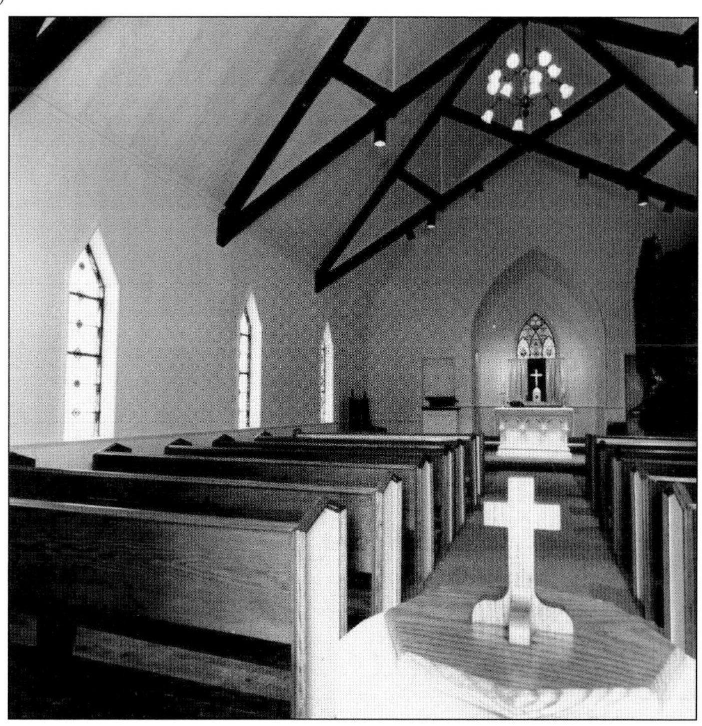

INSIDE TRINITY EPISCOPAL CHURCH. The small church once housed a huge M.P. Moller organ built in 1873. The organ has since been sold, but the building still has its original stained-glass windows, hardwood floors, and carved wooden pews. The wooden baptismal font also remains. (Jefferson Historical Society.)

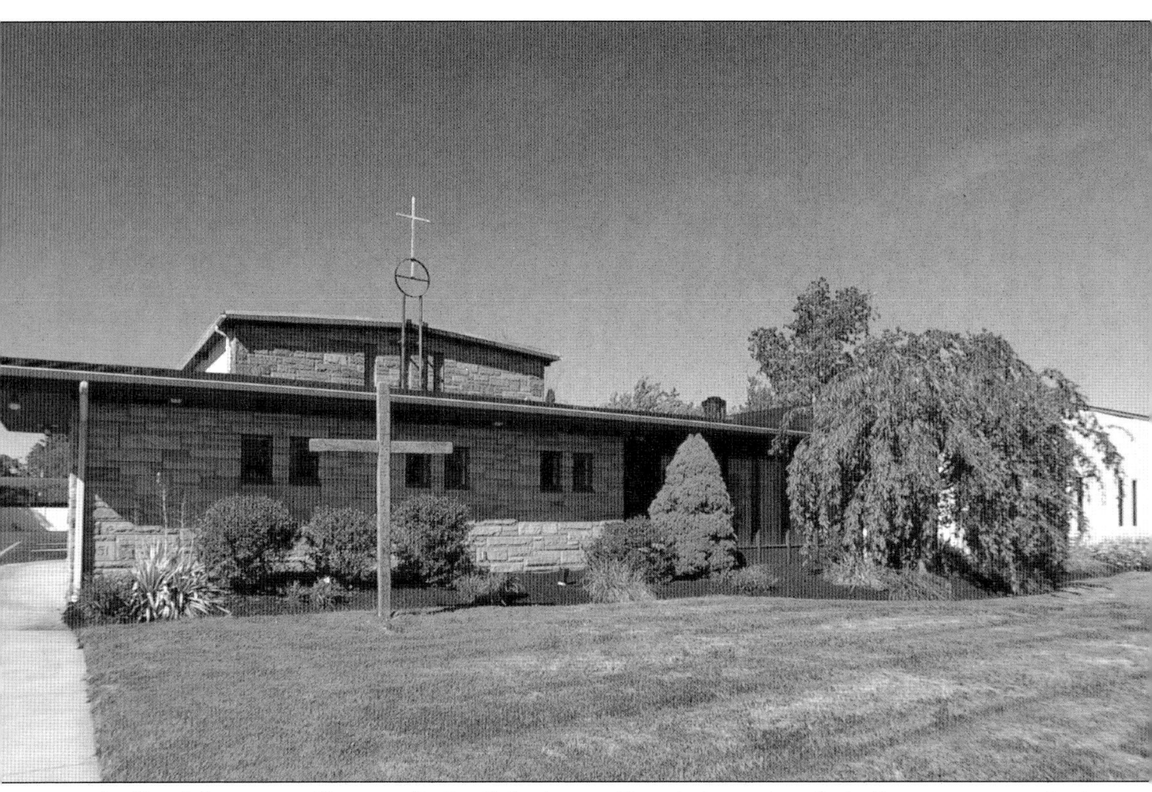

St. Paul's Lutheran Church. St. Paul's Lutheran Church, located on Satin Street, was organized in the 1930s. The current church building, pictured, dates from 1952. St. Paul's current outreach programs include a quilting group that makes items for those in need via Lutheran World Relief, a grief program for widows and widowers, and support of the county's HALO holiday program. (Author's collection.)

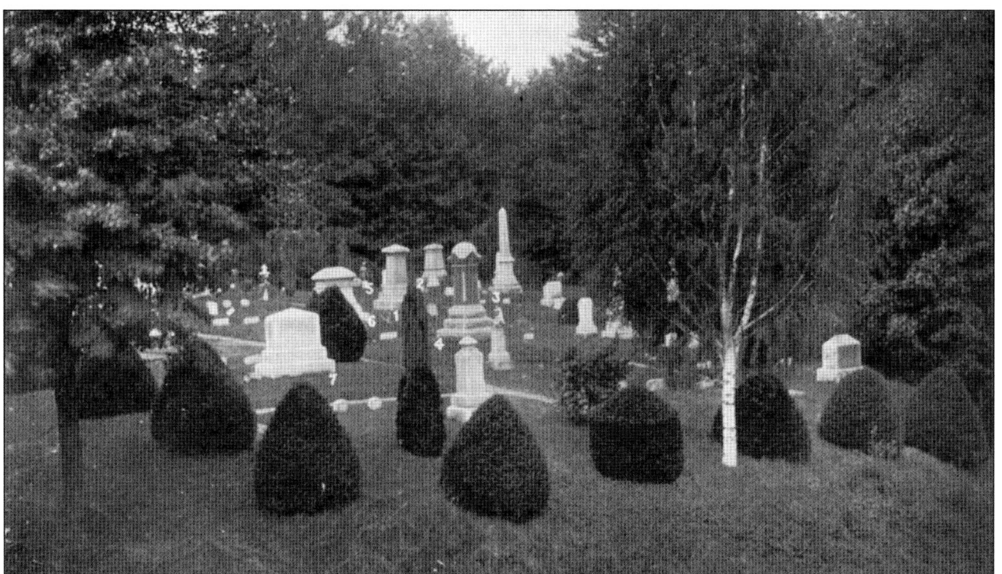

No. 1, B. F. Wade. No. 2, J. A. Giddings. No. 3, H. B. Woodbury. No. 4, Judge Howland. No. 5, Hon. S. A. Northway. No. 6, R. M. Norton. No. 7, E. J. Betts, Jefferson, Ohio.

Oakdale Cemetery. Jefferson's Oakdale Cemetery contains the remains of several notable Jefferson residents. Among these are Sen. Benjamin Wade, the Honorable Joshua R. Giddings, and William Cooper Howells. (Jefferson Historical Society.)

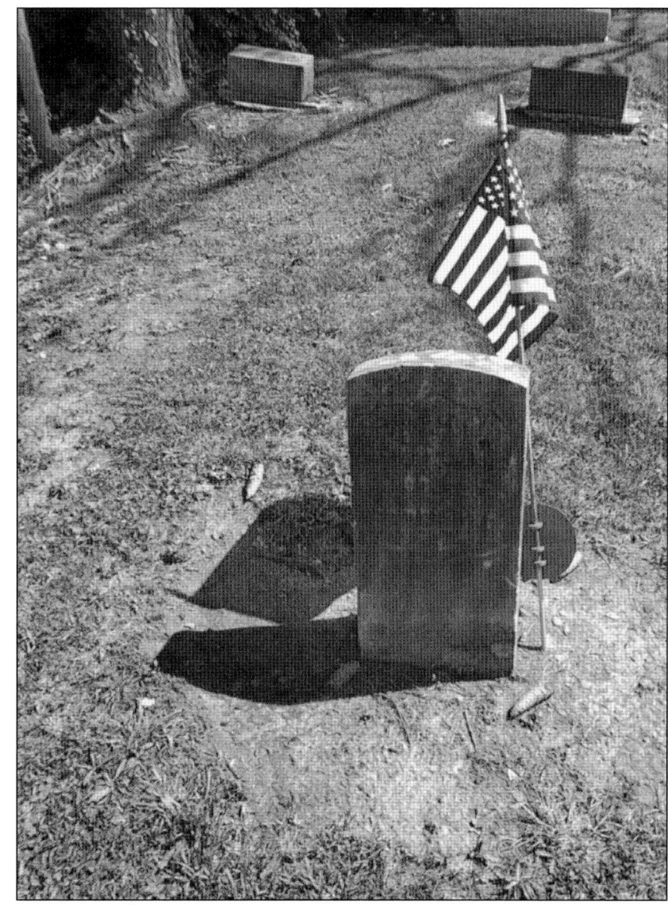

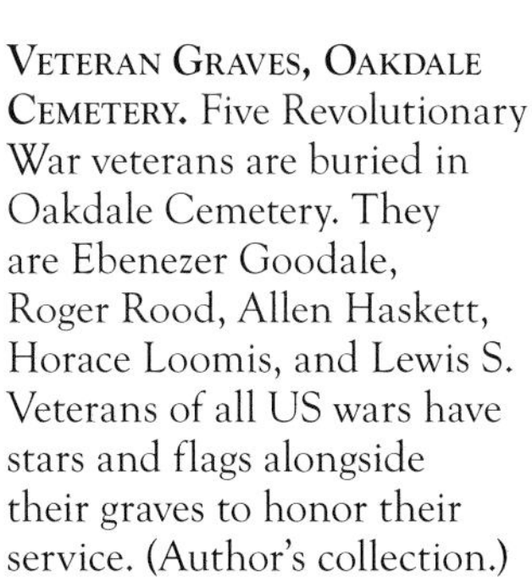

Veteran Graves, Oakdale Cemetery. Five Revolutionary War veterans are buried in Oakdale Cemetery. They are Ebenezer Goodale, Roger Rood, Allen Haskett, Horace Loomis, and Lewis S. Veterans of all US wars have stars and flags alongside their graves to honor their service. (Author's collection.)

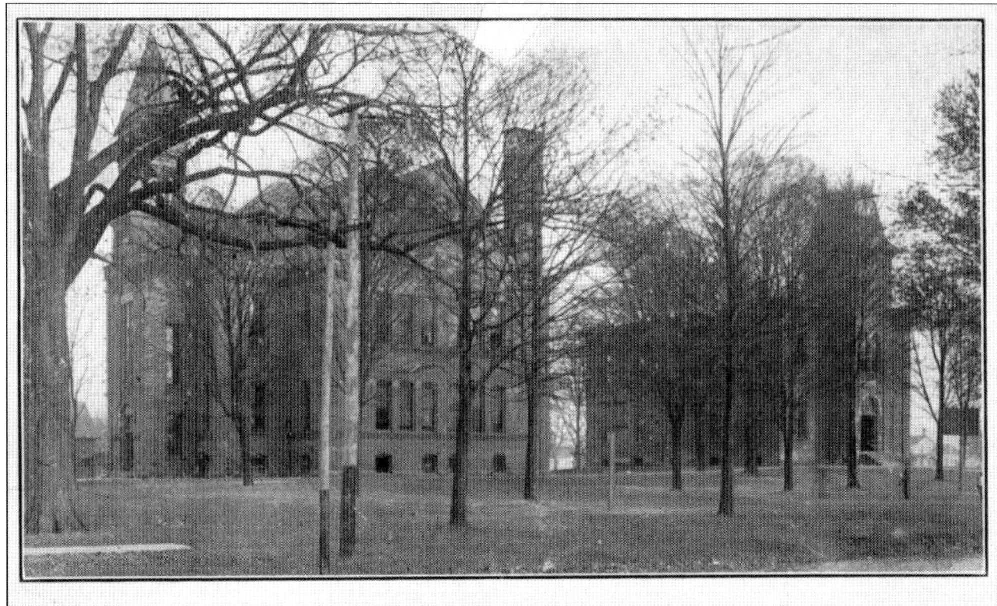

JEFFERSON EDUCATIONAL INSTITUTE, 1909. The Jefferson Educational Institute was erected at the southeast corner of Jefferson and Chestnut Streets in 1870, when the village of Jefferson population was just 869. A high school building was added to the campus in 1888, with students in local grades using the original structure. Jefferson Educational Institute became Jefferson High School in 1910. (Author's collection.)

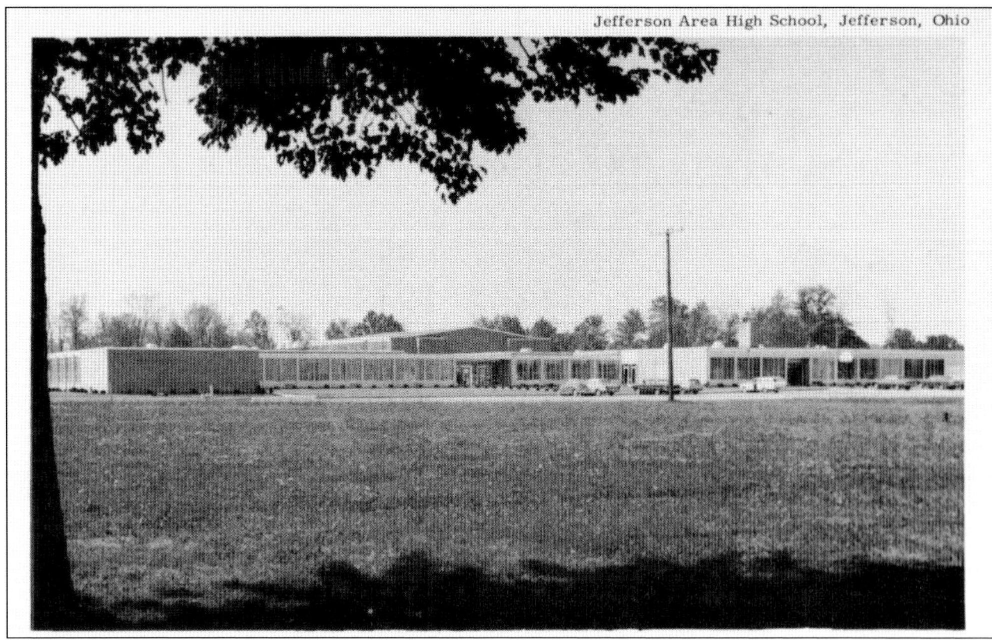

JEFFERSON AREA HIGH SCHOOL. The current Jefferson Area High School, located on the west side of the village, opened in 2009. Before that, a 1962 building (pictured) occupied the space. Jefferson Area High School has a current enrollment of 427 students in grades nine through twelve. (Ashtabula District Library Archives.)

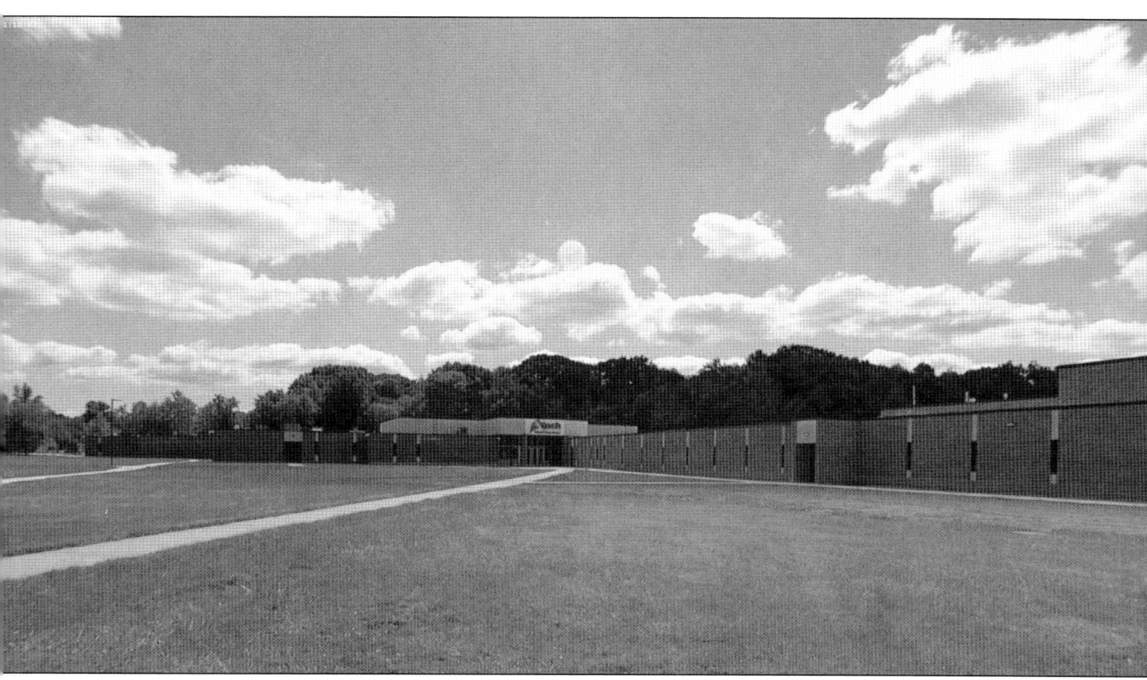

Ashtabula County Technical and Career Campus. Ashtabula County Technical and Career Campus (nicknamed "A-Tech"), located just west of Jefferson, was created in 1965 and opened in 1968 with the mission to offer career training to area high school students who chose not to attend college. It continues to thrive today, drawing students from seven school districts and nine high schools, including Jefferson Area High School. The campus originally offered seven courses of study. That has expanded to 20 programs, including culinary arts, carpentry, auto mechanics, cosmetology, and welding. (Author's collection.)

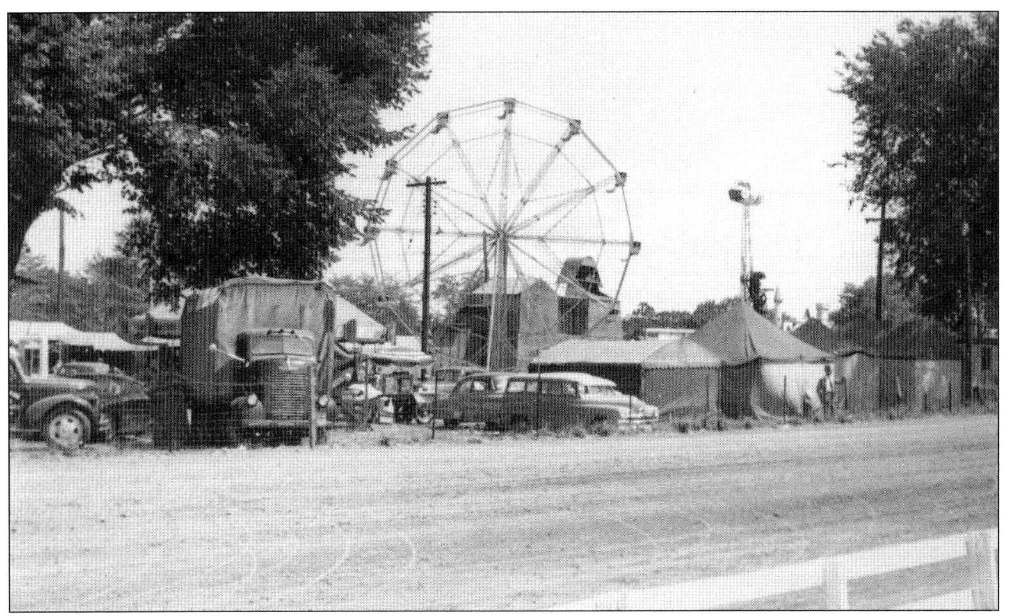

Ashtabula County Fairgrounds, 1958. The Ashtabula County Fair is the second-oldest county fair in the state of Ohio (behind the Geauga County Fair). Founded in December 1822, the fair was first held in Austinburg, then Ashtabula, before moving permanently to Jefferson in 1842. The first Ashtabula County fairgrounds was located across from Trinity Episcopal Church, next to the Jefferson Town Hall building. (Jefferson Historical Society.)

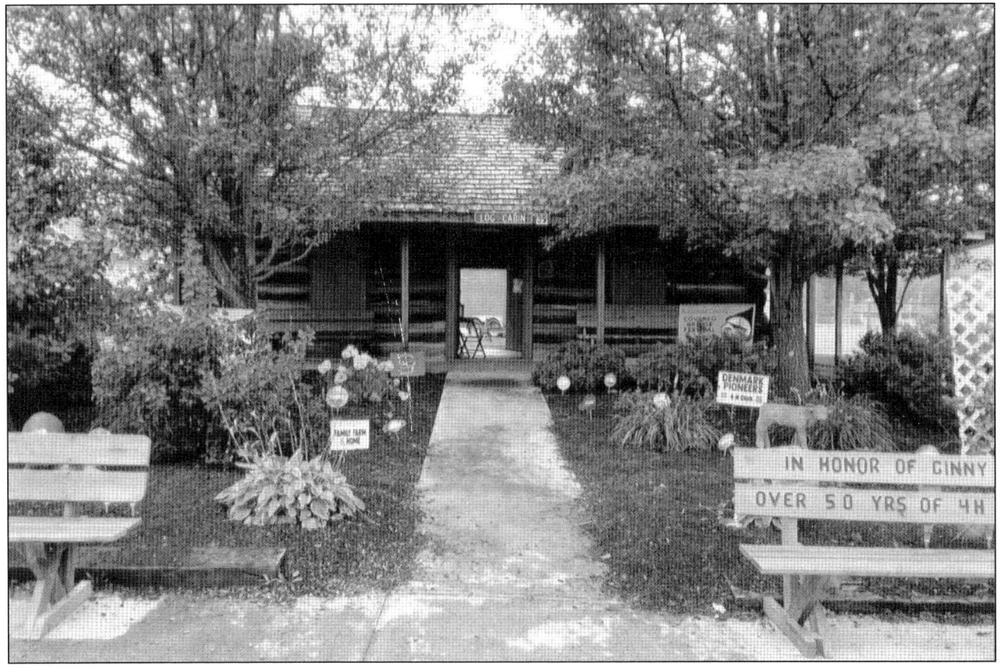

Log Cabin. The log cabin at the fairgrounds is an iconic part of the property. The logs for the structure, which was built in 1915, were given by or in memory of local pioneers who had been born in a log cabin. Today, the cabin houses a variety of historic documents and artifacts. (Jefferson Historical Society.)

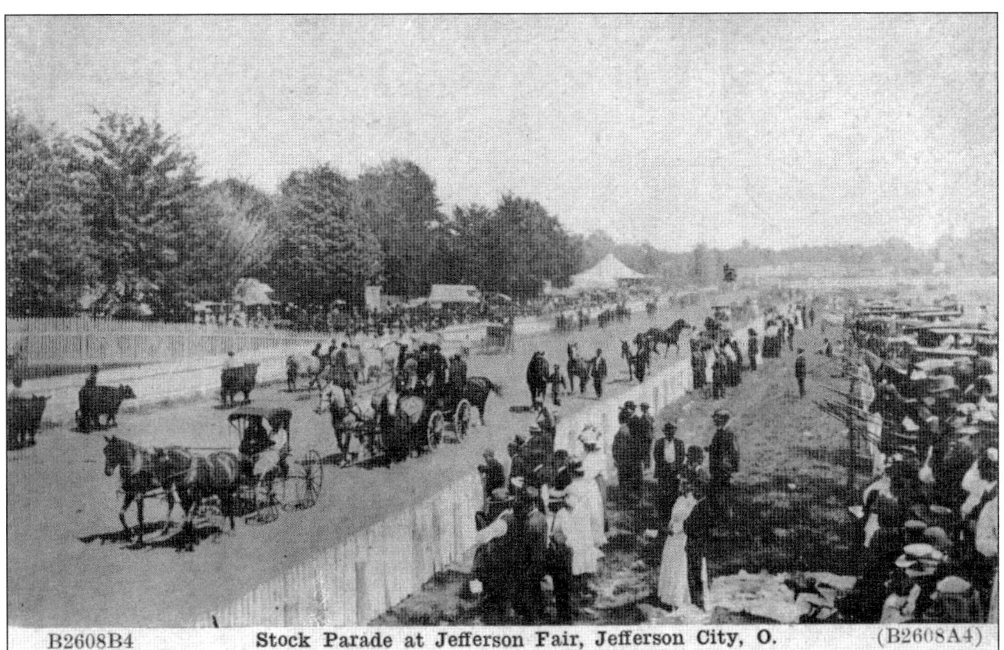

STOCK PARADE, ASHTABULA COUNTY FAIR, 1910. Animals have been an integral part of the Ashtabula County Fair from its beginnings. The Ohio State University Extension Office has helped organize 4-H clubs in the county since 1912. Today, there are fifty-four 4-H clubs in Ashtabula County with more than 900 youth members and 150 volunteer advisors. The highlight of the 4-H season is showing animals at the county fair, which culminates in the livestock auction on the last day of the fair. (Author's collection.)

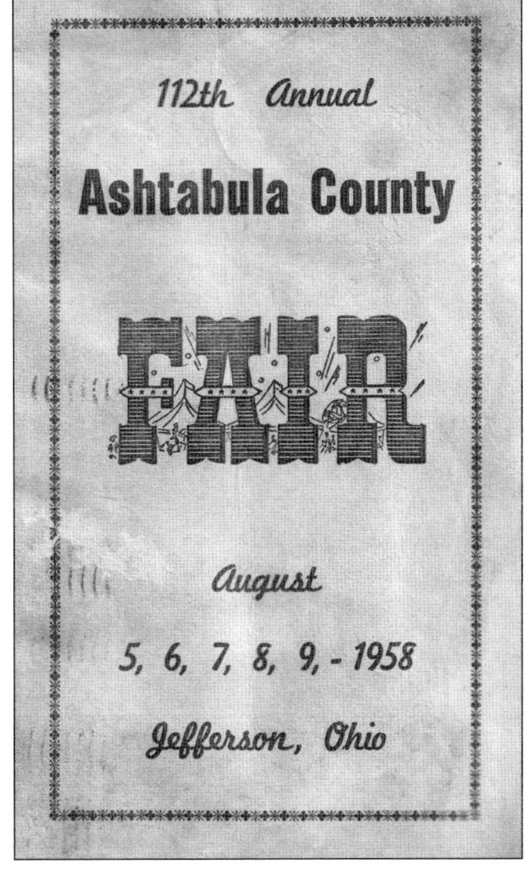

PROGRAM FOR ASHTABULA COUNTY FAIR, 1958. Many people have performed at the Ashtabula County Fair. One of the least expected is a young Burt Lancaster, who performed a trapeze act at the fair in the 1930s while under contract with Klein Attractions. (Jefferson Historical Society.)

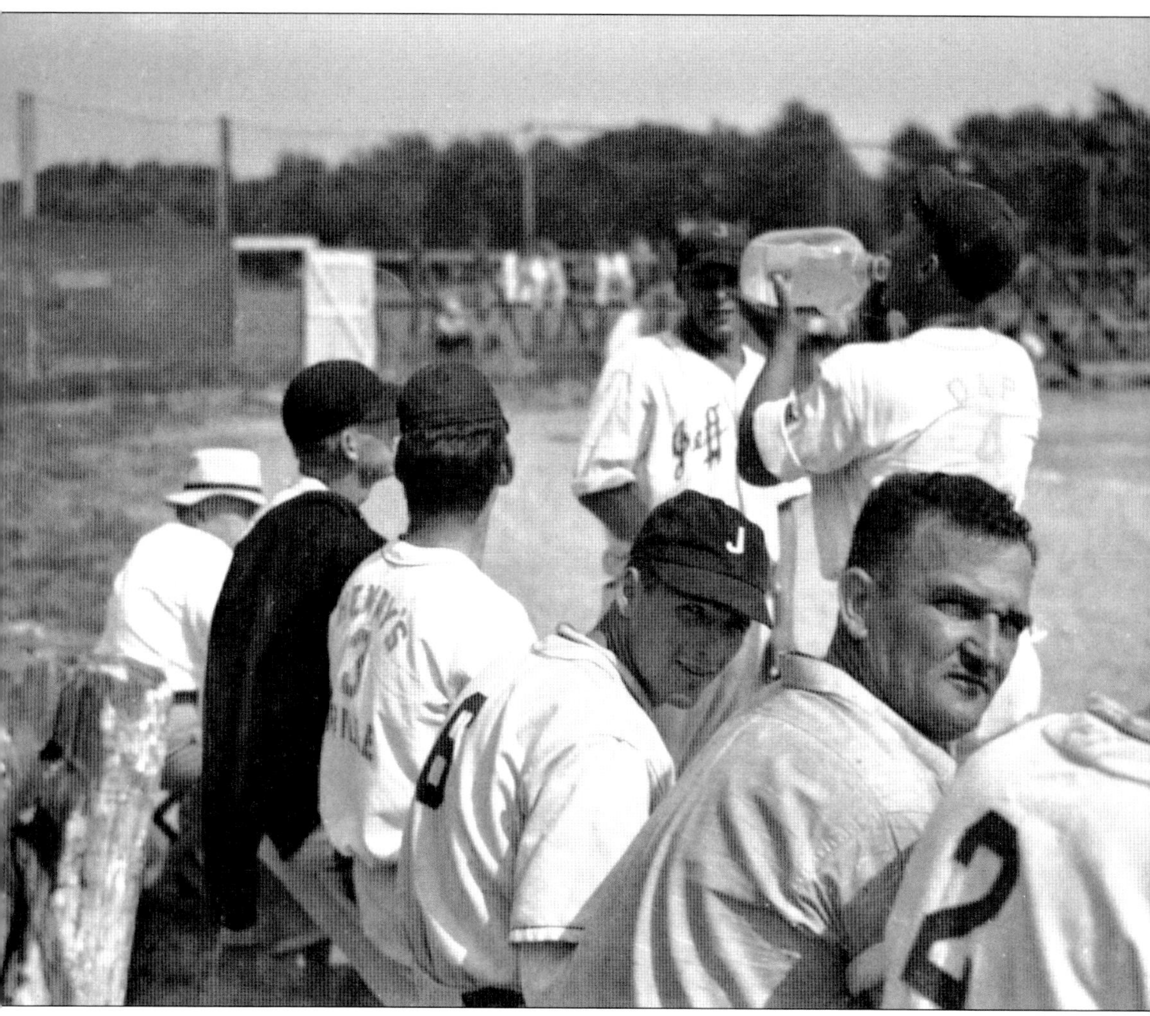

Jefferson Baseball Team. Before television and Internet devices, community sports teams thrived. One such team was the Jefferson baseball team, named the Occidentals in 1875. They first played in an open field near Walnut and Chestnut Streets before a more permanent ball field was created at the fairgrounds. Opponents included the Eagleville White Sox and the Ashtabula Buckeyes. (Author's collection.)

Two

Rock Creek

The village of Rock Creek today is not the thriving community that once occupied that area. The village of Rock Creek in 1880 had a population of 558 persons and boasted three churches, a bank, several newspapers, a sawmill, four steam tanneries, a large hotel with two retailers, a woolen factory, a gristmill, and a cording mill. The railroad stopped in the center of town on its way between Lake Erie and the Ohio River and on to Pittsburgh, making it easy for local factories to get their goods to markets throughout the region. Residents did not have to wait long for a train. Five trains came through town daily.

State Route 45, once a stagecoach route, brought people to Rock Creek on their way from Lake Erie to the Ohio River and beyond. The traffic in the early 20th century supported several hotels as well as two gas stations and multiple restaurants. However, when the interstate highways were constructed in the 1960s, much of this traffic diverted to Route 11, and most of these businesses gradually closed. Loss of these jobs caused Rock Creek to shrink from 731 residents in 1970 to 529 residents in 2010. Since then, the population has rebounded somewhat as the area develops as a wine region and people are drawn to the simple country life in Ashtabula County along the Grand River and Rock Creek.

Despite its small size, Rock Creek has been home to a variety of prominent people. Among these are the artist David Birdsey Walkey, evangelist and theology author Lewis Chaffer, psychologist Theodore Newcomb, and contemporary chainsaw artist Bob Anderson.

Today, Rock Creek is best known for its annual Ox Roast, sponsored by the Morgan Township Fire Department, and its fall festival.

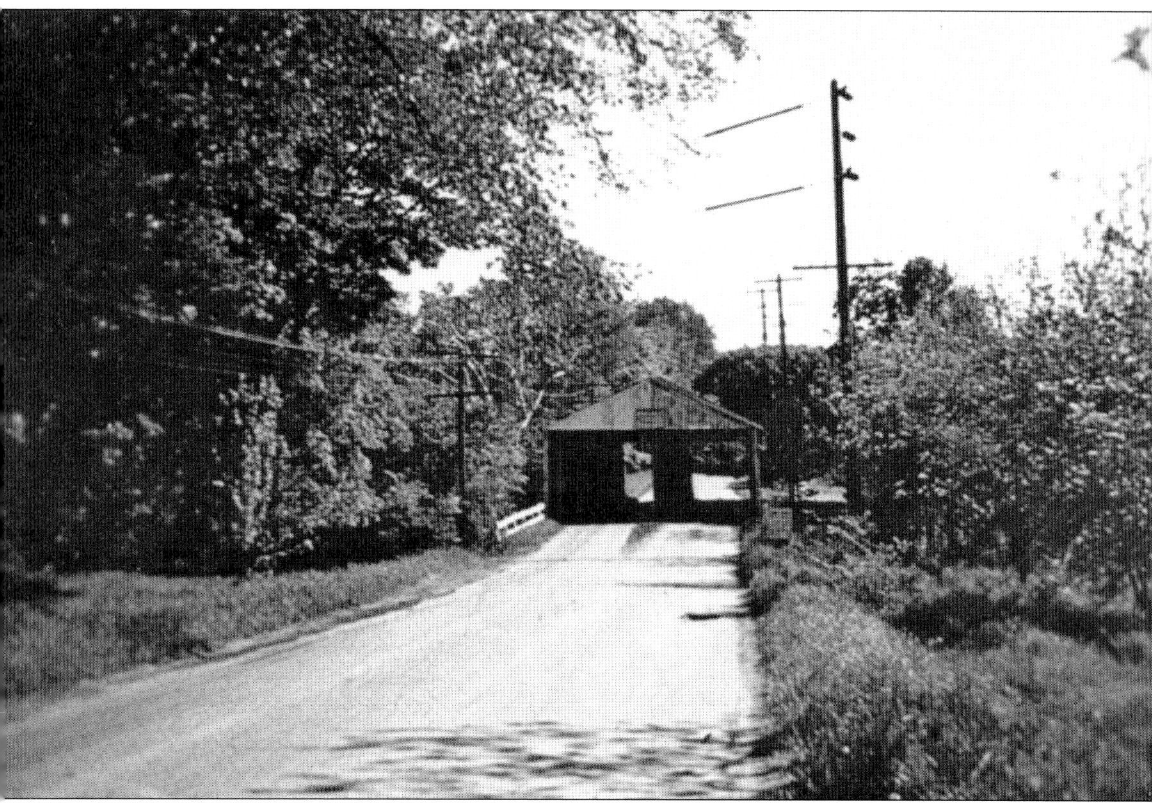

TWO-LANE COVERED BRIDGE. For more than 100 years, a unique two-lane covered bridge was the south entrance to Rock Creek, along State Route 45. The bridge over Rock Creek, built in 1832 and put together by wooden pegs, was designed by Samuel Ackley and George Crowell. It was taken down in 1948 and replaced by the present steel structure. (Author's collection.)

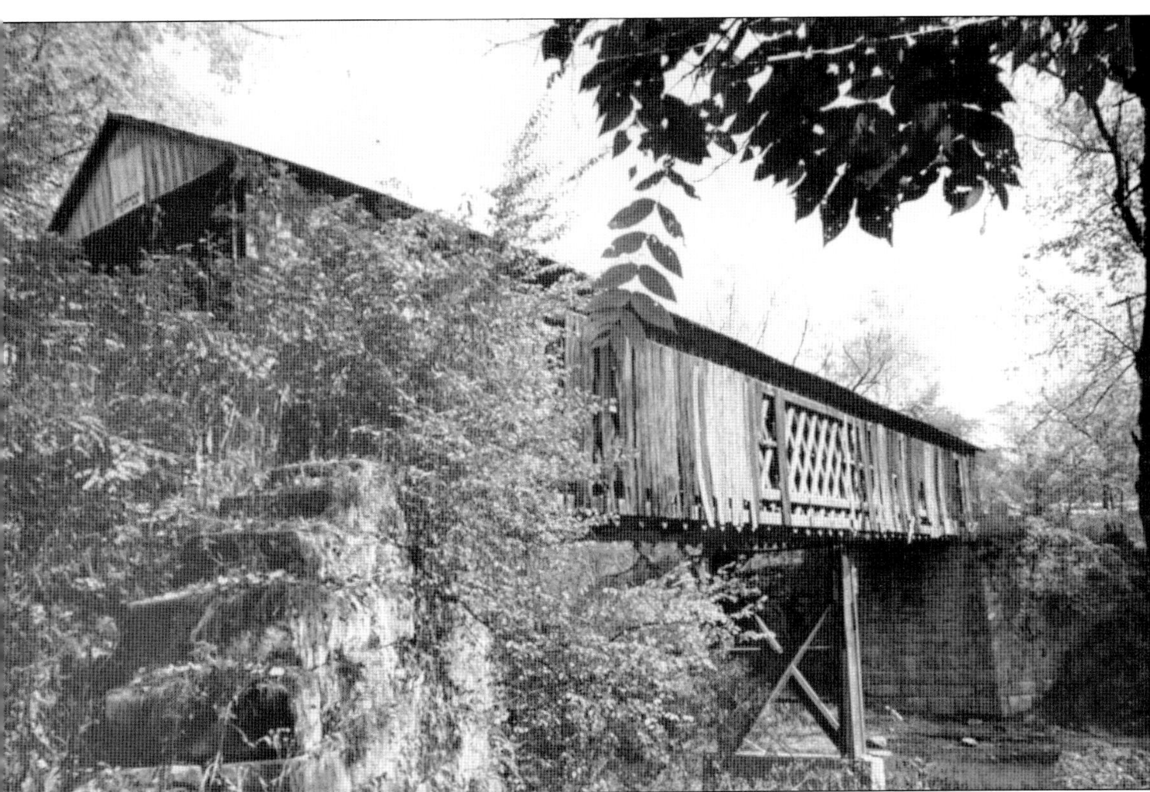

Riverdale Covered Bridge. Riverdale Covered Bridge, located just west of the village, was built in 1874. The 140-foot-long bridge is a single-span, Town truss–style bridge and connects the two banks of the Grand River. Steel bracing was added in 1945, and new wooden flooring was added in 1981. The bridge still stands and is open to road traffic. (Cleveland Press Collection, Cleveland State University.)

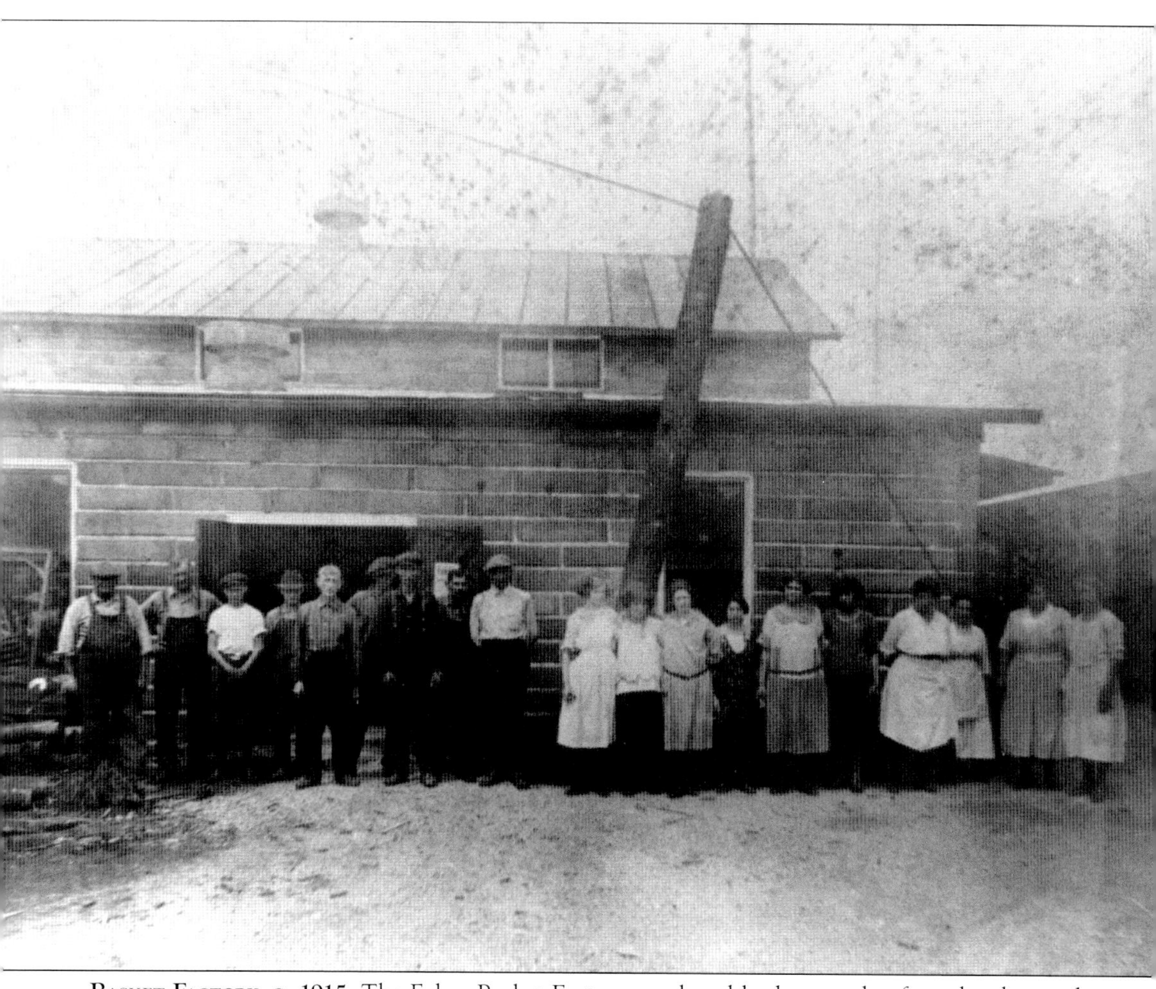

Basket Factory, c. 1915. The Fobes Basket Factory produced baskets made of maple, elm, and beech woods in the early 20th century. The factory burned in 1923 and was never rebuilt. (Jefferson Historical Society.)

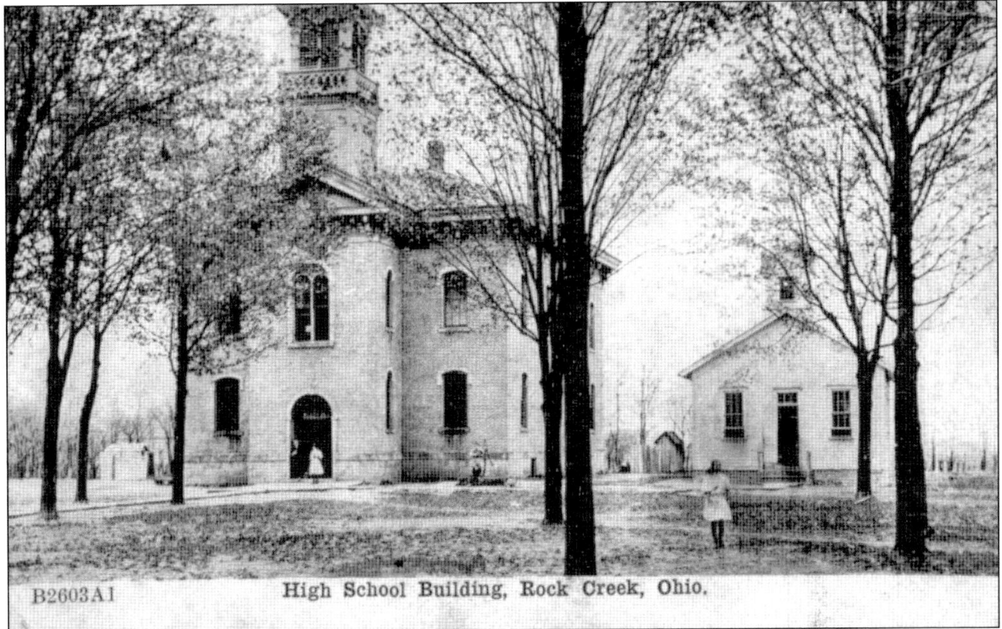

Rock Creek High School. Rock Creek High School, built in 1869 for $12,000, was a two-story brick structure. A new addition was added in 1947 that included a home economics lab, a shop, a science lab, and a cafeteria. (Ashtabula County District Library.)

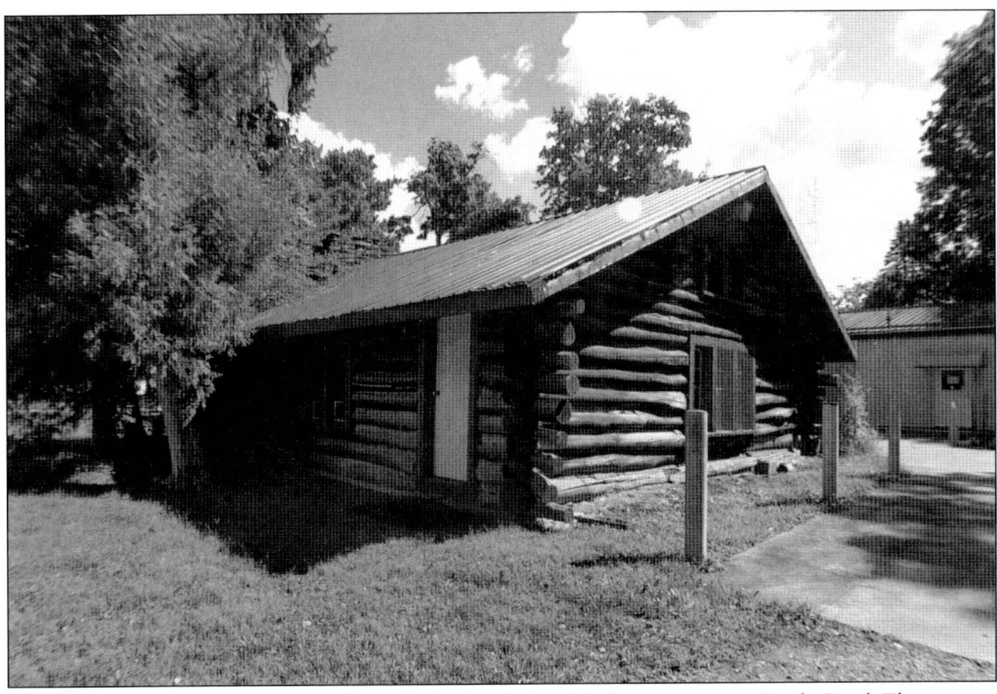

Log Cabin. The log cabin, located beside the Rock Creek Library opposite Rock Creek Elementary School, was built in the 1920s by local Boy Scout Troop No. 43. Prior to 1915, the site was the village cemetery. The cabin was used for decades for village council meetings, but it was turned back over to the Scouts in 1992 when the new village hall building was constructed. (Author's collection.)

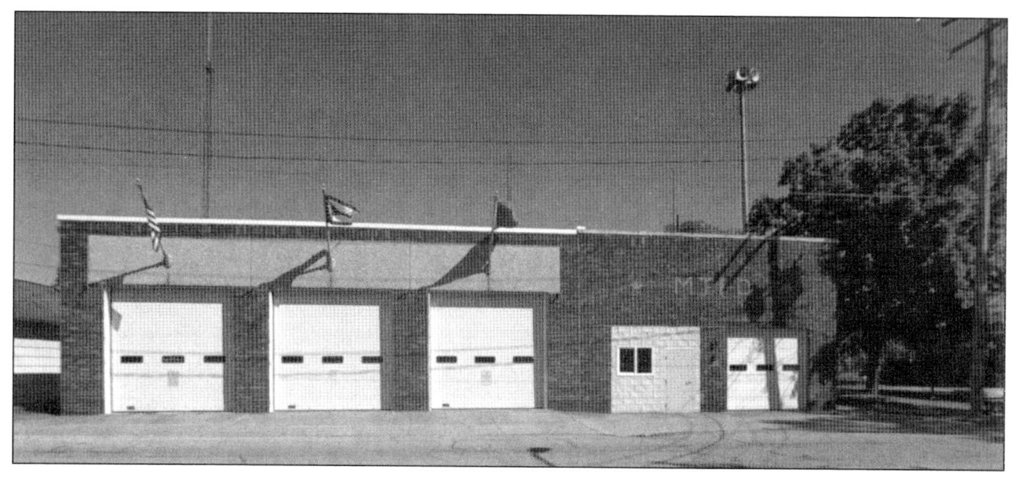

Rock Creek Fire Department (above) and Morgan Township Fire Engine (below), 1949. The original fire station in Rock Creek was a two-room brick structure built in 1939. The three-bay garage structure on the west side of the original section was added in the 1960s. The fire department, originally known as the Morgan Township Volunteer Hose Company of Rock Creek, began with two pumper trucks and 20 volunteer firemen. A 1,000-gallon Ford Tanker was added in 1949. (Above, author's collection; below, Jefferson Historical Society.)

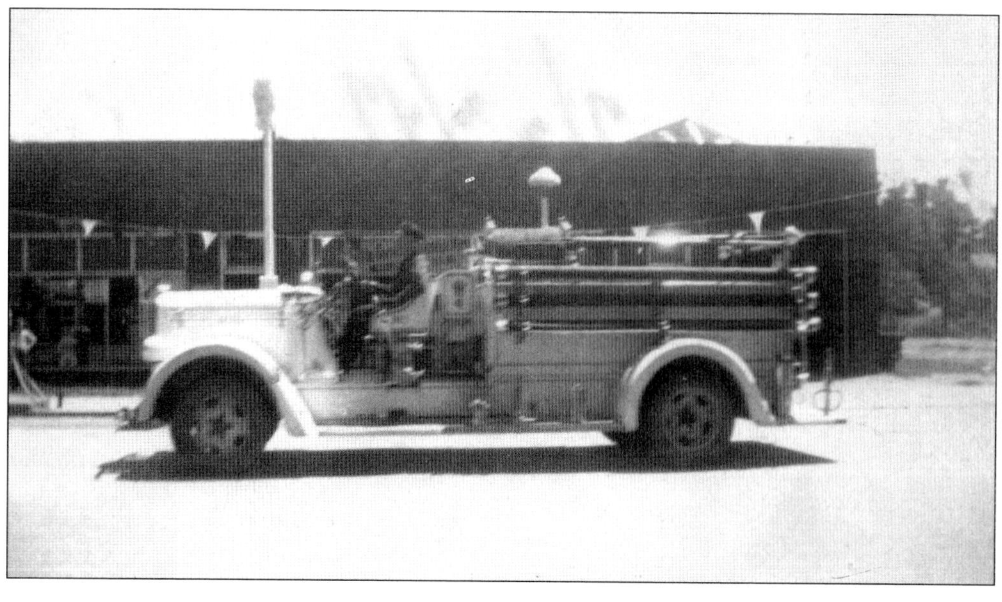

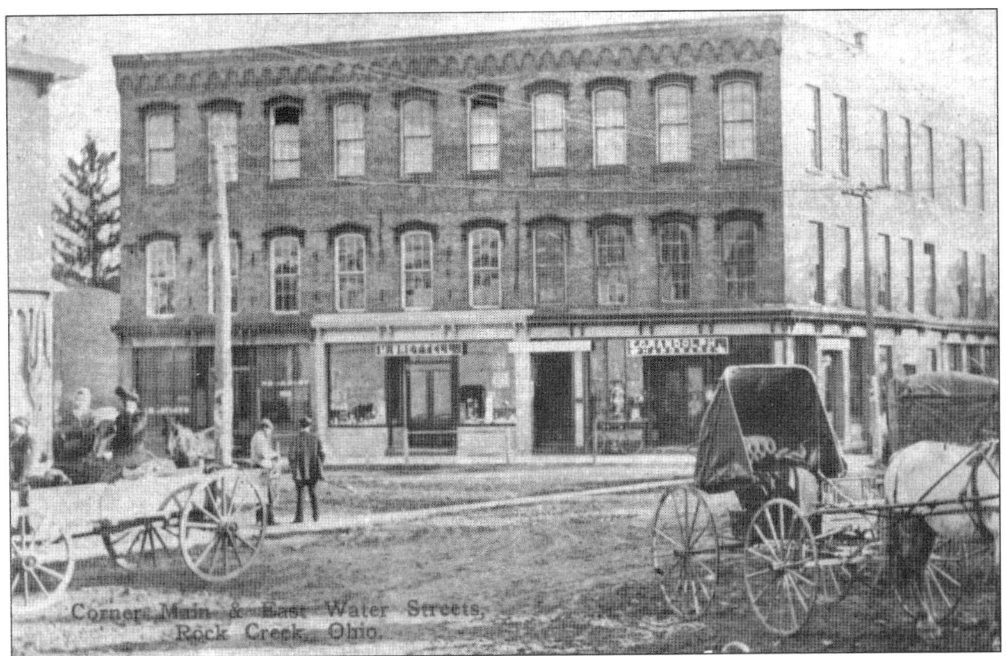

Main and Water Streets. The northeast corner of Main and Water Streets looked very different at the turn of the 20th century when this photograph was taken. The three-story brick building, which housed Randolph Hardware and M. Brettel clothiers, was destroyed by fire. (Ashtabula County District Library.)

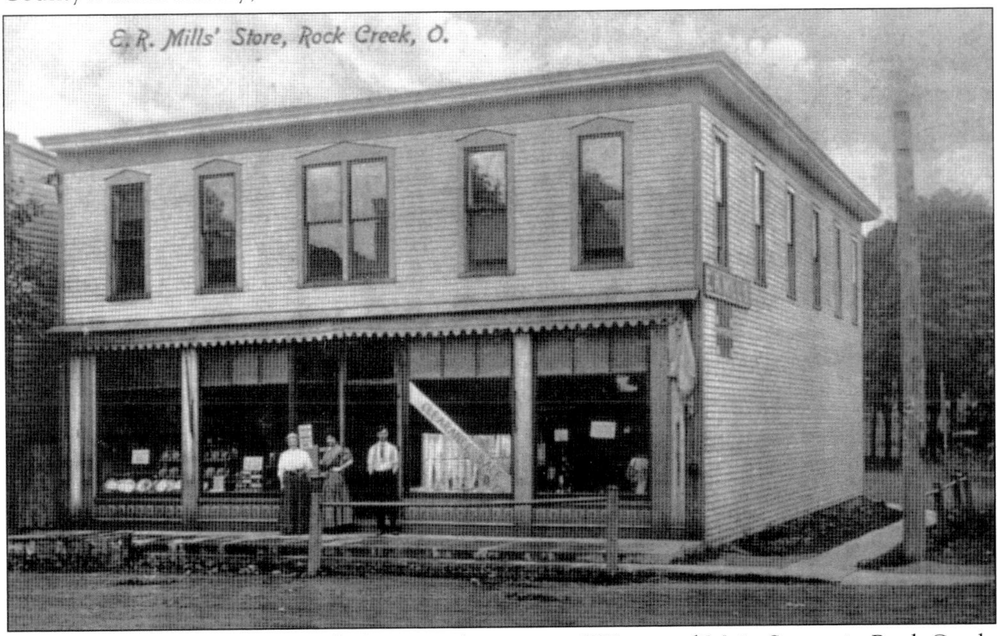

E.R. Mills Store. The E.R. Mills Store, at the corner of Water and Main Streets in Rock Creek, was built in 1898, using lumber hauled from Austinburg. The store, known in its time as the "ready pay store," carried most of what one would find in today's drug and grocery stores. Before it was the Mills Store, this site was home to the village's hotel. In the 1930s, the E.R. Mills Store was purchased by Carl Jones and became a furniture store. (Ashtabula County District Library.)

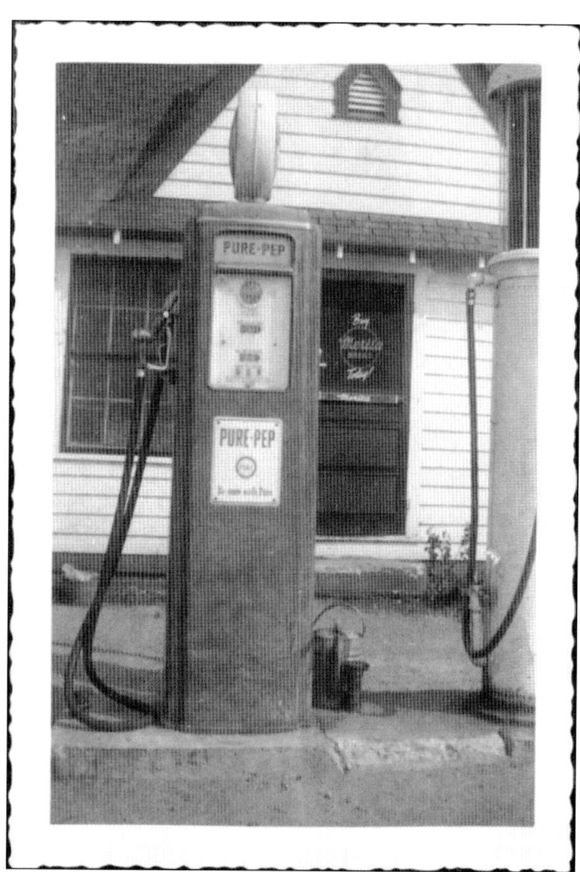

Pure Pep Gas Station (left) and Sohio Gas Station (below), Rock Creek. In the days before interstate highways, Rock Creek was a convenient stop for those traveling by car on Ohio State Route 45, which connects Ashtabula, Ohio, with Orwell, Warren, and ultimately Wellsville, Ohio, along the Ohio River. The traffic supported several gas stations, including the two pictured here. Pure Pep was a popular gasoline station brand during the 1940s and 1950s. SOHIO was a spin-off of the Standard Oil Company that began in 1911 and was acquired by BP in 1987. (Both, Ashtabula District Library Archives.)

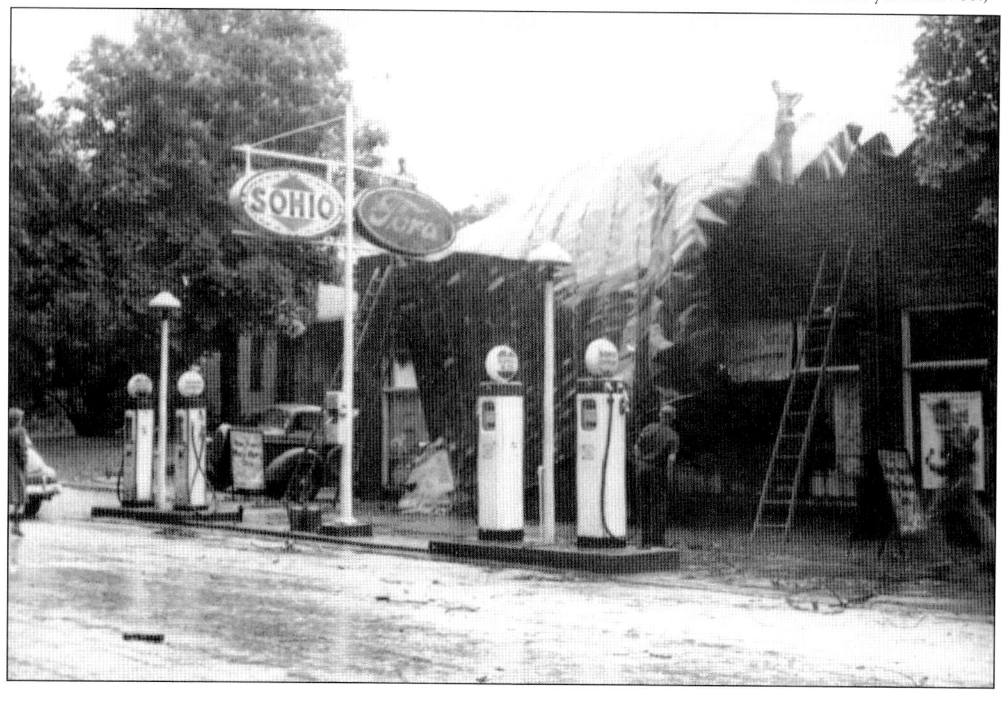

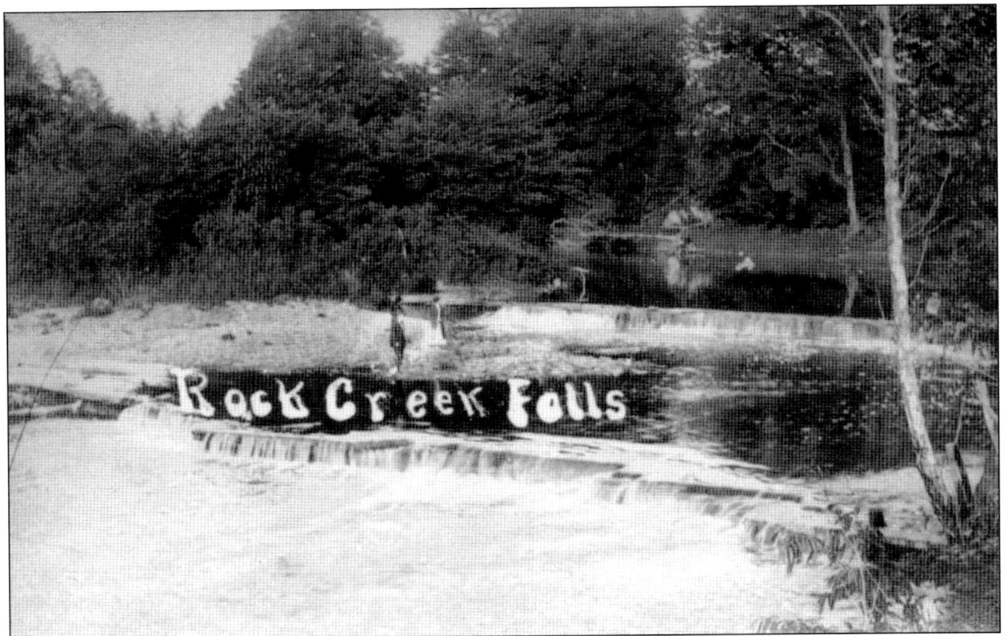

Rock Creek Falls. Rock Creek Falls, one of two waterfalls in Rock Creek, is part of the Ashtabula County Metroparks and is accessible via a short, 1.4-mile out-and-back trail off Rome Rock Creek Road, just before entering the village of Rock Creek. There is parking available near the trailhead. (Ashtabula District Library Archives.)

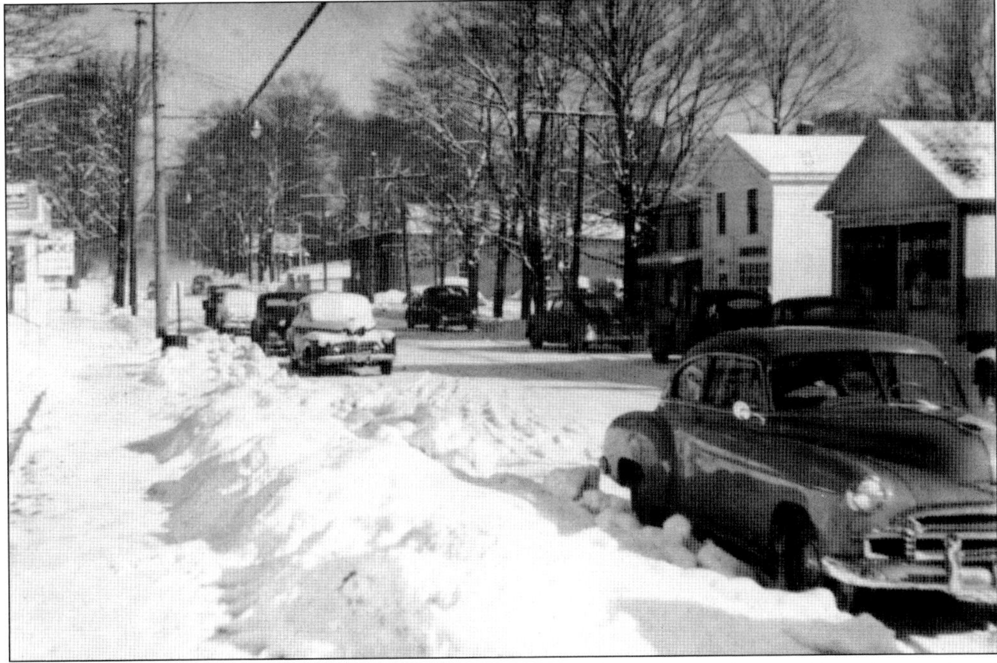

Winter in Rock Creek. The topography of Rock Creek, being located in a valley, often makes it the coldest spot in the county. The average winter low temperature in Rock Creek in January is 23 degrees Fahrenheit, but it is not unusual for temperatures to dip into the single digits during January and February. (Ashtabula District Library Archives.)

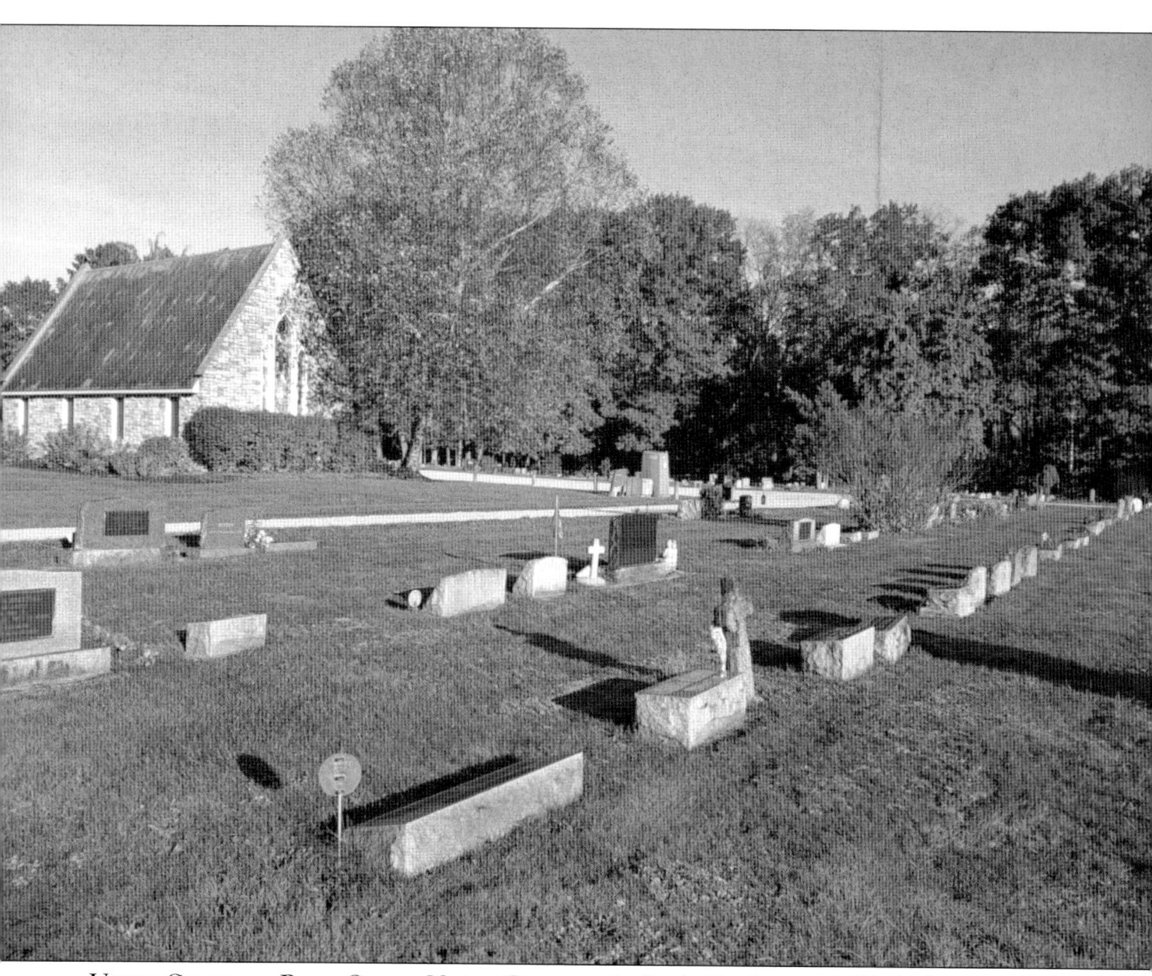

UNION CEMETERY, ROCK CREEK. Union Cemetery in Rock Creek was established in 1867. This hallowed ground is home to the remains of more than 400 veterans, including nearly 100 from the Civil War. The cemetery, located at the end of Stiles Avenue, also includes remains of those interred in the old Rock Creek Cemetery, which was located where the library and log cabin sit today. (Author's collection.)

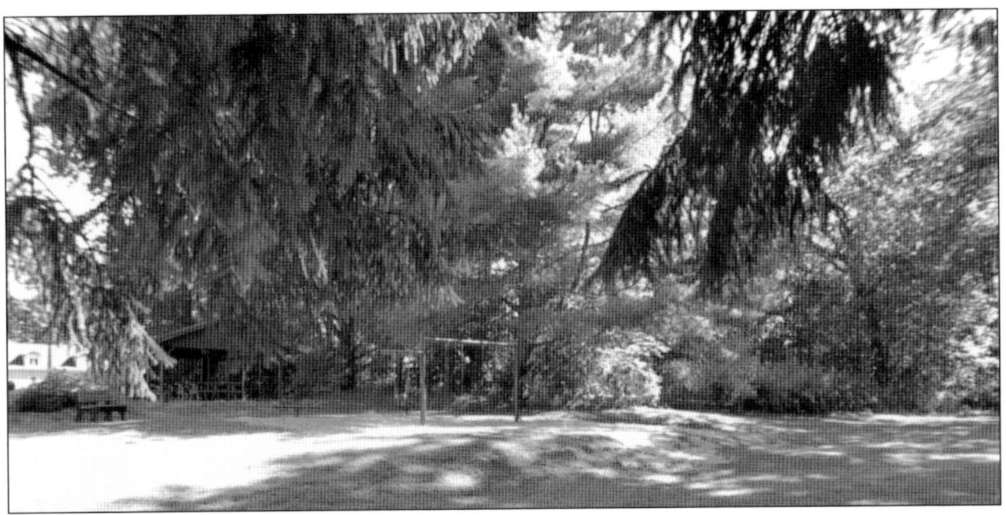

Brandeberry Park and Cobra Helicopter. Located on State Route 45, just south of the center of town, Brandeberry Park sits along Rock Creek. The shale creek bed makes a nice, picturesque, stepped waterfall. The bridge alongside the park replaced the historic double-lane covered bridge that was built in 1832, when what is now State Route 45 was a stagecoach line connecting the Ohio River with Lake Erie. A Vietnam-era Cobra helicopter is on display at the park. (Both, author's collection.)

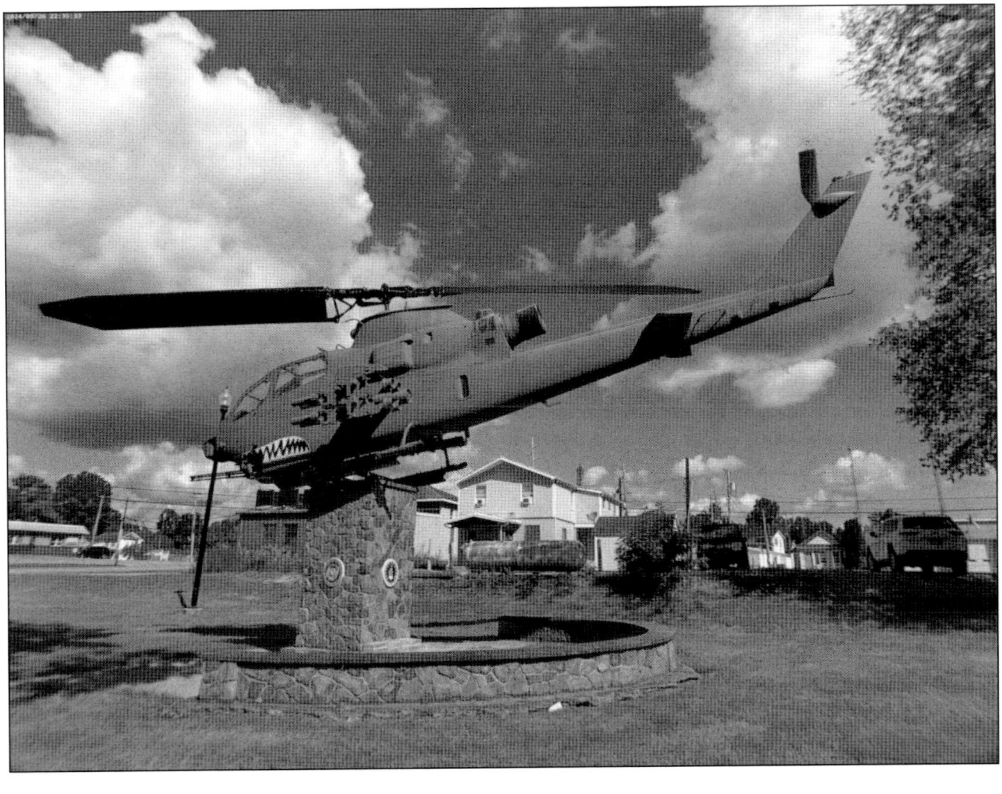

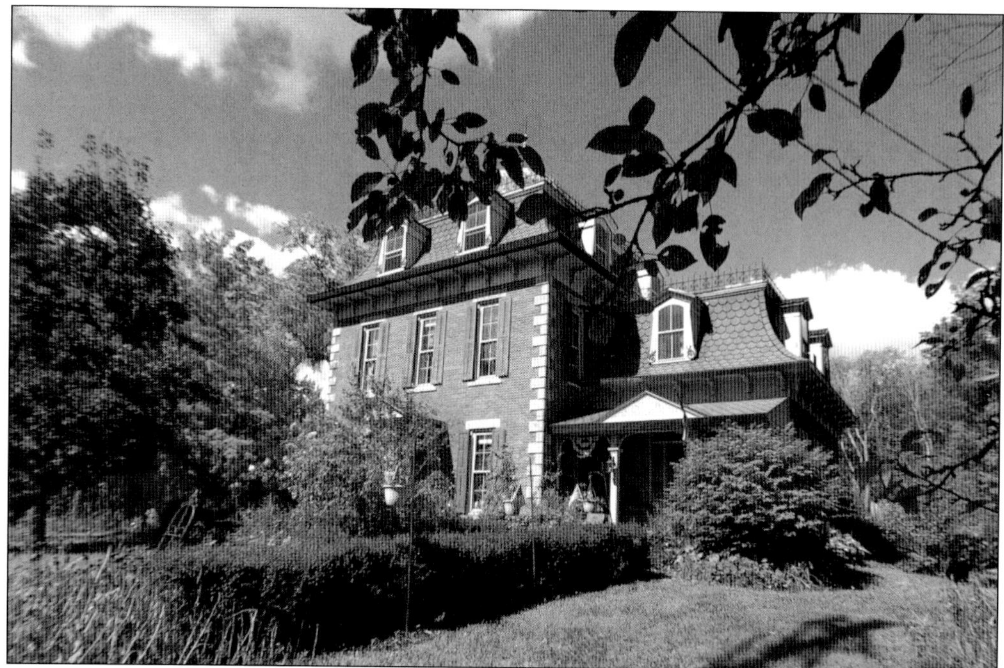

The Wright/Stiles/Crislip House. Located across from Brandeberry Park, on the south side of Rock Creek, is one of the village's most striking homes. The three-story, brick home with the mansard roof was originally the home of Capt. Henry Wright, the owner of the Rock Creek Brick Factory. The home was built in 1867 for the (then staggering) sum of $10,000 by the captain as a last-ditch (and ultimately unsuccessful) effort by him to keep his wife from leaving him. The effort bankrupted him. Subsequent owners include Capt. William Stiles, a lifelong friend of James A. Garfield, and Rev. Rayman Fritz, pastor of the Congregational Church, and his wife (the granddaughter of Captain Stiles), who put in the elaborate gardens. More recently, Gene and Jeanne Crislip restored the home to its 19th-century glory. The image below shows Captain Stiles moving lumber for the house onto his property. (Above, author's collection; below, Jefferson Historical Society.)

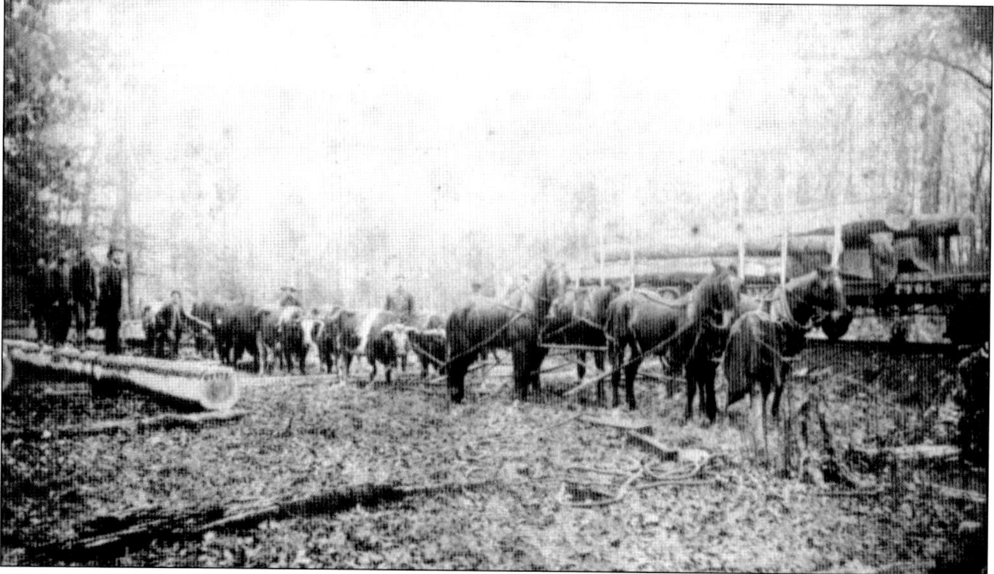

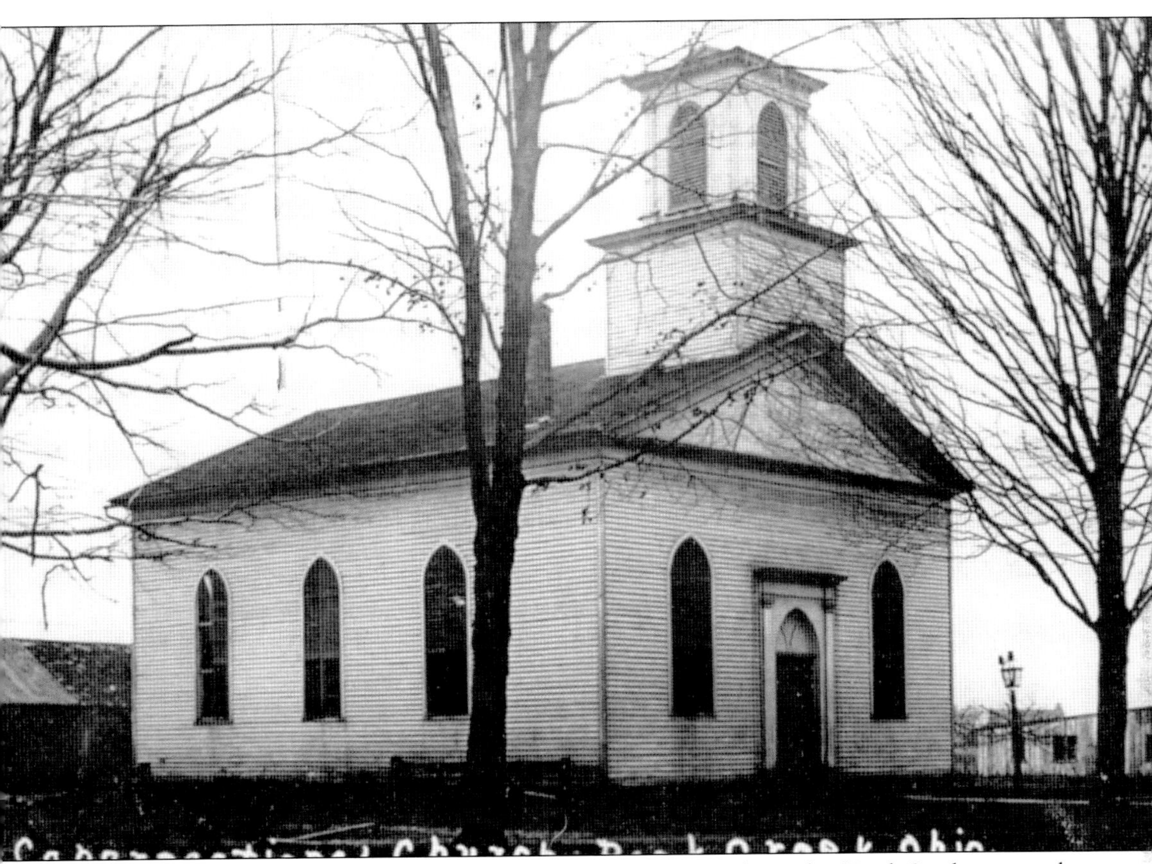

Congregational Church, Rock Creek. Originally located one mile north of Rock Creek, just north of today's Tisch Road, was the Congregational Church, built in 1829. The building was moved to High Street in Rock Creek in 1845. It is now the Rock Creek Church of Christ. (Author's collection.)

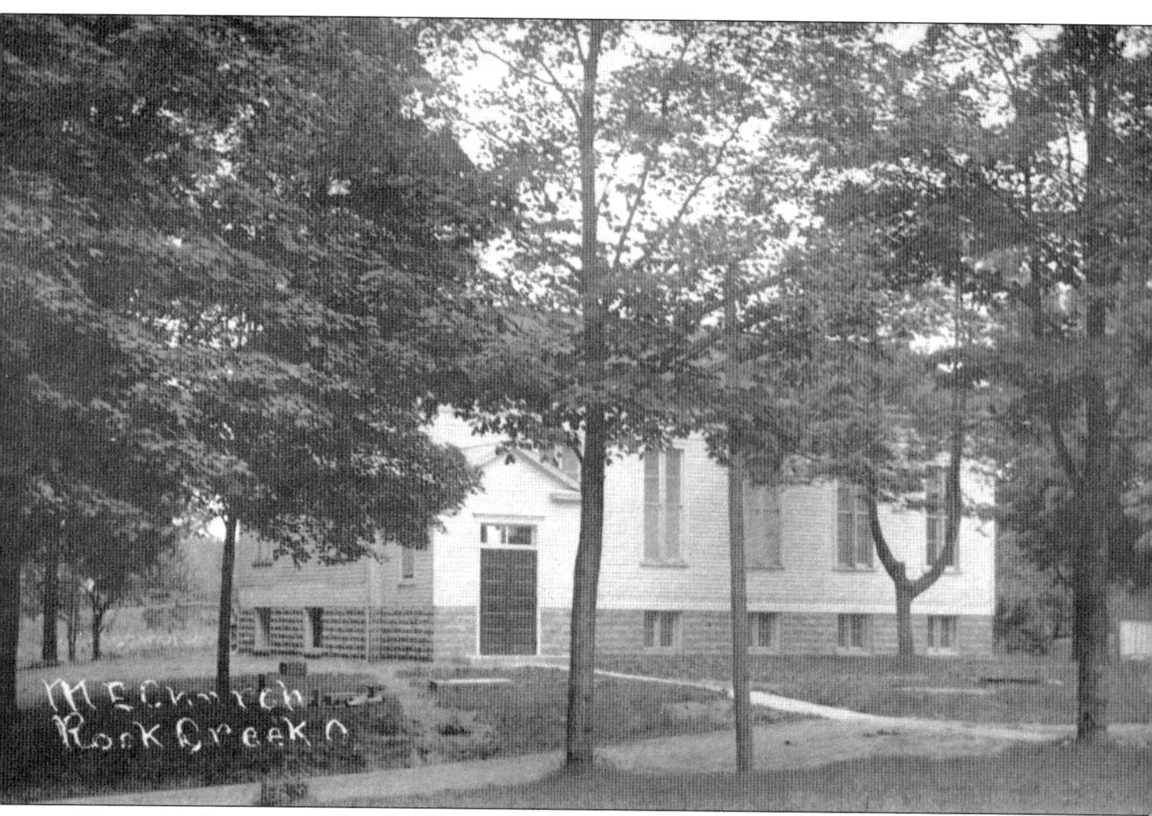

METHODIST CHURCH. Rock Creek United Methodist Church was organized in 1822 as the Methodist Episcopal Church by William Latimer, the father of Methodism in Morgan Township. Services were first held in private homes, including the Latimer home, and a log schoolhouse before the current church structure was built in 1843–1844. Rock Creek Methodist Church closed in 2021. It is now the Rock Creek Library Annex. (Author's collection.)

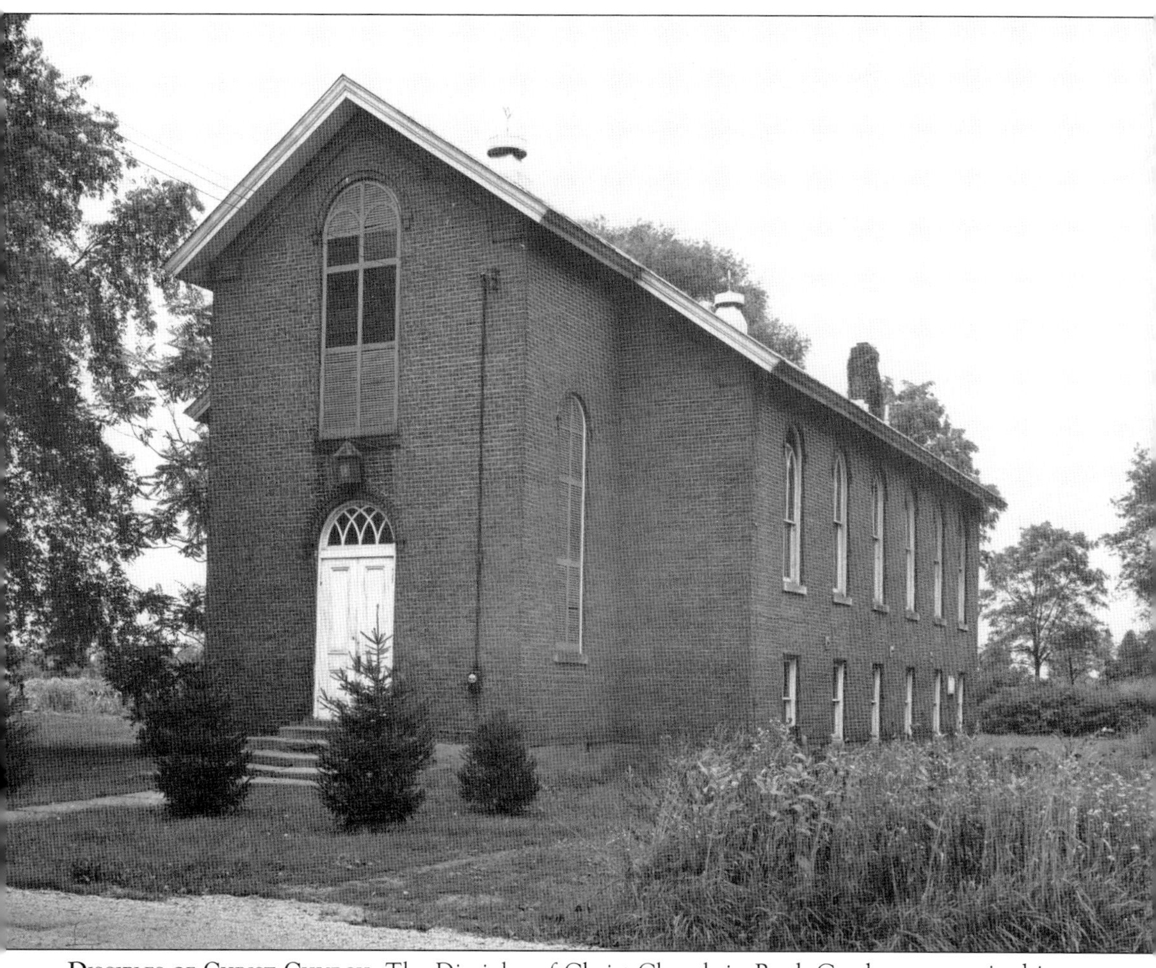

Disciples of Christ Church. The Disciples of Christ Church in Rock Creek was organized in 1858 as a spin-off of the Presbyterian/Congregational Church in Rock Creek with additional members from the Disciples of Christ Church in Eagleville. The church building, located on Lawton Avenue, was built in 1874 for $5,000 and originally had a steeple. A.D. Olds was the first pastor. The Disciples of Christ Church closed in 1924 and is now the Masonic temple. (Ashtabula County District Library.)

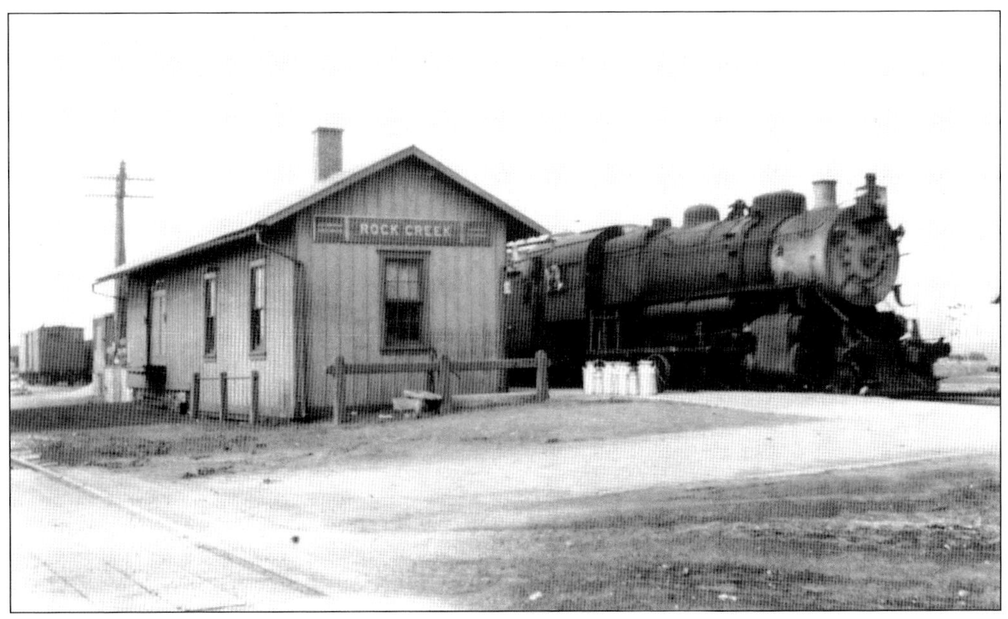

ROCK CREEK TRAIN STATION. Rock Creek was a stop along the Ashtabula & Pittsburg Railroad in the late 19th century. The railroad through Rock Creek was completed in 1872. (Ashtabula County District Library.)

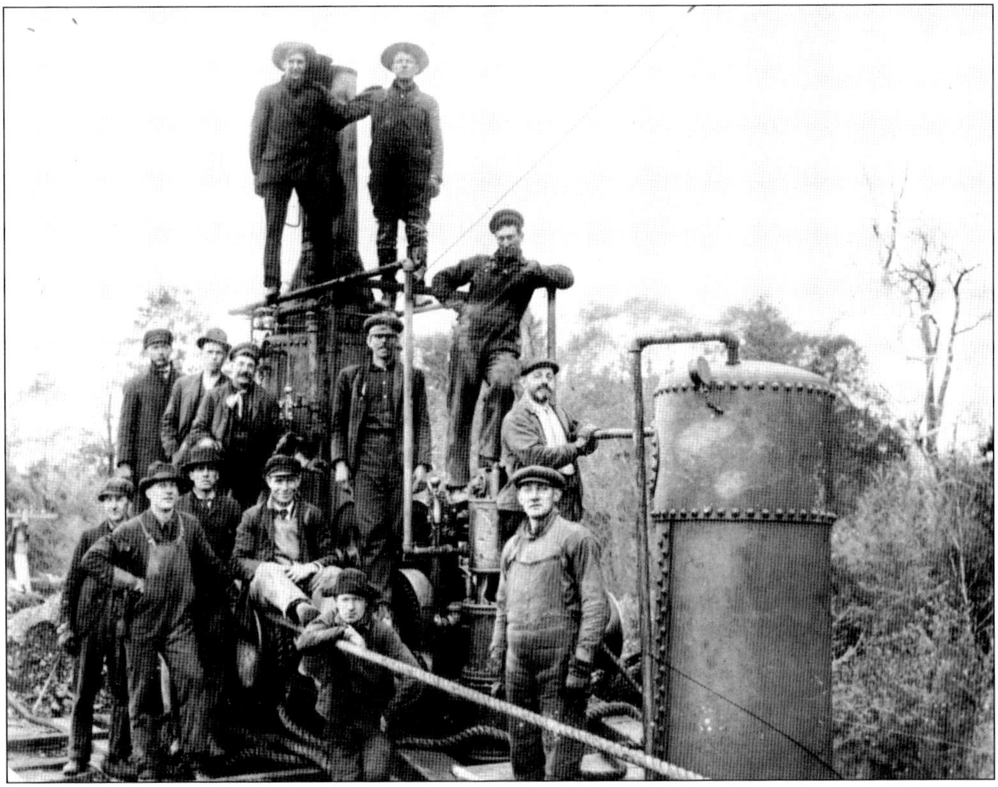

WORKMEN LAYING TRACK, ROCK CREEK. When it was first completed, five passenger trains and two mail coaches passed through Rock Creek every day. Many of the village's industries were located near the rail lines, including Harrington's Feed Mill, Burleigh's Handle Mill, and Van Ormann's Lumber Mill. (Jefferson Historical Society.)

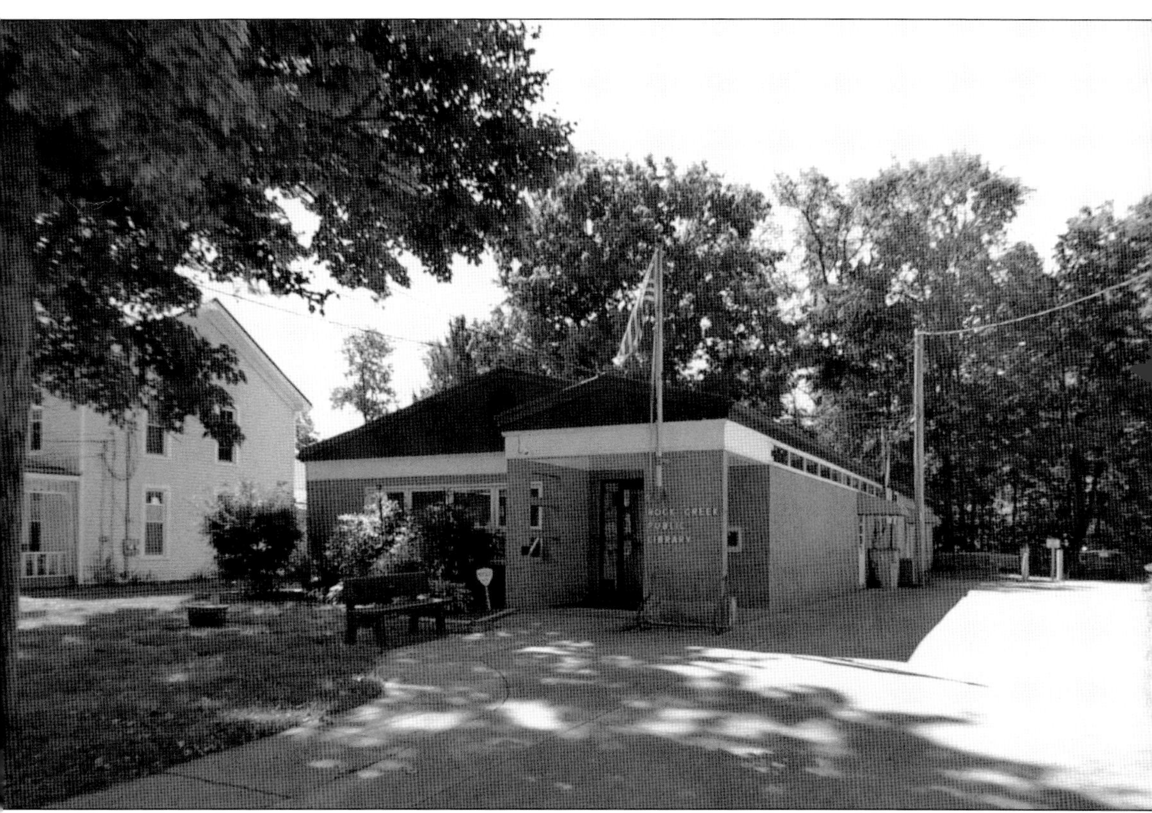

Rock Creek Public Library. The Rock Creek Library once shared space with the village jail. The current library structure on High Street opened in 1965. A 1,400-square-foot addition in 1992 nearly doubled the library's size. The former Methodist church opened as the library's annex in 2025. (Author's collection.)

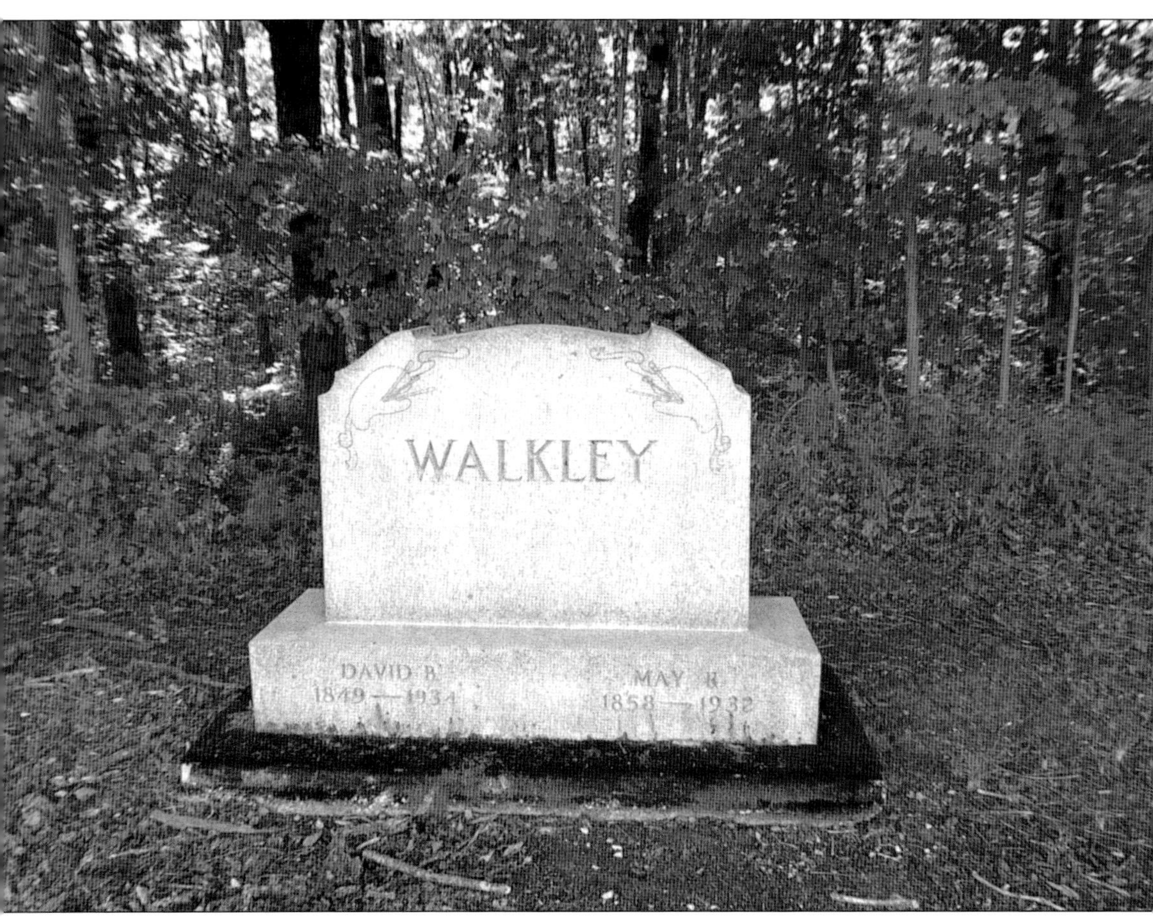

David Birdsey Walkley. Born in Rome, Ohio, David Birdsey Walkley grew up and went to school in Rock Creek. He became a world-famous portrait and landscape artist of the late 19th and early 20th centuries and taught at the Pittsburgh School of Design. Walkley's works have been displayed in galleries in New York City, Philadelphia, and Pittsburgh as well as at the Chicago World's Fair. Walkley died in 1934 at the age of 85. He is buried in Rock Creek's Union Cemetery. (Author's collection.)

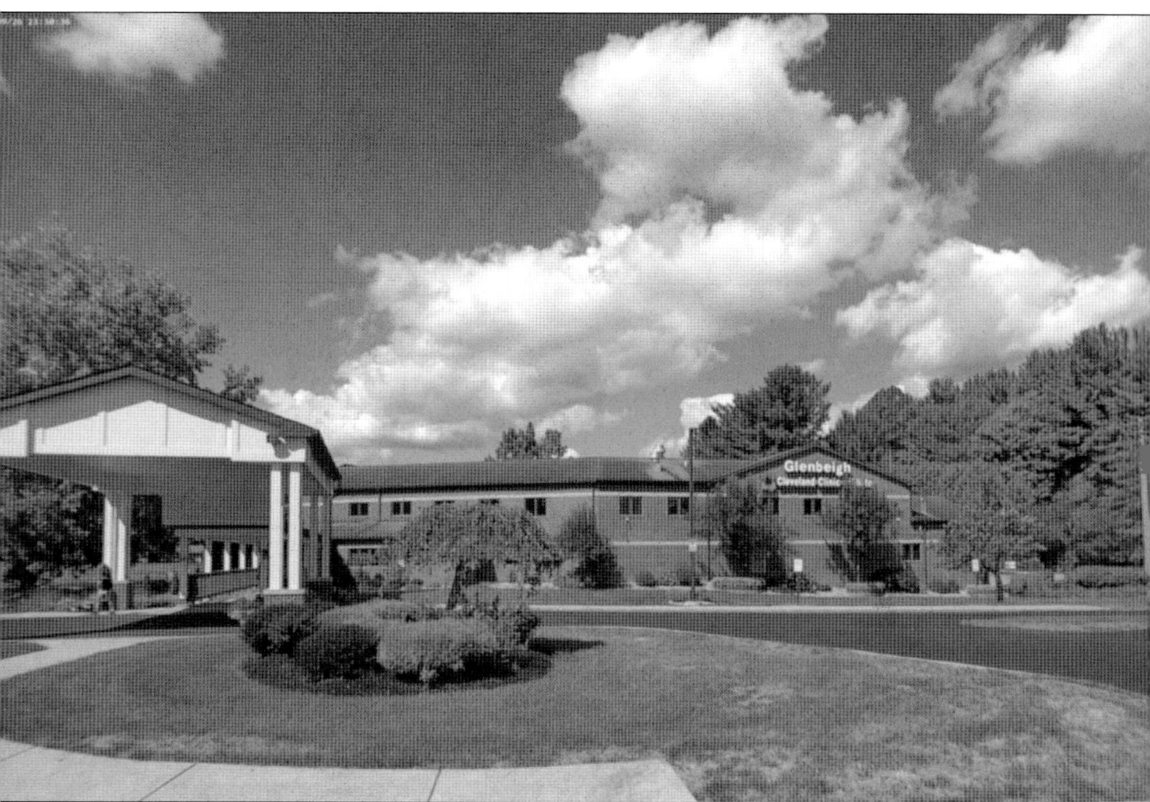

Glenbeigh. Established in 1981, Glenbeigh provides inpatient and outpatient drug and alcohol recovery counseling and treatment. Located just north of downtown Rock Creek, the facility, now a part of the Cleveland Clinic network of health care services, adopts a holistic philosophy toward recovery. (Author's collection.)

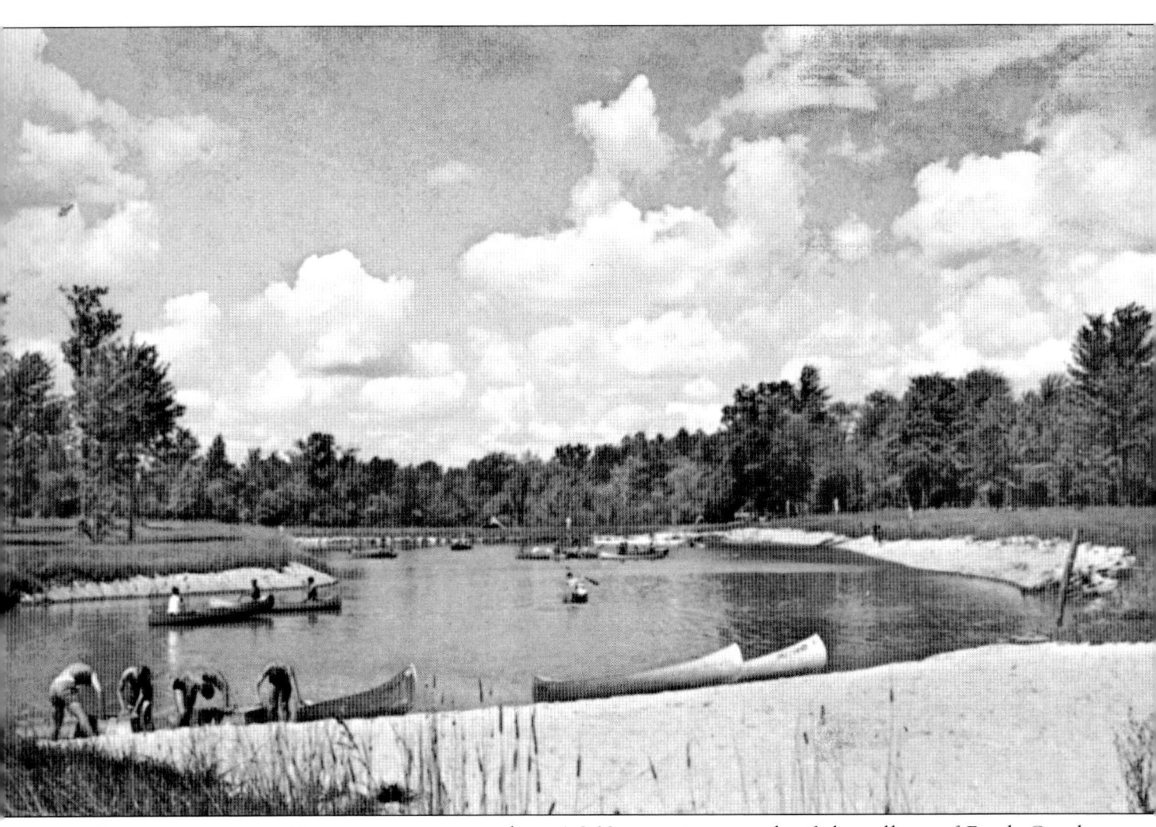

Beaumont Scout Reservation. Located on 1,260 acres just north of the village of Rock Creek is the Beaumont Scout Reservation. Situated along the banks of the Grand River, the year-round facility was founded in 1946 and features five separate camps for families, Scouting troops, and other organizations for day and overnight camping. (Author's collection.)

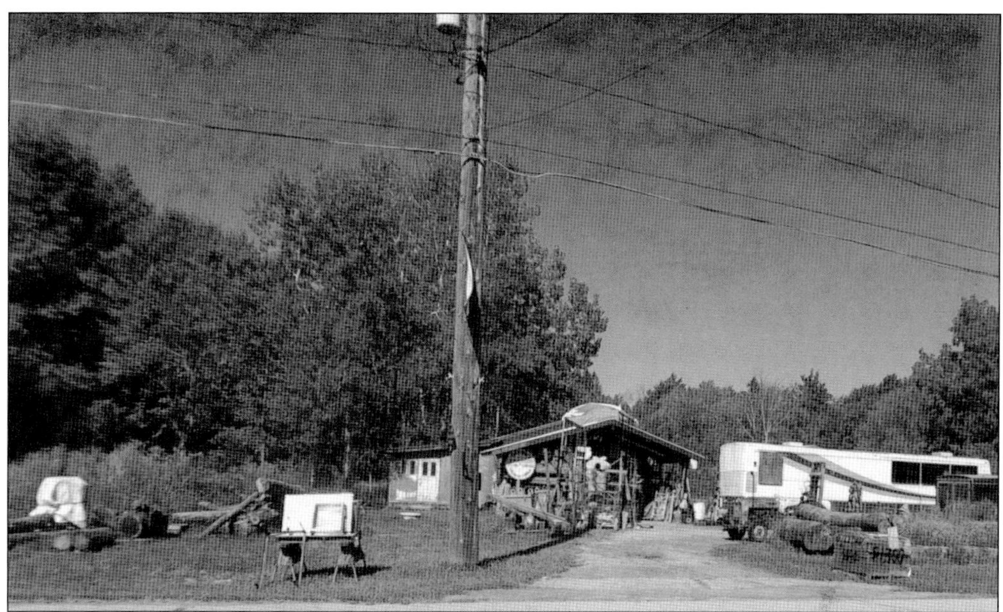

Bob Anderson, Chainsaw Artist. Bob Anderson is another of Rock Creek's creative residents. The 55-year-old retired carpenter has an eclectic workshop on State Route 45 just north of downtown Rock Creek, where he creates bears, Sasquatches, eagles, and other real and mythical creatures, some as big as 10 feet tall. Anderson has been carving since childhood and making chainsaw art since 2008. (Author's collection.)

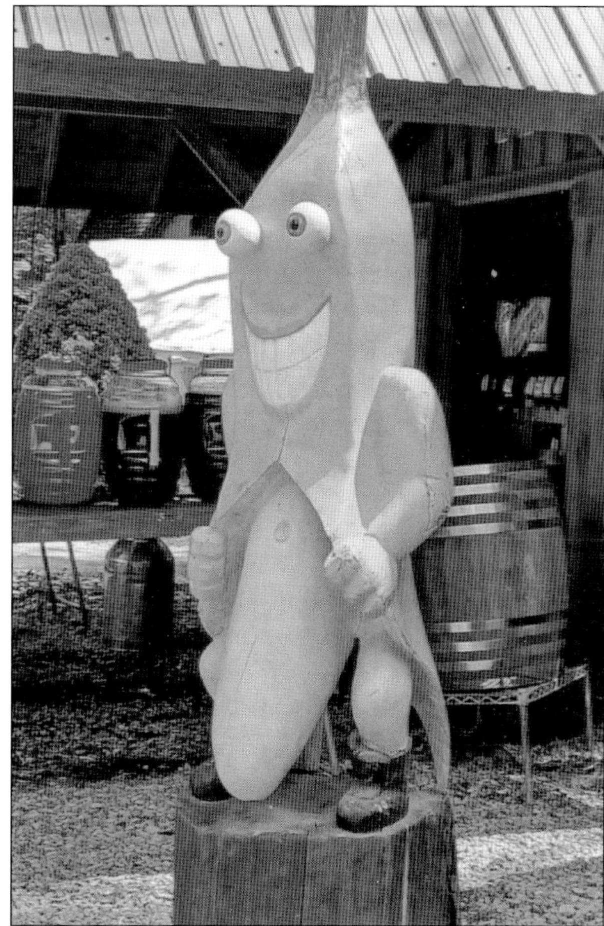

Chainsaw Banana, Great Lakes Medieval Faire. One of Anderson's most unique creations is permanently installed at the entrance to the food court at the seasonal Great Lakes Medieval Faire, located just west of Rock Creek along State Route 534. Other Anderson creations can be found throughout the village of Rock Creek and beyond. (Author's collection.)

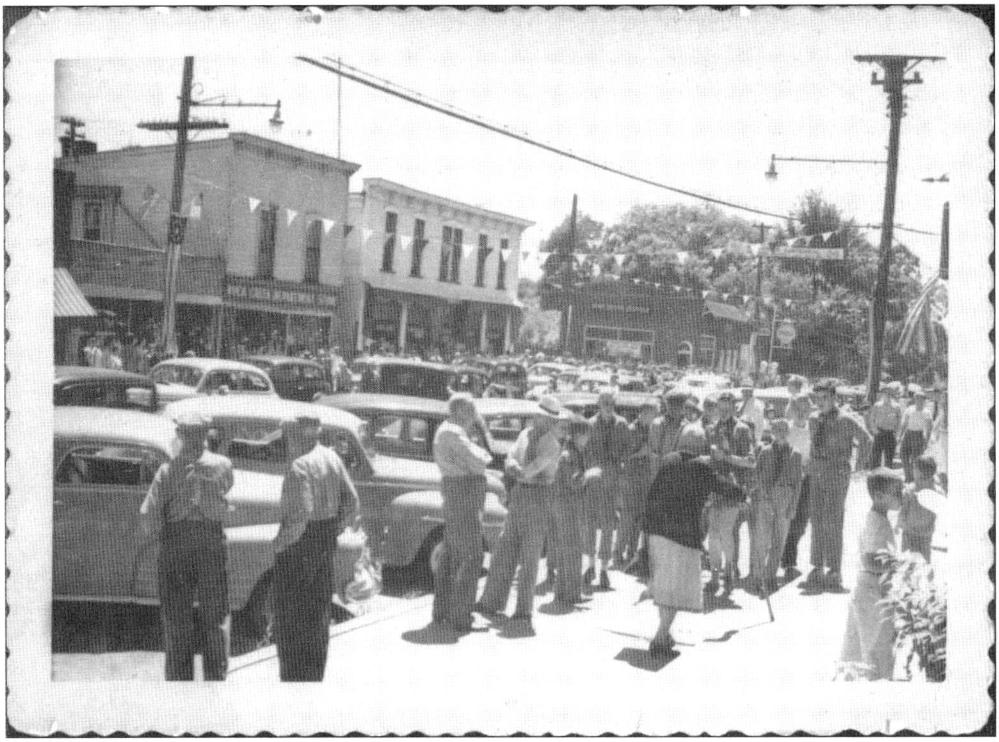

Rock Creek Centennial Parade. The village of Rock Creek celebrated its centennial July 20–23, 1949. The festivities included a parade with covered wagons, fire trucks, five bands, and floats. (Ashtabula County District Library.)

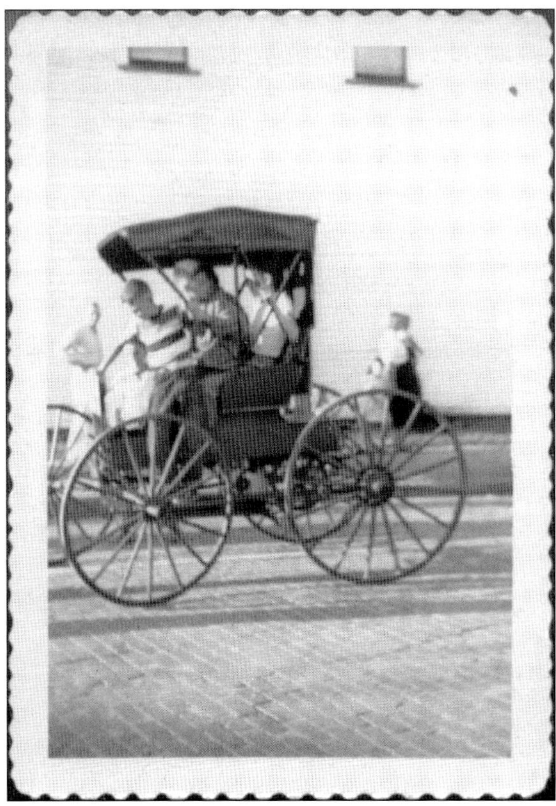

Rock Creek Centennial. Other events associated with the centennial celebration included a dedication of the "new" bridge over Rock Creek south of downtown, a baby beauty contest, a concert, a horse show, and a fireworks display. (Ashtabula County District Library.)

Three

Roaming Shores

People began talking about creating a recreational lake in the heart of Ashtabula County in the 1920s. The idea gathered more support after the end of World War II, when demand for housing in the area increased dramatically. In 1966, Development Services Inc. (DSI) purchased 1,700 acres in Rome and Morgan Townships to create what would become Roaming Shores.

The complicated transaction involved buying out many existing homeowners who had property along Rock Creek. The last part of the deal was completed on June 10, 1966. Dam construction began later that year with Koski Construction in Ashtabula serving as the lead contractor. The Class I earthen dam measures 45 feet high and 730 feet in length. The cost was $800,000 (nearly $8 million in 2025). The 550-acre lake created by the dam features 22 miles of shoreline and has an average depth of 30 feet. The project moved very quickly, and the *Rome Rock News* reported that the first boat was launched on Lake Roaming Rock on January 30, 1967. (It must have been a little chilly that day on the lake.) On September 13, 1971, the *Jefferson Gazette* reported that 167 homes had already been built at Roaming Rock.

Eventually, in 1979, as the community grew, Roaming Rock development was incorporated as the village of Roaming Shores, with its own village administrator, wastewater and sewage treatment plant, and municipal services. Today, Roaming Shores is one of the most sought-after addresses in Ashtabula County.

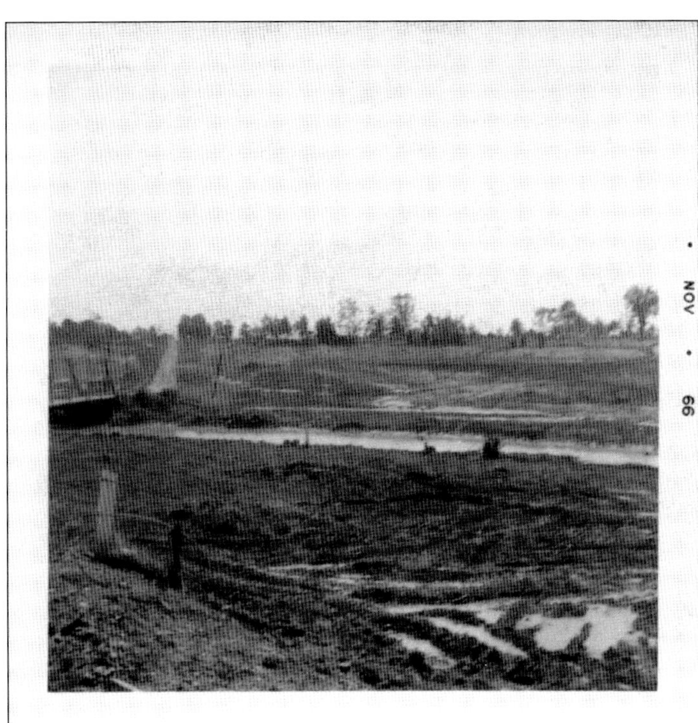

ROAMING ROCK CREEK DAM. The village of Roaming Shores, Ohio, was formed by the damming of Rock Creek in 1966, creating a 1,700-acre lakefront community. Initially, the land was administered by the homeowner's collective. However, the village of Roaming Shores was incorporated in 1979 and elected a village administrator. (Ashtabula County District Library.)

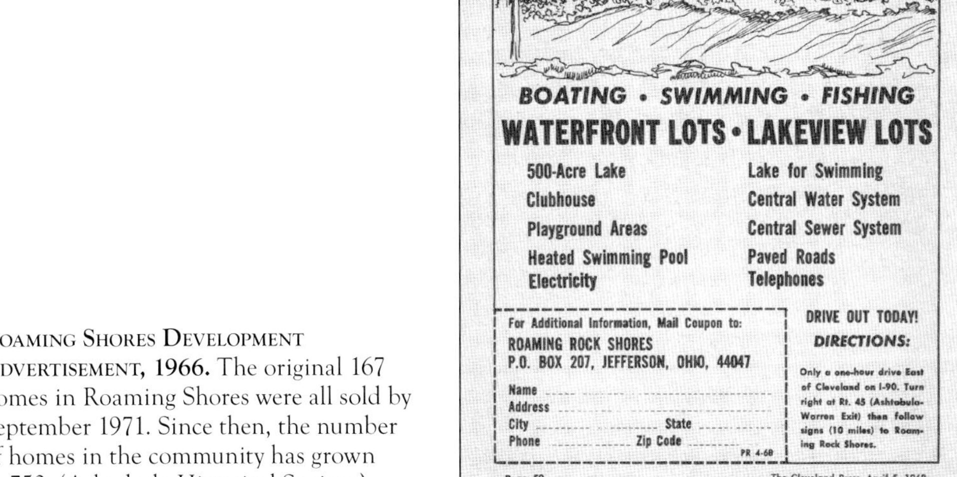

ROAMING SHORES DEVELOPMENT ADVERTISEMENT, 1966. The original 167 homes in Roaming Shores were all sold by September 1971. Since then, the number of homes in the community has grown to 750. (Ashtabula Historical Society.)

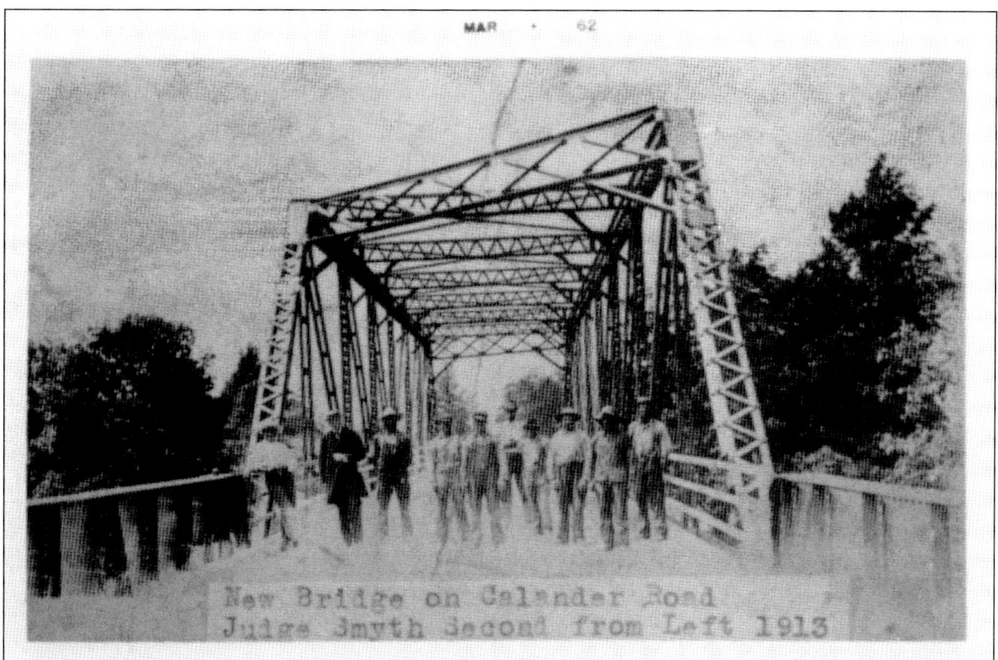

CALLENDER ROAD BRIDGE, 1961. Located just southeast of Rock Creek, the 130-foot Callender Road bridge spanned the Grand River. The steel truss-style bridge built in 1913 was noted for its asymmetrical canopy. The bridge was demolished in 2013. (Jefferson Historical Society.)

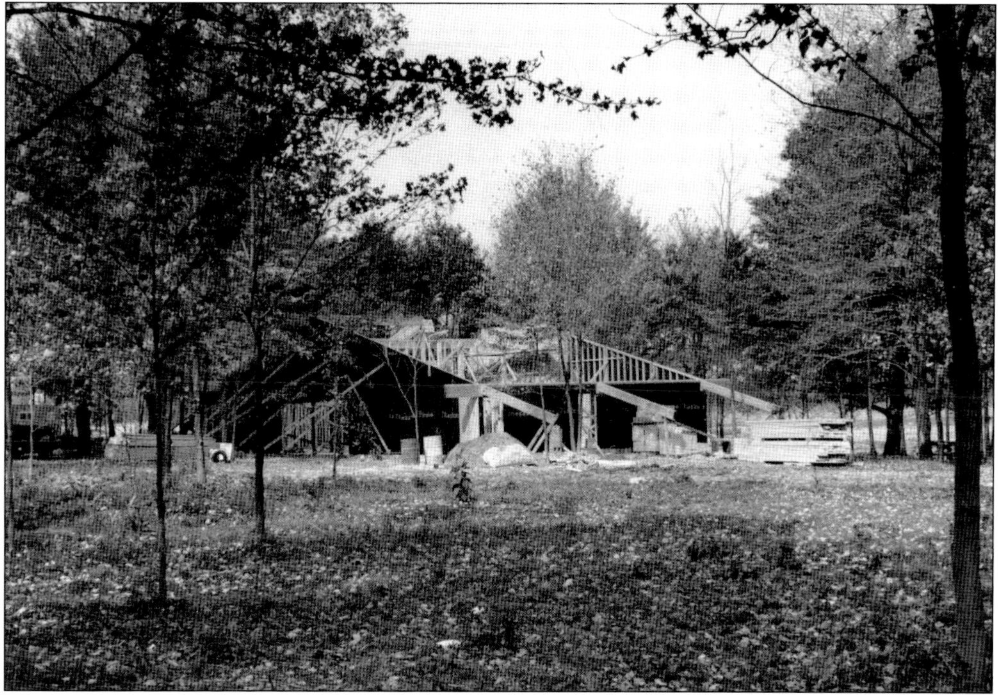

ROAMING SHORES HOME UNDER CONSTRUCTION. Roaming Shores, once called Roaming Rock Shores, was formed by damming Rock Creek in 1966–1967. Many of the 750 homes in the planned community have private docks. Waterfront lots sold for around $7,500 in 1966. (Author's collection.)

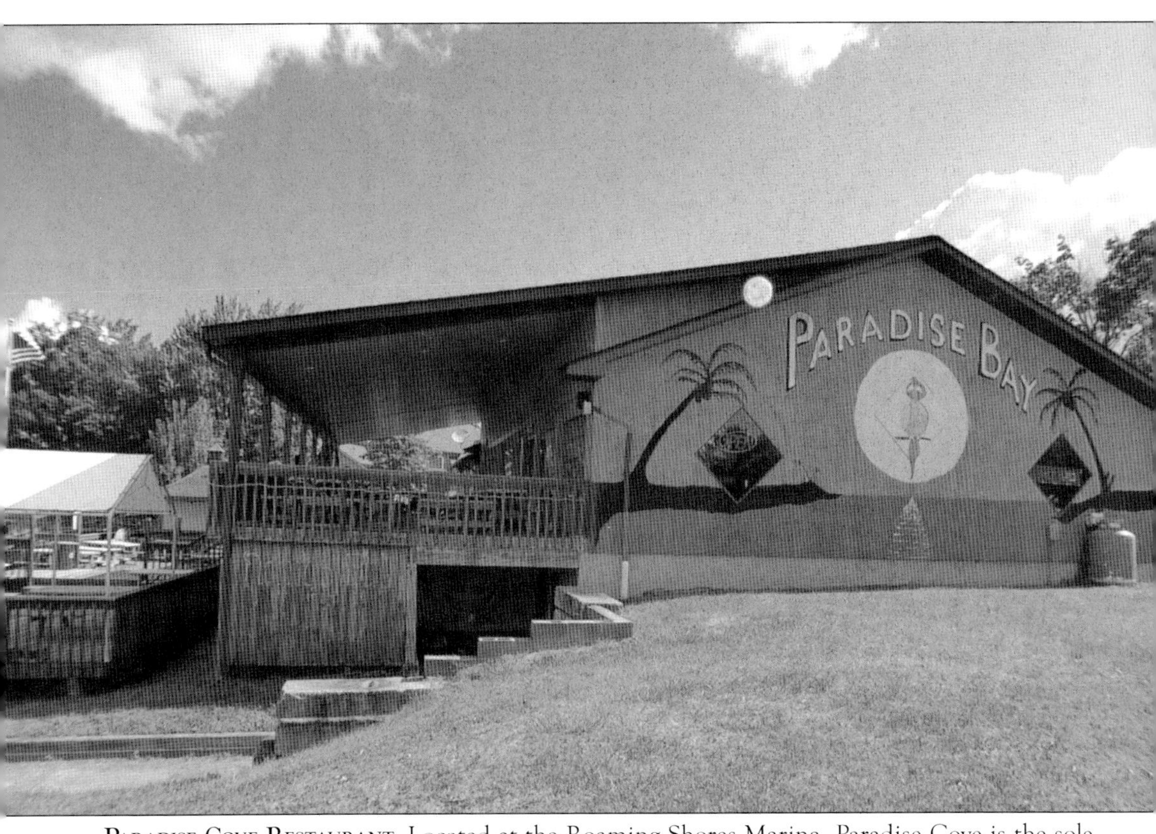

Paradise Cove Restaurant. Located at the Roaming Shores Marina, Paradise Cove is the sole restaurant within the Roaming Shores town limits. The waterfront eatery is open from mid-May through October and has a back patio overlooking the lake. (Author's collection.)

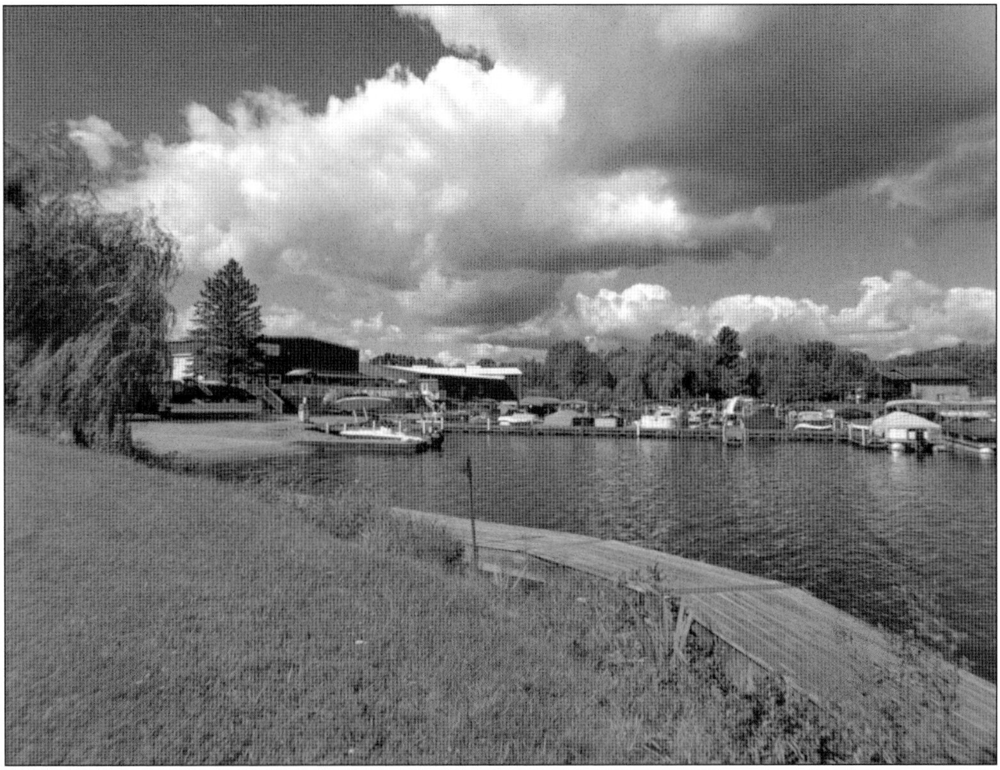

Roaming Rock Marina. Located along the northeast shore of the lake, Roaming Rock Marina is a one-stop resource for Roaming Shores boating enthusiasts. The marina offers boat sales, maintenance and repair services, boat storage, gasoline, boating supplies, and even convenience store items. There is also a boat ramp at the site. Use of the marina is limited to Roaming Shores residents. (Author's collection.)

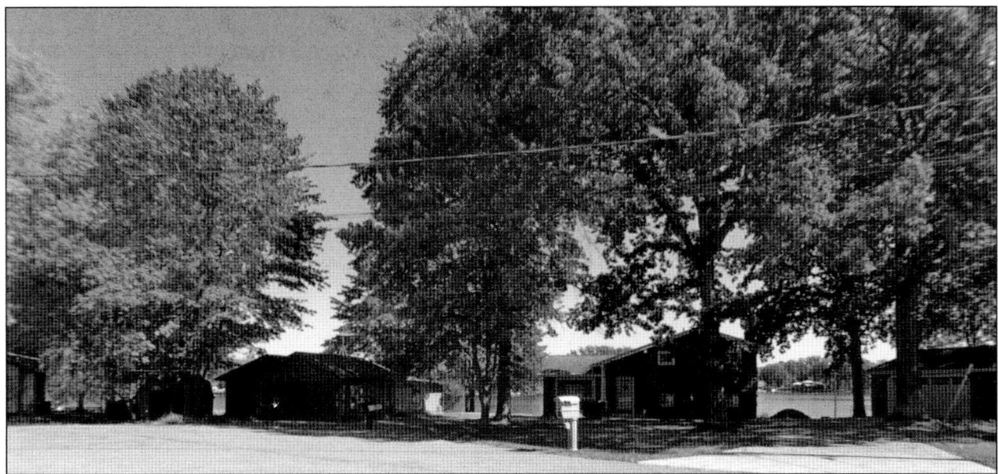

Today's Homes in Roaming Shores. Roaming Shores continues to thrive. As of the 2020 US census, there are 1,586 residents in the community. Homeowner amenities include use of the four swimming pools, eight beaches, a clubhouse, multiple boat ramps, tennis courts, and pickleball courts. (Author's collection.)

Bibliography

Ellsworth, Catherine Trapp. *Historical Sketches of Ashtabula County, Ohio*. Great Lakes Publishing, 1975.

Feather, Carl E. and Ruth. *Ashtabula County: A Field Guide to the historical, natural & curious treasures of Ohio's largest county*. CreateSpace Independent Publishing Platform, 2018.

Feather, Carl. *Hidden History of Ashtabula County*. The History Press, 2015.

Fritsch, James T. *The Untried Life: The 29th Ohio Volunteer Infantry in the Civil War*. Swallow Press/ Ohio University Press, 2012.

Hatcher, Harlan. *The Western Reserve: The Story of New Connecticut in Ohio*. The Bobbs-Merrill Company, Inc., 1949.

Large, Moina W. *History of Ashtabula County*. Historical Publishing Company, 1924.

Riddle, Albert Gallatin. *The Life of Benjamin Wade*. Williams Brothers, 1886.

Udell, Cornelius. *Condensed History of Jefferson, Ashtabula County, Ohio*. J.A. Howells & Company, 1878.

Williams, William W. *History of Ashtabula County*. Williams Brothers, 1878.

Index